OCT 0 5 2018

P9-CRH-685

Middleton Public Library
7425 Hubbard Ave
Middleton, WI 53562

ALSO BY ELIZA GRISWOLD

Wideawake Field

The Tenth Parallel

I Am the Beggar of the World (translator)

AMITY

AND

PROSPERITY

AMITY
AND
PROSPERITY

ONE
FAMILY
AND
THE
FRACTURING
OF
AMERICA

ELIZA GRISWOLD

FARRAR, STRAUS AND GIROUX | NEW YORK

Farrar, Straus and Giroux
175 Varick Street, New York 10014

Copyright © 2018 by Eliza Griswold
Maps copyright © 2018 by Jeffrey L. Ward
All rights reserved
Printed in the United States of America
First edition, 2018

Library of Congress Cataloging-in-Publication Data
Names: Griswold, Eliza, 1973– author.
Title: Amity and Prosperity : one family and the fracturing of America /
    Eliza Griswold.
Description: First edition. | New York : Farrar, Straus and Giroux, 2018. |
    Includes bibliographical references.
Identifiers: LCCN 2017057605 | ISBN 9780374103118 (hardcover)
Subjects: LCSH: Gas wells—Hydraulic fracturing—Environmental aspects—
    Pennsylvania—Amity (Washington County : Township) | Gas wells—Hydraulic
    fracturing—Environmental aspects—Pennsylvania—Prosperity. | Amity
    (Washington County, Pa. : Township)—Social conditions. | Prosperity (Pa.)—
    Social conditions.
Classification: LCC TD195.G3 G747 2018 | DDC 363.7309748/82—dc23
LC record available at https://lccn.loc.gov/2017057605

Designed by Abby Kagan

Our books may be purchased in bulk for promotional, educational, or business use.
Please contact your local bookseller or the Macmillan Corporate and Premium Sales
Department at 1-800-221-7945, extension 5442, or by e-mail at
MacmillanSpecialMarkets@macmillan.com.

www.fsgbooks.com
www.twitter.com/fsgbooks • www.facebook.com/fsgbooks

1 3 5 7 9 10 8 6 4 2

For Harley and Paige

When the poor and needy seek water, and there is
none, and their tongue faileth for thirst,
I the Lord will hear them.

—ISAIAH 41:17

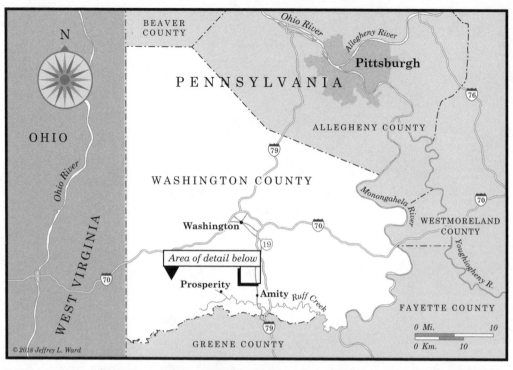

© 2018 Jeffrey L. Ward

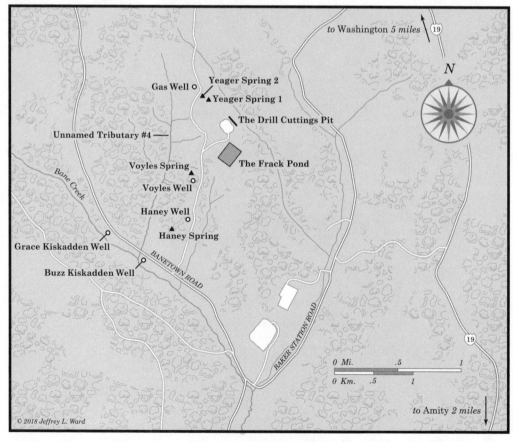

© 2018 Jeffrey L. Ward

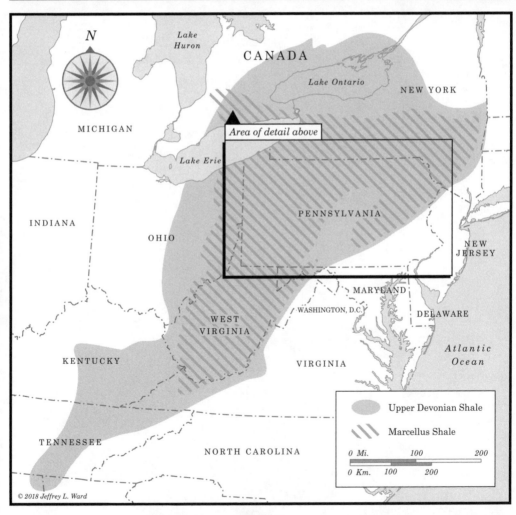

CONTENTS

PART II: BURDEN OF PROOF

PART III: THE RIGHT TO CLEAN AIR AND PURE WATER

AMITY

AND

PROSPERITY

A NOTE

The "Appalachian problem" doesn't seem to me to be political, economic, or social. I believe it is a spiritual problem and its name is greed.

—*OUR APPALACHIA: AN ORAL HISTORY*, EDITED BY
LAUREL SHACKELFORD AND BILL WEINBERG

Four hundred million years ago, dragonflies the size of crows drifted above a giant inland sea. The first sharks swam in its brackish currents, along with algae and other primordial creatures. As they died and sank to the seafloor, their remains petrified, turning into fossil fuel. Oil and gas were trapped in the silt that became a sedimentary rock called shale. Over the next sixty million years, as the sea receded and left behind freshwater bogs, the plants and trees that collapsed into them formed coal, the youngest of earth's fossil fuels. At first these layers of oil, gas, and coal piled tidily atop one another. Then, under tremendous heat and stress, they twisted and buckled, in some places rising to the surface, in others, remaining miles belowground.

In Appalachia, people have employed these fuels for centuries, albeit in unusual ways. There's evidence to suggest that as many as six hundred years ago, the Native inhabitants of what's now Western Pennsylvania dug pits along a riverbank to collect petroleum for the treatment of consumption and venereal disease. When George Washington rode westward before the Revolutionary War in 1753, he found that both coal and natural gas had already been discovered along the frontier. For the next hundred years, coal powered the young country's growth. Natural gas proved harder to harness. It leaked from pits that miners had dug for salt. Some towns figured out how to pipe gas to light streetlamps; others managed only to blow themselves up. In 1859, Colonel Edwin Drake struck oil in Western Pennsylvania. Pennsylvania became the birthplace of the U.S. oil industry—the world's first oil rush whooshed through the state and vanished by the 1870s. It wasn't that the oil was gone; the rest was simply too costly to reach.

America's answer to its energy needs has always been to dig deeper; the question was how. Over the past several decades, a technological innovation called hydraulic fracturing, or fracking, has allowed the extraction of the gas embedded in deep rock. Fracking frees fuel from shale by drilling a mile or more straight down into the earth and then out sideways for as much as another two miles. The straw that Daniel Day-Lewis so fiendishly described in *There Will Be Blood* no longer has to go straight into the milkshake. It can bend and turn in nearly any direction.

A decade ago, fracking kicked off a gas boom, which flooded parts of Appalachia with money. It also took a toll on those who lived where carbon was harvested. In March 2011, I attended a meeting of concerned farmers, who were also retired coal miners and steelworkers, at the airport in Morgantown, West Virginia. There, I met Stacey Haney, a nurse and single mother of two, who invited me to her eight-acre farm just over the border in southwestern Pennsylvania's Washington County. She and her children, Harley and Paige, fourteen and eleven, feared they were sick from exposure to a toxic industrial site next door to their home. All three had low levels of gas-related chemicals in their bodies, but Harley, who'd recently been diagnosed with arsenic poisoning, was the worst off.

When I went to see her the next day, Stacey drove me through the nearby towns of Amity and Prosperity, where her family had lived for 150 years, and around the countryside. Red and white drill rigs dotted the hillsides planted with timothy. Sandy access roads snaked through clover fields. Green condensate tanks shimmered in the distance. This was in the middle of the gas rush that spanned a decade from 2005 to 2015; there were five well sites within a mile of her home. It would be easy to cast the industrial incursion as a blight upon the bucolic, and to many it was. To others, however, the arrival of fracking was the solution to decades of decline.

Amity and Prosperity don't occupy a pristine landscape. The history of energy extraction is etched into Appalachian hollows. The wooden towers of oil wells have dotted Amity's goldenrod fields since 1885, derricks nodding in wild peppermint. Following the Civil War, with wool prices low, sheep farmers sold the rights to the coal under their farms. Pennsylvania's abundance of coal and iron, along with its network of rivers, made it an excellent place to produce steel. In 1875, Andrew Carnegie built the nation's largest steel mill along the Monongahela River, which propelled Pennsylvania to becoming the steel capital of the world.

Rural citizens lived alongside industry for generations, taking jobs and small payouts for mineral leases. Often, they acquired a sophisticated understanding of property and mineral rights, becoming well versed in the history and value of what lay beneath their feet. This arrangement also helped people remain on their land long after farming was profitable. Yet despite these small leases, which might provide free gas and a royalty of a few hundred dollars a year, most of the mineral profits went elsewhere. The wealth fled the land, leaving behind thousands of miles of incarnadine streams ruined by acid mine drainage, artificial mountains of slag heaps, and gutted coal patch towns. Company towns faced mass unemployment, along with the environmental and social problems industry left behind.

Exploiting energy often involves exploiting people. In Amity and Prosperity, as elsewhere, resource extraction has long fed a sense of marginalization and disgust, both with companies that undermine the land and with the urbanites who flick on lights without considering the miners who risk their lives to power them. Today, the fracking boom has reinforced these convictions. This time, a handful of people have made significant amounts of money. With more to lose, they've become still more distrustful of state and federal authorities and environmentalists—as well as of neighbors who speak against the industrial boom. As they see it, the common outsider view that Appalachians are victims of forces they don't understand is naïve and condescending. To them, opposing fracking is an ideological stance couched in a weak understanding of the actual technique and how it can be employed safely.

Split fifty-fifty between red and blue, Pennsylvania is the one purple state in which fracking has flourished. This has rendered the technique as much a political question as a practical one. Fracking has deepened the schism between Democrats and Republicans. It has also brought with it the promise of energy independence and injected much-needed cash into struggling places. Yet it has fractured communities, dividing those making money from those whose water, air, and health are threatened.

Stacey and her kids lost their land and a good part of their lives waging a battle against the oil and gas industry. For the past seven years, amid an ugly public fight, they allowed me to follow their family's intimate challenges—the loss of animals, the nights spent on the bathroom floor, and the travails of a sick kid who doesn't want to leave his basement room. They are among those paying the human cost of American energy.

PROLOGUE

TO THE IGNORANT MOTHERFUCKERS who keep breaking into my house: it's bad enough that my children and I have been homeless for 2 and a half years but now I have to deal with this. Your greediness has cost me over $35,000 in damages and the bank has put a forced insurance of $5000 on my mortgage, so as of jan 1, my mortgage payment goes up $500 a month. I hope you feel good about what you have done and I hope you know that the contamination in this house causes cancer, so keep coming back you fucking losers. I hope you rott with cancer!!! And when your spending all your scrap money I hope you think about what you are taking away from my children.

—A note Stacey Haney posted to the door of her abandoned farmhouse on November 3, 2013

PART 1

HOOPIES

1 | FAIR 2010

Most years at the Washington County Fair, Stacey Haney set up an animal salon outside her blue and white Coachman trailer. She and her younger sister, Shelly, would plug a blow-dryer into a generator and style their children's goats in preparation for the 4-H competition. This year, the salon seemed too much effort, so Stacey readied the animals at home. She'd spent the past two days up to her armpits in a blue kiddie pool of freezing water and Mane 'n Tail soap washing, clipping, and brushing two goats, two pigs, and four rabbits. Then, that August morning, she'd hauled them ten miles to the fairgrounds.

After registering the rabbits, she proceeded to Cowley's lemonade stand with her eleven-year-old daughter, Paige. Thirty miles southwest of Pittsburgh, the Washington County Fairground was composed of two worlds. The lower realm contained the Tilt-A-Whirl operated by strangers, roustabouts who arrived from elsewhere. (Stacey's son, Harley, who'd just turned fourteen, called it Carnyland.) The upper belonged to 4-H and agriculture—"ag"—types, many of whom, including Stacey's family, considered themselves Hoopies, an insider's name for the hill jacks or hillbillies who live in the borderlands of Pennsylvania, Ohio, and West Virginia where Appalachia begins.

These two worlds met midway up the ridge at Cowley's, where Stacey and Paige were waiting for lemonade when they spied two familiar figures trundling downhill from the horse barn. The square woman with frosted hair and the spare man with a snowy mane and a limp were Beth and John Voyles. They lived next door at Justa

Breeze, a fifteen-acre farm where they trained horses and bred high-end dogs. The two families shared a fence and a love of animals. Beth treated her boxers like children. She cooked them angel hair pasta, zucchini, and meatball sandwiches, and dressed them in tiny leather jackets, flight goggles, and scarves for professional photographs. She framed the photos and hung them around the ranch house where she'd lived with John for the past twenty-eight years.

Say what one might about the Voyles, over the past year and a half, they'd proven excellent neighbors. While Stacey, forty, juggled full-time shifts as a nurse in the recovery unit of Washington Hospital and finalized her divorce from Larry Haney, the Voyles kept a quiet eye on her place. Their daughter, Ashley, often brought her new boxer puppy, Cummins, down to distract Harley when he was sick at home. At twenty-two, Ashley still lived at home and raced horses profession-ally. She'd also been teaching Paige to ride since Paige was two.

As Beth and John approached, Stacey could see that mascara was running down Beth's ruddy face. Stacey guessed it was the muggy heat; the air at the fair was redolent with popcorn and musk, which mingled with the scent of baby shampoo from the Mane 'n Tail linger-ing on Stacey's arms. A rash blazed on Stacey's left arm, where it had been erupting on and off for months. Although she was a nurse, she couldn't determine its cause. She studied the welts, and when she looked up, Beth was in front of her, her face smeared with tears.

Cummins is dead, Beth said. Poisoned.

Stacey's head swam. In her mind, she scanned the farmhouses and trailers that wended their way from the top of the valley where she and Beth lived down McAdams Road to the base of the hollow called the Bottoms. She knew nearly everyone. Many families were bound by generations of helping one another farm and, more recently, survive the economic collapse of the past several decades.

No one would poison a puppy, she told Beth gently. Beth thought otherwise. The vet had told her that Cummins's insides had frozen up, she said, crystallized, as if he'd drunk antifreeze. The vet couldn't rule out cancer, either, but Beth suspected foul play. She also thought she knew where the poison had come from: she'd seen the dog drinking from a puddle of water left on the roadside after a truck came through to spray down dust earlier that summer. Wondering what the liquid was, she'd tried to follow with a glass Mason jar, but the driver stopped. Screeching his air brake on the steep dirt hill, he yelled at her to back away.

Later, Beth and Stacey would mark this conversation about Cummins's death as the beginning of solving a mystery. But at the time, Stacey was sweaty and distracted. Paige stood by, crunching the sugar at the bottom of her cup. Stacey hugged Beth and watched her continue down the hill with John toward the field of neon. She wanted to get back to the trailer to check on Harley. She dreaded telling him the news.

Harley loved Cummins, and he was so sick. Over the past year and a half, his stomach had churned with an undiagnosed illness. He'd missed most of seventh grade sitting at home in a recliner watching his dog, Hunter, play with Cummins on the living room floor. Harley had gone from being a shy and handsome basketball player who shambled easily through life to a listless stick figure. At six foot one, he was 127 pounds. A few days earlier, when Harley weighed his goat, Boots, for competition at the fair, she'd weighed nearly the same as her master.

Stacey hoped that this year's 4-H competition would lift his spirits. She and Harley had ambitions for Boots. Instead of being skittish, as most goats are, Boots was friendly. Harley'd spent every day with her since he was home, which may have been why the brown and white Boer goat enjoyed people. When Harley went up to the Haneys' ramshackle barn to feed her, Boots slung her hooves over the wooden pen to lick his face.

With Boots, Harley had a chance at winning a large prize, maybe Grand Champion Showmanship, Stacey thought. She loved the fair and spent most of the year preparing for it, phoning in to goat auctions through the winter and trying to make sure she got her kids the best goats and pigs she could for $150 to $200, which wasn't a lot. Other people spent $600, and she'd heard of a family that paid $5,000 for a pig they hoped would win Grand Champion.

"Even if I could spend five thousand dollars on a pig, I wouldn't," she said. It was flashy and wrong, and went against the spirit of the 212-year-old fair, which had helped to pattern their family's lives for three generations. Her father, Larry Hillberry, whom everyone called Pappy, grew up poor on a small dairy farm nearby. He'd attended but didn't show animals. "We couldn't afford to. We ate them all," he told his grandchildren. Pappy was twenty when he went to work in the local steel mill and then left for Vietnam, returning two years later with feet too riddled with warts from wet combat boots to stand at the steel mill's assembly line. Forced by the condition of his feet to take a few months away from the mill, he came courting at the fair. He played bingo, winning a set of blue-trimmed Corningware dishes for his soon-to-be bride, Linda. A year and a half later, on November 18, 1969, Stacey was born.

By the time Stacey and Shelly, a whip-smart hellion who came along two years later, were old enough to participate in 4-H, the steel mill where Pappy worked was shuttered. With Pappy out of work, the family scraped by. He took every odd job he could find, chopping wood and putting up hay, and Linda, along with a generation of Amity women, left the house to work as a housekeeper, but it still cost too much to let the girls show animals.

Stacey was thirteen when she went to work. She mucked stalls and sold ice cream at the family end of the bar in the Amity Tavern. As soon as she could drive, she got a job as a seamstress in a men's store in the Washington Mall. At seventeen, Stacey graduated from high school and left home for good on a full scholarship to beauty school. It didn't hurt that she was striking, with large blue eyes below a thicket of black lashes. At nineteen, she was married and cutting hair at Some-place Else Salon, where her elderly clients encouraged her to go back to school and join the throngs of young women entering the health care industry. This wasn't just Stacey's personal narrative; this was the story of the region. With steel gone and coal on its way out, communities were turning to "meds and eds," hospitals and universities, now the largest employers. As a nurse, Stacey, in scrubs, would have a demanding but stable place in the sterile halls of a postindustrial landscape.

With two small kids, Stacey preferred cutting hair to the midnight shifts, but steady work as a nurse allowed her to give Harley and Paige the middle-class trappings her parents couldn't afford, the fair first among them. Paige and Harley'd been showing at the fair since they could walk. At five, Harley won first place with his eggs. As the kids grew, their full involvement in country activities also marked a return to Stacey's vision of her family's history. She wanted farming to be once again a way of life rather than the expensive hobby it had become.

As the goat show began, Stacey stood by the ring's steel railing and waited for Harley's number to be called. She scanned the crowd. In front of the silver bleachers, filled with the usual shaggy-haired ag folk in Carhartt overalls and trucker hats, she spied a small group of clean-cut outsiders wearing blue polo shirts that read RANGE RESOURCES. They sat close to the ring in red plastic chairs. Stacey knew who they were: gas executives had recently arrived in the region with the shale gas boom.

In 2004, Range Resources, which was based in Fort Worth, Texas, had successfully fracked the first well in Washington County. Now, six years later, the billion-dollar company was the largest producer of natural gas in the southwestern part of the state. *Forbes* magazine was calling Range "the King of the Marcellus," the gas-rich shale deposit that stretched from New York State to West Virginia and contained enough natural gas to power America for a decade. Range's stock price reflected its success in the Marcellus, rising from just under seven dollars in 2004 to fifty dollars in 2010, as the natural gas boom approached its apex. With its sudden bounty and low price, natural gas was a great bet for the future. It also burned cleaner than coal, releasing

less carbon into the atmosphere. And soon, Pennsylvania would be pro-
ducing one-fifth of America's supply.

The Washington County Fair provided a place where companies
could speak directly to farmers whose mineral rights they coveted.
Range Resources began to attend in 2006, thanks to Ray Walker,
who'd graduated with a degree in agricultural engineering from Texas
A&M and now headed the company's new Marcellus Division. Walker
was known to be a man of principle. He seemed less concerned with
Range's public appearance than with simply enjoying the fair. He also
bid on pigs and goats.

Most locals saw the gas company's involvement in the fair as a gesture of neighborliness. They cheered industry's return. It marked a new
era in a long-depressed place, and the lease money Range and other
companies paid helped people replace roofs, build fences, and hang on
to their farms instead of being forced to sell to developers. Corporations were also generously filling the pockets of Washington County's
kids, including Harley Haney's, buying up their animals at auction.

Stacey was skeptical. It made her uneasy to watch these corporations come in and toss money around, and she suspected that Range
Resources wanted something in return for its mini water bottles and
freebie seat cushions. Stacey was convinced that the animals that
fetched the highest prices tended to belong to the children of large
landowners whose farms were most attractive to oil and gas companies
looking to sign leases. Stacey had signed her own lease with Range
two years earlier, but that hadn't turned out like she'd planned.

When Harley stepped into the ring with Boots, however, Stacey's
irritation vanished. In his red shirt and dark jeans, Harley led his
goat on a short leash without having to tug her along like the rest
of the kids did. The goat heeled as a dog does and then stood on
command as Harley set her feet squarely in the sawdust. When the
judge took her back leg in his hand to examine her, she stayed still.
Harley smiled down at her and at the judges, not the ear-to-ear grin
of the boy showman, but the self-conscious half smile of a young man

proud of his animal. Together, he and Boots won Grand Champion Showmanship.

The 2010 fair marked a good year for the family. Pepsi and Phantom, two of Paige's rabbits, tied for second place. Paige also took second in the junior SPAM-cooking contest with her southwestern-themed Mexi-SPAM Mac and Cheese. Pappy won a blue ribbon for his butternuts for the second year running.

Packing up the trailer at the week's end, Stacey was relieved. The fair had gone better than she'd dared to hope. In addition to the kids' wins, there was the successful visit by her friend Chris Rush. Chris, who was six years younger, had grown up in Amity. Although they'd been dating nearly a year, she wouldn't call him her boyfriend until she was sure that he was going to stick. At the fair, he'd shown up for Harley's and Paige's events. In his reticent way, he offered support by just being there, and that pleased her. She was also so happy with Boots and the rabbits that she decided not to sell them. Although, as a Boer, Boots was raised for meat, Stacey now wanted to breed her with their neighbor's billy. Selling the babies would bring in some helpful cash.

After five nights in the camper away from home, Harley had improved in both body and spirit. Striding around the fair with ease, he was still a scarecrow, but a happy one. He clearly felt better, and Stacey hoped that she was watching his illness recede for the last time, returning him to the boy he'd been before he got sick.

2 | WHEN THE BOOM BEGAN

Stacey had long wanted to replace the battered lean-to that housed their animals, exposing them to wind, rain, and snow. But on the six hundred dollars she made a week as a nurse, the dream barn remained a dream. When oil and gas leases began to appear in people's mailboxes in the early 2000s, she thought that this lease money might finally pay for it. No one knew what these new leases would yield, but at work at Washington Hospital, her fellow nurses told stories—rural myths really—about this or that elderly hayseed with hundreds of rocky acres who'd suddenly become a shaleionaire.

Talk of who was cashing in and how they were doing it became part of daily chatter in the recovery unit, a fourteen-bed open bay hung with pale green curtains, which Stacey and four other nurses on duty kept open unless they were emptying bedpans or changing a catheter. Patients arrived directly from the operating room, asleep or emerging from sedation's murky depths. The nurses' main job was to make sure that no one stroked out, which was rare. More often they woke up nauseous and confused. Clad in scrubs of blue bottoms and white V-necks, the nurses moved among their patients as machines monitored vitals automatically. Every fifteen minutes, the machines issued a series of bleeps measuring blood pressure.

Stacey was happiest working a shift alongside her best friend, Kelly Tush, a soft-spoken redhead. Both liked their jobs, although they complained about the long hours. A shift could last from twelve to twenty-three hours straight with no breaks. Still, even when exhausted,

Stacey possessed a natural tenderness with patients, an empathy with the infirm. There was something about a vulnerable person lying in bed, often a neighbor or someone she knew, that elicited a calm in her. She was also that way with animals and small children.

The nurses kept their voices low until they were in the break room, where amid the lingering aroma of urine, bleach, and blood they ate lunch and talked about whatever was going on in their lives. Stacey often entertained her colleagues with tales of farm life, which involved the latest antics of her animals—stories of her donkey, Bob, who kept breaking down the fence between her place and the Voyles' farm next door. Bob was in love with their high-class mare, Doll, and kept trying to mount her.

Since Stacey lived farther out in the country than most, where leasing was at its peak, she was the first with the chance to sign. When the shiny SUVs of the land men who negotiated the leases appeared on the back roads of Amity, Stacey plotted a course of action. In 2004, as the buzz of Range's groundbreaking success with fracking in Washington County trickled down to its residents, few locals understood what fracking was, or what these leases entailed. On signing, people could earn a bonus from five dollars to seven thousand dollars an acre; there were few rules governing such deals, and Stacey, with eight acres, was hoping for the going price of a thousand dollars each, nearly the nine-thousand-dollar price tag of the barn she wanted to build.

Yet signing a lease wasn't just about money. Stacey also saw it as her patriotic duty. She, like many Americans, was tired of the United States sending troops to fight wars for oil. Her father had served the country's dubious needs in Vietnam, and she saw the war in Iraq as more of the same. Once again, poor Americans were fighting on behalf of the rich. "My dad lived through Vietnam," she said. "I'm totally about getting soldiers home, and not relying on foreign oil."

It wasn't just about ending wars. Relying on domestic energy could also help restore America's place in the world, possibly returning

Amity to its former standing. She'd heard the news reports about how natural gas could revive the region's industries, and thought of her father and those of his generation who'd lost their jobs. And although Stacey had her doubts about the full-throated corporate messaging, this had little effect on her desire to sign a lease. These new leases sprang from the ground—a rare win in a place that had been losing for generations.

She also hoped that signing a gas lease might block the coal company from undermining her farm. She, like others, didn't want Amity to become like Prosperity, the village seven miles away where a kind of industrial coal mining called "long wall" had cost many farm families their water by damaging the aquifer below their land. In response, the coal company bought up people's property and some residents left. Once empty, the houses were stripped of their copper wiring by scrap metal thieves, which made them unlivable and risked turning Prosperity into yet another coal patch ghost town. Maybe, Stacey and others thought, the gas companies would trump the coal operators, and drilling would stave off mining. The unknown realities of drilling for shale gas seemed preferable to the familiar toll coal mining levied.

Stacey first asked her neighbor Rick Baker for advice on leasing back in 2006. He lived a mile from the Haneys' farmhouse and taught Harley guitar. He also cut an unusual figure in Amity: a mild-mannered church-choir director who wore wire-rimmed glasses, he was a registered Democrat. As he grew older, he grew more committed to progressive politics, mostly around social issues, including gay and transgender rights. Historically, being a Democrat here wasn't unusual, due to the legacy of the coal and steel unions that once held sway. Over time, however, many union members had moved to the right out of hostility to the federal government, which they felt was both failing them and invading their lives. Baker was one of the few he knew who voted for Obama.

Although Baker had some concerns about the environmental hazards related to fracking, he was pro-gas. As he saw it, the benefits to the country outweighed the potential personal costs of contaminated water. Every industrial practice came with risks. "If we don't take chances we're not going to continue to be the greatest nation in the world," he said. He also believed it was time for landowners to share some of the risks that coal miners had borne for centuries. Those who campaigned against fracking were mostly environmentalists who had no experience with extractive industry and stood to make nothing off of leases. They knew nothing of what it meant to live atop a coal mine, of poisoned streams, of how a coal company's bankruptcy devastated a town, of how a farm could lose its water when the coal was mined from beneath it.

Baker also had other reasons to favor fracking over his region's legacy of coal: he stood to make hundreds of thousands by leasing his land for a compressor station. The station would place the gas under enough pressure that it could hurtle another fifty to one hundred miles toward the East Coast markets of Philadelphia and New York City. From the start, Baker had enjoyed good relations with Range Resources. He found the employees who came out to survey his pastures to be up-front, and liked it when the higher-ups took him into confidence regarding their plans. For a time, the money would change the lives of both Baker and his wife, Melinda, a housekeeper. Melinda was able to stop cleaning houses. Baker, like others, wasn't going to rush off to Florida with a big wad of cash. He would stay on the land, and continue to live his steady life, giving guitar lessons.

He was confident enough in Range Resources that when the company approached him to ask if he'd make a television commercial for their "My Range Resources" campaign, Baker said yes. On radio and television ads, Range wanted to show local people enjoying the outdoors while talking about the benefits of leasing. In his spot, Baker wandered his land against a backdrop of his own guitar picking. For the ad, he was paid two hundred dollars. Baker was bright: he knew the fee was a pittance. But he loved composing, and hearing his music on TV was enough to make him happy. There were others, far more vociferous than Baker, who made public salvos on the company's behalf. "Farmers around here couldn't afford a tractor," Mary Dalbo, a Range leaseholder said in her "My Range Resources" advertisement. "Now since they leased their farm to Range Resources, they're driving tractors with air-conditions. It's wonderful they got this opportunity, because, believe me, them boys worked hard just to survive."

Baker was happy to share what he was learning from Range with Stacey. Through Baker and others, Stacey learned that the companies were looking for larger lots to make it easier for them to consolidate leases and infrastructure. The bigger the plot, the more the company might be willing to pay per acre. So one summer evening in 2006, Stacey drove up and down her dirt road to speak to her neighbors. She stopped next door at Justa Breeze to see Beth and John Voyles. Outside their ranch house, a miniature white picket fence surrounded a life-sized statue of a boxer. The dog sat beneath a sign that read BOXER HEAVEN. The Voyles didn't intend the rock garden to look like a cemetery, just a tribute to the dogs they considered family. Beth moved around a lot as a child; her father was in the military, and she'd originally come to Amity to visit her grandmother's farm. Now she stayed put, leaving only for horse shows, veterinary appointments, and trips to the Giant Eagle supermarket in nearby Washington. Beth loved to cook, and she usually had a stew pot bubbling on the stove.

When Stacey pulled into the drive, Beth, surrounded by a swarm of slobbering boxers, came out of the basement and greeted her warmly. Stacey explained the virtues of signing a lease together: more money and greater influence than going it alone with a corporation. To Beth, this sounded like a smart idea. She went out to the garage, where her husband liked to retreat to the quiet of a chaise longue. The farm had been in his family for seventy-five years, and this was his refuge. He sat beneath a ceiling fan and next to an antique Ford tractor, which he'd restored himself and painted with the confederate flag. John said yes, as he always did. Whatever Beth wanted was fine by him. A kind and taciturn man, he'd lost his leg at seventeen when he was hit by a car on the way to school. Then he'd worked as a mechanic for seventeen years before getting hurt on the job. Between this incident and a fight with Beth's half sister, the Voyles had been involved in two personal-injury suits, which gave them a reputation for being litigious. The story was that the Voyles were always suing somebody, but this story, like another about Beth shooting a man in California, was untrue, nothing more than country prattle. John Voyles attempted to avoid such gossip, preferring the solitude of his farm, his family, and his bees.

"Keep to myself kind of," he said later under oath. "And that ain't working too good."

To continue their discussion about signing a lease together, Stacey invited Beth and John down to her farmhouse one evening. She baked sugar cookies for John Voyles, his favorite. Over cookies and coffee, Stacey, the Voyles, and Derrick Puskarich, who lived with his wife down McAdams, discussed the advantages and possible pitfalls of selling off the right to the gas beneath their property.

Stacey was most concerned about protecting the quality of their water, since she'd grown up without any. Her family had relied on rainwater to fill a giant cistern outside their house, or they hauled water. This involved loading a huge plastic tank called a water buffalo onto the bed of a pickup and driving ten miles to fill it at the nearest water station, in a village called Ruff Creek. She hated hauling water; growing up, it had symbolized all her family lacked. When Stacey went looking for a home of her own, the quality of its well and an abundance of clean water had been her top priorities. In any lease she was going to sign, she wanted to include a clause that guaranteed that if anything went wrong with their wells, the company would pay to fix the problem and to supply them water. The Voyles and Puskarichs agreed. So Stacey called Range Resources to discuss the group lease and the clause she wanted to include. After she went back and forth on the phone with Range's leasing agents, the company drafted the following provision, which Stacey approved: *Lessee, at Lessee's expense, agrees to provide Lessor with potable water until such time as Lessor's water source has been repaired or replaced with a source of substantially similar quality.*

On December 30, 2008, their lease was ready to sign. That day, the families planned to meet together at Range's corporate offices in Southpointe, the industrial park twenty miles north of Amity, which served as headquarters to nearly every major oil and gas player in the region. Beth and Stacey wanted to start in the morning, so they'd have plenty of time to read the lease carefully. Instead, they were given an appointment for late afternoon, which miffed Beth. She didn't think they could review legal documents at 4:30 p.m. if the office closed at 5:00. When the families arrived, both Stacey and Beth felt they were being rushed through the stack of documents on the conference table between them. They'd risked not hiring an attorney to keep their costs low, and now Stacey regretted it.

Stacey glanced at Beth to assess whether she looked uneasy too. She wanted to speak to Beth privately, but there were Range employees in the room. She didn't want to seem rude, so she kept quiet and turned the pages of her lease looking for the water clause. It was missing. When she asked, however, an employee went to fetch a copy of the addendum.

Across the table, Beth also felt they were being treated shabbily. There was no notary there to countersign in front of them, which Beth thought was another indication that the company took them for bumpkins. She considered putting up a fuss and not signing, but there was a risk. All of their neighbors were signing leases, and she was concerned that their little collective plot might get left out. If Range could get what they wanted from others, the company might not need their land. So, reluctantly, she signed. By 5:00 p.m., they were back in the freezing parking lot, unsure they'd done the right thing.

Weeks later, when their fully executed leases arrived in the mail, Beth and Stacey discovered another problem. Now that they had the chance to comb the fine print, they realized the royalty rate in the contract was lower than the one they'd remembered discussing on the phone with the company before signing. According to the contract, they were going to receive a 15 percent royalty rate only after the company had deducted a list of expenses the two women didn't understand. "It's so complicated and confusing, you just rely on them that they're doing the right thing," Stacey said. She and Beth wondered if the hasty appointment and the practice of rushing them through might have been a tactic for screwing them out of percentage points.

Beth told Stacey she thought they were dealing with "crooks." She'd anticipated receiving a signing bonus of nearly fifteen thousand dollars for their acreage, but it arrived in installments. "They told me some blame excuse," as Beth put it. She often misused words— mistakenly substituting one that fit even better. Meanwhile, Stacey's dream barn would have to wait. Her eight-thousand-dollar signing bonus was also divided. After taxes, each payment dwindled to about half; then she had to split that with her ex-husband, Larry. And there always seemed to be more pressing needs for that last few hundred dollars than putting it aside for the barn.

By the spring of 2009, a few months after signing the lease, Stacey's initial suspicions gave way to open frustration. Next door at Justa Breeze, John Voyles had taken to counting the number of trucks that rattled by in a day. He told Stacey that he'd counted 250 trucks passing her farmhouse, which sat 30 feet from the narrow dirt track of

McAdams. It was like living next to a highway. Stacey couldn't believe how much dust the trucks kicked up. The dirt, grimy with diesel oil, settled on the glass hummingbird feeder on the wraparound porch that Stacey kept filled with sugar water. It coated the wooden railings until, by week's end, it was half an inch thick. The dust gathered on the relics of childhood in the front yard: a tire swing, a trampoline, and an abandoned red tricycle. Stacey had passed her love of little children on to Harley and Paige, so they kept toys on hand for young visitors even after Harley and Paige had outgrown them.

The grime caught in their throats. The goats Harley and Paige raised for the fair began to cough so much that Stacey feared they might not make weight. Harley, Paige, and Stacey coughed too. Their noses ran and their eyes watered. Although Stacey was annoyed, she figured this was the temporary price one paid for progress. They had no choice but to tough it out, as inside, the judder of trucks shook the house, tilting the Sears baby pictures of Harley and Paige, fat-legged and grinning, hanging on the living room wall and rolling Stacey's antique sock darner off of the shelf and onto the rag rug.

The foundation of Stacey's house cracked. Vibrations rutted the road with industrial-strength potholes that punctured nine tires on her gold Pontiac G6 and cracked a rim. In her deepening ire, she wasn't alone; in Amity, and all over the drilling epicenter of Western Pennsylvania, the weight and number of trucks destroyed bridges and roads, imperiling some small farms and dairies that struggled to get their milk to market. And according to state records, nearly half of the industry's trucks were in such poor condition they had to be removed from use. It wasn't all a disaster. The companies also paved back roads, which pleased inhabitants, issuing bonds to finance the repairs. But the bonds covered only 10 to 20 percent of the cost, so companies ended up passing most of the bill on to the county and state, which paid between $8.5 million and $39 million for repairs in 2011 alone. This was one of the hidden ways in which the industry transferred its costs to the public.

And small towns were powerless to stop the traffic. "These water trucks would come through town in a caravan and one would run a red light, so they all would," Blair Zimmerman, a former mayor in the neighboring county of Greene, told me. "They'd go up on sidewalks, they'd drive through residential areas. At three a.m., one traveled at seventy miles an hour right through town." Incensed, Zimmerman called for a meeting with the gas companies. "I want money to fix my sidewalks, my streets," he recalled telling them. "I want to hire more police officers for arresting your butts for being where you shouldn't be." The corporate representatives paid little attention, he said. "Environmentally, who's going to clean this up when they leave?" he asked. "Some of these farmers become millionaires, but the majority of the costs are going to be passed on to other people."

As one of these people, Stacey was dealing with the damage to her car from ruined roads. To register her complaints, Stacey called Range Resources and the company sent out Tony Berardi, an affable land man whose job it was to negotiate between the company and landowners like Stacey—"to put out fires," he told me. Berardi prided himself in being straight with people: "My motto is, I'm going to show you the ugly, the bad, and the good in that order." At first, Stacey appreciated his honesty and he appreciated Stacey. He figured that as a single mom she worked hard to keep things together. And Berardi believed he was helping people like Stacey who lived "on the front lines" of the gas rush. That was the term for such places, "frontline communities," as if they were at war with extractive industries. "Aside from what the common people think, that these companies are out to screw them, they're not," he told me. Stacey and her neighbors up and down McAdams took to calling men like Berardi "yes men." Their eagerness to please was often little more than hot air, they thought. Yet Berardi did manage to get Stacey some money from Range: $1,500 for dust cleanup and car repairs, and $650 for doors in the house that wouldn't shut anymore.

Range didn't pay to repair the farmhouse foundation; Stacey couldn't prove the trucks had caused the damage and she couldn't afford to do anything about it. It was a matter of hanging on, and that required muscles she was accustomed to using.

3 | THE MESS NEXT DOOR

The trucks were only the first sign of trouble. After they passed Stacey's house, then Beth and John's, they made a sharp right and lumbered up a steep hill belonging to their neighbor, a cattle farmer named Ron Yeager. Sallow, with a face as wrinkled as a dried tobacco leaf, Yeager could often be spotted slouched over the black wheel of his green John Deere, riding up and down his hilly alfalfa fields, a trucker hat pulled low over his eyes.

Ron Yeager was as shrewd a businessman as anyone in Washington County. After retiring from Verizon, he'd taken to working hard on his farm, leaving home early in the morning with a packed lunch, returning in the late afternoon. He was constantly repairing his high-tensile wire fence, which shined on his hills. Before fracking arrived, and plunged his hillside into controversy, he'd clear-cut old-growth trees on his farm—trees "as old as America," one of the farm's former owners lamented. The land had belonged to her family since at least 1804, and its woods had been full of cherry, oak, and walnut.

Yeager's farm sat atop the Ten Mile Creek watershed, the source of sixteen underground springs that flowed downhill into a network of streams. These streams eventually ran into the Ohio River basin, which supplies drinking water to 8 percent of Americans. The Yeagers drank water from these springs. So did the Angus they raised for human consumption.

Ron Yeager was considered to be among the wealthier and larger landowners who'd signed leases. Neither Stacey nor Beth knew what he'd been paid. Neighbors didn't tend to discuss the size of their sudden windfalls, since people often felt they were competing with one another to wangle the highest price they could from the handful of companies staking mineral leases. This newfound secrecy strained ties that stretched back generations.

The leasing money could be decent, but the real money lay in industrial infrastructure, in allowing companies to drill wells and store waste on one's land. With the promise of abundant shale gas deep below, the Yeagers' land was highly desirable, and Range wanted to drill at least three wells, in addition to digging a waste pit and pond on their farm. As a result, those alfalfa fields took on a new identity. The property came to be known as "the Yeager site"—a subject of debate over which Ron and Sharon Yeager had little control. This was the case despite the Yeagers' fervent desire to have their private lives remain out of the public limelight. When I asked to speak to them over the course of seven years of reporting, driving past their farm and stopping on occasion, or running into them at local events, they responded with a polite but adamant no.

Unfortunately for the Yeagers, a litany of troubles small and large, unavoidably affecting the lives of their neighbors, arrived along with the industrial site. Even if the Yeagers never sought or expected any of the controversy, and were not directly responsible for the many adverse impacts, their name was inevitably linked to the local fracking debate. It was the Yeager site—though not the Yeagers—that became a subject of great and ongoing public concern.

Beginning in 2009, workers sheared off the top of the Yeagers' hill to build a sandy three-acre lot where they could park trucks and drill the gas wells. It was common practice to remove the top of a hill: this was the easiest way to make a flat space for a well pad. Then Range and its subcontractors began to dig two waste pits deep into the ground. The first was much smaller, slightly larger than an Olympic-size swimming pool. This pit was designed to hold the rocks and mud that came off the drill bit, like pencil shavings, as it bore down more than a mile. Called a drill cuttings pit, it was insulated with a single plastic liner, which looked like an oversized garbage bag. The larger, at a little more than four acres, was really a pond. It could hold thirty Olympic pools' worth of flowback, the potentially toxic sludge that returned to the surface after the frack. The pond, called a centralized impoundment, had much more traffic than most, since the fluid within it was trucked in and out to other sites to frack elsewhere. When viewed from above, the waste pond was half as large as Stacey's farm, which sat a quarter of a mile below.

On September 11, 2009, a seventy-five-foot air rig began to drill the vertical leg of the first well. Range was going to conduct what a petroleum engineer called "major science projects"—running diagnostics on an unexplored layer of shale. This layer, the Upper Devonian, sat three to five hundred feet above the much better known Marcellus. Since it was younger and closer to the surface, its ocean of gas could prove cheaper and easier to reach.

As the vertical rig worked its way down, lengths of pipe were inserted into the earth and cemented into place. Yet some of the cement intended to secure the casing was lost in the earth. Then, a second, bigger rig 175 feet high drilled the horizontals. These kicked out sideways and ran for another mile. Three months later, the frack began. Range's subcontractors pumped a total of 3,343,986 gallons of water and chemicals into the perforated pipe. Some of the chemicals were as harmless as soap; others carried greater risks. These included ethylene glycol, a neurotoxin, and elements of BTEX, the shorthand for benzene, toluene, ethylbenzene, and xylene. Employing pressure approaching a shotgun blast, they drove this fluid, along with a total of 4,014,729 pounds of clay pellets, downhole to crack the shale.

Once the pressure and fluid splintered the rock, the clay pellets propped open the new fissures so that gas could flow up to the surface. But gas wasn't the only thing that rose: 10 to 40 percent of the water and chemicals used in the frack returned too, as did radioactive materials, both natural and synthetic, and bacteria that hadn't seen daylight since the giant dragonflies roamed the earth. The larger waste pond wasn't yet finished. So the operators pumped this flowback into the smaller pit, which contained only that single liner. Within months, there were indications of trouble in the smaller pit. The Yeagers' grass was dying.

One day in March 2010, three months after the frack, Ron Yeager caught a worker known as a mud man standing next to sludge seeping out of the hillside. He asked what the mud man was doing as he watched him pump the seep back into the pit.

Down the hill, during that month of March 2010, Harley was ill. For much of his seventh-grade year, he'd been waking up sick to his stomach, stricken with diarrhea. Because of his stomach pains and the canker sores that kept appearing in his mouth, he didn't want to eat. To coax him, Stacey cooked his favorite foods, chicken and stuffed shells, grilled cheese. Still, he only picked at meals. Finally, he'd missed so much of seventh grade that she enrolled him in a home-bound program. Once a week a teacher came to the house with his homework. Stacey'd tried everything she'd learned over twenty-three years of nursing to figure out what was wrong. They'd made trips to Children's Hospital in Pittsburgh and the ER at Washington Hospital, where she worked. Harley was tested for appendicitis, Crohn's disease, irritable bowel syndrome, cat scratch fever (after one of the Haneys' three cats, Cheyenne, scratched his lip), Rocky Mountain spotted fever, mononucleosis, swine flu. All came back negative.

Then one March night, he woke calling for his mom. Stacey struggled awake and felt by the bed for her crutches. She was recovering from routine surgery for a cut on the bottom of her foot. (She'd jumped off of Harley's top bunk and sliced a tendon on a glass jar.) Hobbling to the bathroom, she found him crumpled on the floor. Sweat had darkened his chestnut hair, and in the quarter-light near dawn, his pupils were so large his eyes looked black. She crouched on the floor and tried to comfort him, then called Chris for help. She didn't need to tell him what had happened—Harley'd been sick so many times. Within twenty minutes, Chris had arrived, and he scooped Harley into his arms and slid him into the Pontiac's back seat.

Stacey, in pajamas, climbed into the driver's seat and hauled down the hollow toward Washington Hospital. In the ER waiting room, Harley couldn't lift his head out of her lap. Admitted for severely sensitive bowels, he was confused and disoriented, his lymph nodes extremely swollen. He spent six days in the hospital, so gravely ill that his dad paid an unusual visit. Larry looked down at his son, gray and drawn, with concern. He lived only a few miles away, in the town of Washington, but he and Stacey weren't on speaking terms, so he vanished as quickly as he appeared. Harley was too sick to notice. The doctors found that his liver enzymes were elevated and kidney function was off. His liver didn't look inflamed on ultrasound, however. Maybe it was celiac. Stacey started buying gluten-free.

Meanwhile, her foot refused to heal. Since her nursing job required twelve-hour shifts on her feet, she had to stay home, parked on a couch. Slumped next to Harley, she felt like she was coming down with a milder version of whatever he had. She abandoned the daily battle against the dust from the ongoing truck traffic. Even in winter, with the windows closed, grime crept in the house. Some days she could feel its grit in her teeth.

One late-winter day, Beth called. Bob the amorous donkey had broken through the fence and was up at Justa Breeze again. Bob's escapades were a rare point of contention between Stacey and Beth. In his perennial efforts to mount Doll, Bob risked impregnating the valuable quarter horse.

Stacey apologized and said she'd be right up. Still on crutches, she hobbled up the ridge through the snow, cursing Bob. His antics were more than she could handle. Bob mounted everything, even a friend's goat once, which frightened Paige. She asked her mother if Bob was "a sex offender."

Finally, Stacey decided she had to geld Bob. Since she wasn't working, she didn't have the hundred dollars to pay for a vet to do it, so she found a farmer who would castrate Bob for twenty-five. The procedure didn't go as she hoped. There was so much blood that Stacey raced home towing Bob in the horse trailer as fast as she could, hoping her speed and the cold air might stanch the bleeding. In the end, however, Bob healed so well that he still snuck up to Justa Breeze. He didn't seem to realize what he'd lost.

Over the rest of that winter and early spring of 2010, the trucks kept coming. Stacey finally got off the couch and made it back to work, but Harley stayed parked in the recliner as the school year drew to a close. By June 2010, the dust on the porch was so thick Stacey thought she'd have to cancel the kids' joint eleventh and fourteenth birthday parties. Born nearly three years apart, Harley and Paige shared a party every year. Stacey invited as many children as she knew, hosting horse rides on the thirty-five-year-old Duchess and filling water balloons, which were a rare luxury thanks to their abundant well. She even fashioned a homemade contraption she called a redneck Slip 'N Slide, rigged from a tarp, dish soap, and a hose.

But she couldn't host the party in the midst of the dust bowl, so she called Tony Berardi to ask if the company might water the dirt road, maybe even cut down on the traffic for a week or so before the party. The trucks thinned. The dust settled. The party was a success, and Harley, now fourteen, was thrilled with his 154-piece Craftsman tool set, and even more so with his new guitar. Watching him fiddle with the strings, Stacey thought maybe he was ready to start up lessons with Baker again. On that June day, with the farm's air clear like it used to be, a return to life before drilling seemed possible.

But a few weeks later, in July, a stench began wafting over Beth's and Stacey's farms. They weren't sure if the sewage odor was rising from their pipes or descending the hill from behind the high fence. Sometimes it seemed to be coming through the plumbing. The stink mortified Stacey. After she or the kids took a shower, she sprayed the entire house with Febreze, especially on weekends when Chris was around.

One afternoon in August, Stacey was out by the goats' kiddie pool when she caught a whiff of the rank stink drifting down the hill. Her eyes began to water and her nose burned. It was the kind of fugitive scent that made Stacey feel paranoid and alone. Later, they learned that one Range employee was calling it "shitty beef jerky." She went inside to phone Beth and ask if she smelled it.

Beth also smelled it, and knew what it was. For months, Beth had been phoning the state Department of Environmental Protection to register complaints about the Yeager site. Finally, in August, she'd received a call from Vince Yantko, a water quality supervisor at the DEP. He explained that the larger waste pond on the hilltop, now filled with the sludge used in fracking, had gone septic, like an infected wound. A bacterial outbreak was off-gassing hydrogen sulfide, a colorless gas. Open-air waste ponds were already of mounting concern to landowners, to responsible drillers, and to the DEP.

This was a problem.

Beth and Stacey didn't know that some companies avoided using the shoddy ponds, nor did they know the potential health effects of hydrogen sulfide gas. According to Beth, the DEP told her only that hydrogen sulfide was naturally occurring. But "naturally occurring" didn't mean harmless, as she and Stacey would soon learn. Low levels of exposure to hydrogen sulfide inflamed the eyes and could cause depression; high levels could be lethal, especially in children. She and Beth weren't the only ones to complain about smells. Later a neighbor over the valley on Headley Road called to say that her young child was throwing up from one.

Stacey went back outside and kept clipping Boots in preparation for the coming fair. Later, she and Beth would learn that they were being exposed to more than hydrogen sulfide. Up at the waste pond, workers in hazmat suits and respirators were applying 819 pounds of a liquid carcinogen and biocide to the sludge in an effort to control the outbreak, while just hundreds of feet away, the women worked outside in T-shirts. At much higher concentrations, the biocide, named Acrolein, was used to make chemical weapons.

4 | ARSENIP

From the basement, Chris called up to Stacey in the kitchen. He'd gone downstairs to change the water filter on her well, and wanted her to see what he'd found. The silver filter was coated with sludge. The hot water heater was also full of the stuff. The sludge crept into the dishwater, soiling her dishes, and water ran black from the tap.

She and the kids had just returned from the 2010 fair awash in pride bred by Boots's big win. She'd hoped that Harley's victory would carry him happily back to school for eighth grade. They'd been absent from the house for two weeks: one at the fair, a second camping with her sister's family in Emporium, Pennsylvania. Away from the dust and odors, Harley had continued to improve. Stacey had felt better too, a sudden surge of well-being brought about by relief, and maybe also by falling in love.

But the black water ended that immediately. She called Range Resources, and instead of sending out Tony Berardi, who said he'd been pulled off her case when her complaints grew more serious, the company sent a young man so soft-spoken and polite he seemed almost afraid to speak to her. By the time he arrived, the sediment had acquired a smell worse than sewage—rotting sewage maybe, if Stacey stopped to describe it. She guessed it was the source of some of the mysterious stink that had pervaded the house for months. She told him that the sludge was also leaving a ring in the tub and toilet. But he reassured her that the black sediment and the bad smell were nothing to worry about. She should boil the water before drinking, but otherwise cooking with it was okay.

Stacey wasn't sure what to do. In Pennsylvania, private water wells aren't subject to regulation. Some people liked it that way, viewing government intervention as both useless and expensive.

Stacey didn't think that the company would lie if the sludge was truly dangerous, so she followed Range's instructions and boiled the water until the odor grew so nauseating that her mother, Linda, found a twenty-five-gallon water jug in the *PennySaver* used for washing dishes and clothes. Their animals kept drinking the sulfur-stinking water, and the stench still filled the house, so she kept up her Febreze spritzing and a potpourri campaign around the commode, the word many in Amity used for toilet.

Stacey was also wrestling with whether to send Harley back to school. He'd gone back to the recliner, watching *MTV Cribs*. When Harley had returned from the camping trip, he'd discovered his dog, Hunter, was missing. After searching for days, they'd finally found Hunter dead in a hay pile up in the barn. It was impossible to know exactly what had happened, though it looked like Hunter might have fallen from the rafters and smothered to death in the hay. Hunter was Harley's best friend, and he took it hard. As she watched his brief advances slip away, Stacey didn't think she could take another winter of watching Harley curled up in front of that TV.

It wasn't like Harley was mean; he was hollowed out, absent. He'd always been shy, preferring the company of animals. But now he was drawing inside himself to a place she often couldn't reach. Gone were the days of basketball, the one sport Harley liked. He'd stopped riding four-wheelers with Aunt Shelly's sons, his first cousins J.P. and Judd. Since Harley wasn't much of a talker, he'd relied on being active alongside other boys as a means of belonging. Now that he didn't feel well enough to play, he felt more and more isolated.

Dr. Fox, their family doctor, wondered if Harley might have a rare autoimmune disorder called Behçet's disease. Its symptoms included eye irritation, rashes, and mouth ulcers, all of which Harley had. The doctor referred him back to Children's Hospital in Pittsburgh. Once, again, however, the tests came back negative. When school began, Stacey didn't see how she could get Harley to go. So he stayed home.

Lying in bed at night, Stacey couldn't sleep. Instead, she replayed scenes from Harley's childhood, experiences she'd worked so hard to create. A decade earlier, when Harley was four, his favorite activity had been collecting eggs from their chicken coop. Stacey loved to watch him watch the eggs warm beneath the incubator she kept in their farmhouse basement. They began thin-shelled, nearly translucent, darkening as the chicks' bodies grew inside until they ran out of room and had no choice but to hatch.

He'd wanted to become a veterinarian, the first person in his family to attend college. Stacey encouraged that dream, and she raised him on stories of their family's ties to the land. She drove him to her sister's house three miles away to play Cowboys and Indians with his cousins. Their woods were rife with stories of Native Americans battling early settlers over land, small bands of Delaware and Shawnee fighting the white men who arrived from New Jersey and Virginia. Harley loved the old stories. He was proud of being "a little more backward" than other kids, as he put it, rooted in a frontier past he imagined as noble and strong.

So that Harley could learn to track animals, Stacey hand-stenciled hoof and paw prints of deer, bear, and wild turkey on the walls of his bedroom. At night, he lay in his bottom bunk and followed their paths around his room. When Harley was nine, Pappy rounded him up, along with J.P. and Judd, and took them to a cattle farmer's hillside infested with groundhogs. Groundhogs were pests; a Hereford could catch a hoof and break a leg in one of their holes. The boys lay on a blanket in the shade cast by Pappy's truck. Passing a pair of binoculars between them, they peered at the greasy creatures scampering in and out of their burrows. Then Pappy gave them turns with his gun. That summer, the boys learned to be excellent shots.

Stacey grew up following her father in silence through the woods, where he'd seemed most comfortable since returning from Vietnam. She knew that Harley also loved hunting, in part, because it necessitated quiet. When Harley was thirteen, Stacey took him deer hunting. In the dawn frost, he fell asleep. Shaking him awake, she pointed at a buck. He was shaking as he took aim, and Stacey told him to stay calm. Breathe. Find the buck through the scope. He squeezed the trigger. The buck bolted and started downhill for the creek. Harley raced after him as Stacey shouted for Harley to stay back. Wounded animals could be dangerous. By the time he reached the creature, the three-pointer lay dead by the stream and Harley cradled its head in his lap.

Now the guns in the basement scared her. In her darkest moments, she feared Harley might hurt himself. She lugged the half-dozen shotguns and varmint guns she kept in the gun safe up the stairs and into her car and drove them to her parents' house in Amity.

As the fall of 2010 wore on, Stacey worried about Boots too. A few days before Halloween, Boots came back to the farm pregnant. Yet by November, Boots, like her owner, was listless and dropping pounds. Stacey tried to coax her to eat too, but she refused. Between the goat and her son and daughter, Stacey felt she'd returned to parenting small children, her life devoted to filling mouths.

Her farmhouse kitchen was her command center. From her place at the sink, she could turn and see Harley's feet propped up at the end of the plaid recliner in the living room, and through the window over the sink she could see the dragon, the wood burner she and the kids fed to heat the house. Up the scraggly rise, the goat barn she couldn't afford to replace stared back at her as an indictment.

One afternoon, Stacey was standing at the sink, looking out at the dragon and worrying about Boots. Her phone rang. She glanced down at the number and saw it was Beth. Shit, she thought. Bob must be out again. Ready to apologize, she picked up. The Voyles had just returned from Louisville, Kentucky, where Ashley had competed in the world finals for barrel racing, a fast-paced country sport in which horses race a cloverleaf pattern around barrels in fifteen seconds or so.

This year's competition had gone poorly, Beth told Stacey. Ashley's horse Jodi, a world champion sorrel quarter horse, had stayed at home, too sick to travel to Kentucky. She'd stopped eating. From Kentucky, Beth called the vet six times a day. Jodi was severely dehydrated, so Dr. Cheney administered IVs, steroids, pain medicine, and penicillin. At first, he thought she had myelitis, an infection horses contract after exposure to possum droppings. He ruled that out, but couldn't determine the source of her illness. Her back end was weak, which meant that Jodi was struggling to stand.

Stacey knew that horses that can't stand don't live long.

By the time Beth and Ashley came home, Jodi was having seizures and foaming at the mouth. She was beating her head against the ground. Dr. Cheney told Beth that a lethal injection was the most humane option. They buried her on the farm below the horse paddock. Her blood tests showed that Jodi had liver damage and a condition called blood dyscrasia, a killing-off of white blood cells. Dr. Cheney thought that this kind of toxicity likely indicated she'd consumed something poisonous. His findings were consistent with metal poisoning— exposure to mercury, lead, or arsenic.

"Arsenip," Beth called it, but Stacey knew she meant arsenic. Dr. Cheney told Beth to call the Pennsylvania Department of Health. The Department of Health told her to call the Department of Agriculture. The Department of Agriculture told her to call the Centers for Disease Control. On call after call, Beth felt she got a bureaucratic runaround. Meanwhile, she didn't know what to do about Ashley. Rawboned and athletic, Ashley was a loner like her father. She relied on her animals as companions. She'd already lost her puppy, Cummins, and now Jodi, the horse she'd ridden for the past fifteen years. Ashley was despondent. She wouldn't get out of bed. After missing a week's work, she went out and got a winged cross tattooed up the left side of her torso in Jodi's memory. It read *"I can do all this through Christ who gives me strength." Philippians 4:13.*

Boots is sick too, Stacey told Beth.

Cummins. Jodi. Boots.

Maybe whatever was sickening the animals was sickening her son, Stacey thought. She hung up immediately and called Dr. Fox, repeating to him what the veterinarian had told Beth. Maybe there was a link between the sick animals and the drilling next door. Maybe the noxious water was more than a nuisance.

She listed their ailments: her foot that wouldn't heal, Paige's nausea, her fatigue and rashes, their nosebleeds and headaches. For the first time she thought to talk to Dr. Fox about the foul-smelling water and that the company had instructed her to boil it. He listened in disbelief. This family had been through the wringer, he thought. Dr. Fox told her that Harley needed to be screened for metals. From now on, when children came into his office with flu-like symptoms, he was going to ask immediately if they lived near fracking and if it had affected their water.

Stacey called Pappy next. She asked him if she could borrow a water buffalo, and if he could help her start to haul water.

Then she texted Chris at the warehouse where, for ten to fourteen hours a day, he unloaded pallets of nails made in Bangladesh. He'd gone to college and majored in environmental science. All his life, he'd wanted to work as a warden in the U.S. Fish and Wildlife Service, but the job didn't pay enough to support him.

Soon after, the *Dukes of Hazzard* theme blared from her phone. It was Harley's ringtone, which she'd also recently bestowed upon Chris. Stacey recounted to Chris what Beth had told her about Jodi and how she thought it might be related to whatever was making Harley ill. At first, Chris doubted that the drill site could have sickened Harley. He listened to the radio on his way to and from work and had heard the "My Range Resources" ads. Hearing his neighbors talk about their experiences with fracking had helped to convince him that it must be safe. And it wasn't in Range's interest to make people sick.

Still, he'd seen Harley at his worst. Under normal circumstances, a proud fourteen-year-old boy from Amity—from anywhere, really— would've been mortified to have his mother's boyfriend carry him to his mom's car, cradling him like an infant, but Harley'd been too sick to care. Those moments stuck with Chris. So did the water filter full of black and gray chunks.

They waited a week for Harley's test results. On November 18, 2010, Stacey's forty-first birthday, she was out back feeding the dragon when her cell phone rang. It was Dr. Fox's office. Harley's urine contained 85 mcg/g of arsenic. A favorite poison of the Borgias, arsenic is naturally occurring and can be found in rice. Levels of up to 25 mcg/g are normal in an adult. Harley's levels concerned the pediatrician, and he diagnosed him with arsenic poisoning.

Oh dear Lord, Paige probably has it too, she thought to herself. Paige had been whining about her stomach when she got out of the shower. She wouldn't eat breakfast. She'd kept telling Stacey that her belly hurt while Stacey scooted her off to school. Maybe it wasn't just Jodi; maybe the Voyles were sick too.

"I could kick myself for not recognizing this sooner," she told me later, "but no one was asking about our water. No one had ever seen anything like this." The nurse informed Stacey that the doctor wanted her to call Range Resources again and demand they supply an alternate source of water. The company agreed. The same day, she called the Department of Environmental Protection and the Department of Health. "The Department of Health told us they didn't know what to do," she said. "If this was lead poisoning, they'd have a protocol, but they have no protocol for this."

That evening, having already planned to celebrate her birthday with her parents, she drove the kids five miles to Amity. Stacey stood in the kitchen with her mother and sister, piecing together the story of Beth's sick animals with Harley's illness. Harley sat at the kitchen table listening to the three women talk. He didn't know what arsenic poisoning was, but it sounded serious. In addition to Cummins, Jodi, and Boots, there was Hunter. It seemed so odd that a dog would fall into a hay pile and smother to death, unless maybe he was already disoriented by illness.

At home that night, Stacey sat down with a piece of loose-leaf paper. In the childlike block letters she used to chart as a nurse, she began a journal: *Thurs. 11/18/10 Harley tested (+) for high levels of arsenic 85 mcg/g co-pay $40.* The next day, Range sent the local water purveyor, Dean's, which was owned by a family in Amity, to deliver a 5,100-gallon water buffalo to the Haneys' farm. It sat just outside the dining room by the crack in the house's foundation.

From the day of Harley's diagnosis, Stacey began to gather every fact she could about what was happening to her family. First, she had Paige's arsenic levels tested, along with her own. Stacey's came back 64 mcg/g and Paige was negative. Relieved that Paige was in the clear, Stacey wondered why her daughter would show no signs of exposure if they were all living in the same house. Then she thought of all of those days that she'd pushed Paige onto the bus—days that Harley'd stayed on the recliner. She thought of that brain fog she'd felt descend over her too when her foot wouldn't heal and she stayed at home along with him. She realized that keeping Harley homebound might have compounded his exposure.

Within days of the buffalo's arrival, she and the kids began to feel better. After two weeks, a spray of acne over Stacey's cheeks and nose cleared up, as did the rash on her arm. At three weeks, when Harley went back to Dr. Fox's office to have his arsenic levels retested, the results came back negative. Soon, Harley felt well enough to return to school. Late that fall, he began playing basketball for the first time in a year and a half. Yet some of their symptoms persisted. All three still had headaches, and Harley's mouth was riddled with ulcers. He kept refusing food, so his doctors prescribed Zofran, an anti-nausea medication for cancer patients undergoing chemotherapy.

5 | AIRBORNE

One day that fall, Paige's sixth-grade teacher assigned the class the task of finding their houses on Google Earth. Paige came home from school and pulled up what she'd found on the family laptop. A black void eighty times the size of their house sat carved into the hilltop across the road. It looked like a pond: its surface shimmered as if filled with something wet. Around it sat a handful of trailers and another smaller pit. There appeared to be oversized black plastic garbage bags around the sides of the pond. The connection was poor and the image fuzzy; Stacey couldn't see clearly, but there were white polka dots spread across the pond's surface. She wondered what the dots could be.

As the fall days shortened, Stacey came home from her shifts at the hospital in darkness. At the back door, she kicked off the white Brooks sneakers she had to wear to work. Even though nine months had passed, her foot was still aching from surgery, and she feared the slowness to heal had something to do with chemical exposure. Still wearing scrubs, she went through the mounting stack of urine tests with a yellow highlighter, noting what she thought might be a problem and what she didn't understand. She also sifted through scant medical information online to parse what she could. There was almost nothing reliable to read. It was too early in the Marcellus Boom for peer-reviewed medical studies to be completed, let alone published. So she combed the Centers for Disease Control website for the health effects of arsenic and other metals on children. What she found disturbed her. Given their small bodies and developing nervous systems, children were at higher risk of being affected by exposure.

And the water tests Range was performing didn't reassure Stacey either. Although the company claimed to hire independent laboratories to ensure homeowners received objective results, Stacey worried that the results might not be so independent, since Range was paying for them. She found and hired her own hydrologist, Bob Fargo. Fargo had little experience with oil and gas contamination, but he taught Stacey how to perform rapid arsenic testing on her well. At different times of day, she lowered into the well a strip of paper, which turned color, like pH paper, in the presence of arsenic and other metals. Regularly, when she went down to the basement to test, the results showed low levels of arsenic but nothing too startling. That was part of the problem, as Fargo explained it. All of these samples could capture only a moment in time. They were the equivalent of taking a photograph. To learn how an aquifer worked, Stacey pulled one of Chris's college textbooks off the shelf. She'd always assumed that groundwater sat still underground, like a lake. But she discovered that an aquifer was more of an underground river. Water was always on the move. What if a plume of arsenic had passed by and she'd missed the main event? What if her test methods were too rudimentary to capture what was really going on?

Fargo also told Stacey that he wondered whether the arsenic wasn't only in the water but also in the air. That might be why she and the kids weren't feeling entirely better. Maybe, while showering, they were breathing in arsine gas.

Stacey puzzled over these and other issues aloud among her fellow nurses at the hospital. For two years now, her colleagues had listened to stories of Harley's sickness and seen it firsthand when he arrived at the ER ashen and doubled over. None of the other nurses or even the sympathetic doctors at the hospital knew where to point Stacey for answers. No one had any experience with these deep wells.

The ordinary shallow gas wells, which some farms still had, were small affairs where people put in pumpjacks on the weekend. The scale of this industry itself was new, and Stacey didn't know where else to turn besides Kelly Tush, her fellow nurse, and her sister, Shelly, who was in charge of surgical instruments at Advanced Surgical Hospital nearby.

Kelly swapped shifts and spent hours talking to Stacey about Harley's sicknesses. She looked up to Stacey. The two had been close ever since Kelly had nursed Stacey's grandparents in the hospital's geriatric unit. Then Kelly transferred to recovery and also became a stepmother to three rambunctious boys. Stacey coached her into the new job and into parenthood. Now the roles switched and Kelly became Stacey's emotional mainstay. She sent Stacey supportive texts and e-cards. "Friendship isn't about who you've known the longest," one read. "It's about who came and never left your side."

Shelly was already accustomed to helping her sister balance life and work. When Stacey was in nursing school, Shelly watched Harley alongside her two boys. Now, as Stacey shuttled urine samples to Dr. Fox's office, Shelly drove the kids to 4-H and hauled water with Pappy for Stacey's animals. Shelly wasn't doing great herself: she too was working full-time at the orthopedic hospital, as well as suffering from diabetes and being in the throes of a crumbling marriage. Still, she showed up for Stacey because that's what sisters did. Shelly kept asking the doctors she worked with if they knew of anyone who could help her sister's son, until finally an orthopedic surgeon told her about a Washington County man named Ron Gulla.

Gulla lived about an hour's drive from Amity in Mount Pleasant Township, the epicenter of Range's leasing and drilling activity. It was here, in 2004, that Range drilled and fracked its first well in Washington County. The gas wells on Gulla's farm were among the first to be fracked, and things hadn't gone as he'd expected. He was in the midst of a legal battle with Range Resources over everything from fish dying in his pond to workers defecating in his woods. Gulla, who'd become the local lightning rod in the unfolding debate around fracking, was obsessed with the issue, and when Stacey called, she found it was nearly impossible to get off the phone with him. He began to ring her with updates and requests from the flock of reporters descending on southwestern Pennsylvania, their arrival a symptom of the boom. Stacey declined. She wanted no part of the spotlight in a greater fight against fracking. She didn't trust strangers who had their own agendas.

Also, where she came from, no one liked a complainer. Stacey was well aware that Amity's most respected citizens held some of the most lucrative leases. But her greatest concern was that if she spoke out against Range Resources, the company would take her water buffalo away. Without it, she and the kids would have to move, and they had nowhere to go and no way to afford the $1,200 mortgage and again as much rent for another home.

Gulla introduced Stacey to a Mount Pleasant family much like her own. Stephanie and Chris Hallowich had built their dream house on ten acres of farmland, which they said had become a toxic waste site. Their children, Allie, six, and Nate, nine, were suffering from symptoms a lot like Harley's and Paige's headaches and nosebleeds. The Hallowiches believed these problems resulted from exposure to a waste pond like the one by Stacey and a compressor station on their farm. For two years, they'd been trying to move, but no one wanted to buy their land.

The family was stuck, Stephanie Hallowich told Stacey. Through a series of late-night phone calls, the two became friends. In addition to suffering illnesses, the Hallowiches were ostracized for opposing an industry that was bringing so much money into the community. But that hadn't stopped the family from suing Range Resources, and they were now in the middle of a contentious lawsuit. Eventually, in order to move away, the Hallowiches sold their home to Range and settled with the company for $750,000. In exchange, the family signed a gag order that initially seemed to prohibit the parents as well as their two

children from commenting on Marcellus shale or on fracking, report-
edly for the rest of their lives. Although the settlement was sealed, the
Pittsburgh Post-Gazette fought in court to make it public, and won.
When the agreement was unsealed, it kicked off a nationwide controversy over the First Amendment rights of children, and eventually a
new attorney for Range backed away from a previous claim that the
gag order extended to the kids.

No one in Amity would dare say Stacey and her kids were inter-
lopers looking for money and a way out of town. They weren't going
anywhere. They would outlast the drilling, as people in Amity and
Prosperity had always done with extractive industry. Let the company
supply water, and they'd sit tight on the family farm until Range was
gone. For now, she'd stay put to keep fighting, gathering proof of harm
as quickly as she could.

Up at Justa Breeze, the Voyles were contending with their own problems. Beth and John lived 800 feet down the hill from the waste pond.
(The Haneys, at 1,530 feet, were nearly double that.) The Voyles'
drinking water also came from the underground springs flowing off
the Yeager site. They relied on that spring water for themselves and
for their horses and dogs. When Range had started digging the waste
pond earlier that year, the Voyles' spring water flow had dropped off to
a trickle—"a sprinkering," Beth called it. She'd phoned Range, and the
company paid Dean's to deliver water. Range had also paid for Beth
and John to drill a new well. But Beth didn't trust that water either,
as tests they conducted on their own came back saying it was full of
E. coli. The buffalo couldn't supply enough water for the Voyles' twenty-
one horses. So Beth parked herself in the basement, its walls hung
with John's horseshoe art, a cross reading FAITH, and Ashley's trophies,
to call buyers and auctions until she'd found homes for fifteen of them.

Beth's boxers Smoke and Presley each gave birth to a litter of puppies that fall. One, black and white, was born with a cleft palate. The puppy had trouble drinking milk, which kept getting into his lungs, and he died. In her seven years as a breeder, she'd never seen this kind of defect. She wrapped the puppy in a plastic baggie and placed him in the basement deep freeze. She hoped to test the corpse for clues about his deformity—perhaps a genetic mutuation linked to exposure. But she'd already learned when Cummins died that such tests were inconclusive. They could also cost two thousand dollars. Now, with Jodi and the puppy dead in addition to Cummins, she called Range to tell them about her animals and her fears that they were being poisoned with ethylene glycol. Laura Rusmisel, a Range employee, then phoned Beth's vet. She informed him that Range didn't use ethylene glycol in fracking, which he recorded in his notes. When Beth found out that Range had called the vet without her consent, she threw a fit. It seemed to Beth a backhanded attempt to undermine her claims. And, in fact, Rusmisel turned out to be wrong.

The incident left Beth deeply suspicious. Feeling that she had nowhere else to turn, Beth kept calling the Department of Environmental Protection, the state agency that investigated all such complaints. Since its creation in 1995, the DEP's main role was to enforce Pennsylvania's environmental laws. For a decade the agency had been understaffed and underfunded. Yet since 2008, things had gotten substantially worse, and the agency's shortcomings were a symptom of a larger problem of public poverty. As fallout from the Great Recession, the Commonwealth of Pennsylvania faced a budget shortfall of $1.6 billion. Governor Ed Rendell, a Democrat, sliced the DEP's budget of $217,515,000 by 27 percent, one of the biggest cuts in its history. The governor also shaved 19 percent from the $113,369,000 budget of the Department of Conservation and Natural Resources, the agency tasked with maintaining state parks and forests. To plug the hole in the budget, he also started leasing oil and gas rights on public land. In three separate sales, the state made $413 million by leasing 138,866 acres. This marked the beginning of one of the largest public sell-offs in Pennsylvania's recent history.

The DEP also had a dismal record of responding to homeowners' complaints. Poor communication, missed deadlines, giving homeowners confusing and incomplete test results—the DEP had failed at its most basic duties in protecting the public, a 2014 report by the inspector general found: "Undoubtedly, these shortcomings have eroded the public's trust." And due to the current rush, the agency was flooded with operators applying for permits. The DEP almost never said no. Of the 7,019 drilling applications received since 2005, the state had rejected only 31.

Despite Beth's urging, Stacey didn't call the DEP very often. At work, on the rare days that she had even thirty minutes for lunch, she spent them on the phone trying to return doctors' calls. She didn't want to waste time trying to reach a human being at the DEP. Even when she did, no one had any answers. To be fair, health issues were beyond their mandate, so she was left on her own, giving the kids specimen cups to pee in first thing in the morning and performing inconclusive water tests in her pajamas. She told her new friend Stephanie Hallowich that she needed more help. Hallowich suggested that Stacey alert the federal government. If the DEP wasn't going to do its job, then maybe the Environmental Protection Agency would step in. Their mandate was larger and ostensibly more powerful. When President Nixon and Congress founded the EPA in 1970, its purpose was to wage a "coordinated attack" on pollution that crossed state lines. Since then, the EPA had been tasked with everything from laying out ground rules for large-scale cleanups to investigating serious environmental crimes.

Stacey wasn't sure that she wanted or needed the feds traipsing through her home. She believed she stood a better chance of working with the company to make things right if she didn't call in the cavalry yet, so she waited. At least they had clean water now. Although she and the kids were drinking from the buffalo outside the dining room, they needed more water for the animals, so Pappy kept hauling water. It was hard to keep up with the demand and sometimes the animals drank tainted water.

At the end of November, Boots went into labor and Stacey prepared to deliver the kids up in the lean-to. The goat was having contractions but struggling to push, so Stacey had to reach in and pull the babies out. The first emerged in three pieces; the second intact. On Christmas Eve, Boots started having seizures. On Christmas Day, after opening presents, she and the kids checked on Boots. The goat was still seizing, so Stacey wrapped her in a blanket and carried her down to the house. Stacey called the vet, who prescribed steroids, pain medication, and antibiotics. Nothing worked. The day after Christmas, the vet came to put Boots down.

Upsetting loss for our whole family. $76.60, Stacey wrote in her notebook. She was beginning to keep a running ledger of every expense, emotional and financial, that she could attribute to the ordeal. Boots's death also marked a turning point: she was now willing to work with the feds. The next day, Stephanie Hallowich brought an EPA criminal investigator named Martin Schwartz to Stacey's house. Bald and ex-military, Schwartz had served as a police officer for twenty-five years. He worked much as police detectives do, he explained, gathering evidence through tips, interviews, search warrants, and subpoenas. Unlike the state's environmental inspectors, Schwartz carried a gun, which Stacey took as a sign of the EPA's seriousness. As he sat in her kitchen, Schwartz found Stacey credible. "As a cop, you develop a feel for people," he said later. "She wasn't some quack or tree-hugger." And she was also a nurse. Yet whether or not she was telling the truth wasn't the question. Schwartz wasn't sure what he'd be able to prove. Take the animals, he told her. With sick animals, there were usually too many environmental factors to make any real link between toxic exposure and sickness.

That morning of December 27, Stacey wrapped Boots in a sheet and placed her in the Pontiac's back seat for the three-hour trip to

Penn State. Although Stacey knew the tests were rarely conclusive, she wanted to do them anyway. And the university would pay. The results showed an extreme number of parasites in the goat's blood, which could mean anything. Animals can contract parasites in many ways, but Stacey learned that the condition can be common in animals affected by metal poisoning: metals replace calcium in an animal's bones, and the immune system can no longer fight infection.

When Boots's test results came back, Stacey placed them in her thickening binder as evidence for the federal government. Since the Hallowiches could no longer speak publicly about their experience, Stacey feared it was going to be her job to expose what was happening in Amity. Maybe she could do so quietly; attention brought nothing but trouble. That she could see from the lives of the Hallowiches. She dreaded the idea of going public, of waging a fight. For now, in private, she'd write down every vet bill and co-pay in the corner of her polka-dotted journal.

6 | HOOPIES

Growing up Amity, as Stacey called it, meant growing up poor. Stacey was in the third grade when her father's steel mill closed. She and Shelly were raised as children of the Bust. They grew and pickled as much of their own food as they could from a large garden, chopped firewood for fuel, and fetched drinking water. Although southwestern Pennsylvania is one of the most water-rich regions in the world, due to its rivers and the frequent rain that falls in the shadow of the Allegheny Mountains, many people who live there have no access to the municipal supply they call city water.

In lower Amity, where Stacey had lived with her parents, whether a house had water or not was largely a matter of luck. Some people dug successful wells in their backyards. For others the wells cost too much to dig or the aquifer proved too deep to reach. Stacey's family relied on storm water to do laundry or bathe or to fill the large concrete cistern that sat outside the brown house with a black and white POW/MIA flag where her parents still lived.

Sometimes, since Pappy was a volunteer fireman, he could use the Amity fire truck to pump creek water into their tank for bathing and washing. For drinking water, the girls took turns crossing the driveway to a neighbor's outdoor pump with eight empty plastic milk jugs balanced in their arms. They lugged them home two at a time, running so the jugs wouldn't have time to slip from their hands. The chore fell to girls the world over. In many places, it could be perilous: requiring venturing alone far from home. Shelly and Stacey were only crossing a driveway; still, the memory lodged within them. Shelly remembered with delight when she was eleven and could manage four jugs at once. She'd always been less of a primper than her older sister, and still described herself as "a dirty tomboy." The hardest part for her about their childhood dearth of water was that they'd never had water balloons, or water guns, or a sprinkler.

"Water was too precious for play," she said. Now thirty-eight, Shelly favored John Lennon glasses, a bandana, and a T-shirt that said MY KID SHOT A DEER WHILE YOUR HONOR STUDENT WAS AT SCHOOL. She made moonshine and tended a hive of feral bees in a hollow log behind the two-hundred-year-old farmhouse she'd bought for $25,000. In the middle of the unfinished living room, she kept a whirlpool tub she'd found at a rummage sale. The tub served as a kind of hopeful joke that they might one day have water. It was also loaded with laundry, which she and her boys washed when it rained.

"We're not fresh sheet washers," she said. She called the oversized tub "a time capsule"; her son's football uniform from three years back was still in there somewhere.

Stacey, in contrast, liked keeping her hair clean and her legs shaven, which was hard as a teenager, when taking a shower longer than ninety seconds was verboten. "By the time the pump switched on, you'd better be out," Stacey said. Back then, the water wasn't the problem. Water was cheap: fifty gallons cost twenty-five cents, so filling a five-hundred-gallon buffalo cost only $2.50. But filling the gas tank and finding the time for the half-hour drives back and forth to Ruff Creek placed a strain on her family.

Since 1970, the Dean family had made a business of hauling water. They also owned the Amity Laundromat, a hardware store, and eventually a gas station and convenience store, but before fracking arrived— and with it an insatiable demand for water—the Deans weren't rich. They lived in a tin-sided trailer behind the Laundromat, and their son, Richard, like every other boy in town, had had a crush on Stacey. When they were teenagers, to be nice, Stacey went with him once as his date to the fair.

Although Stacey's parents were poor, they were well respected. Money mattered much less than reputation, and her parents and their parents before them were admired for their integrity. On Stacey's mother's side, they traced their history in Washington County back to Stacey's great-grandfather Oliver Mankey, the grandson of a German immigrant by the name of Mannchen. Oliver Mankey was born near the town of Nineveh, ten miles from Amity, in 1865, and moved to Prosperity to farm. He lived on land that the Delaware had once called Anawanna, the path of the water. Now the land belonged to a Boy Scout camp and the Anawanna Club, which Stacey called "a redneck country club." Although the club was little more than a muddy pond stocked with catfish and a soda machine stocked with beer, members voted on prospective members by placing white or black balls in a box. One black ball and you were out.

Stacey's father's family also lived in Washington County, but most of the Hillberrys, who were also originally from Germany, had settled in West Virginia. This was the original Hoopy country, where during the last century hill people wove hoops out of saplings and carried them down to West Virginian ceramics makers to fashion into barrels for shipping plates and cups. In West Virginia, people still joked that the initials of the Homer Laughlin China Company stood for "Hoopies' Last Chance." And now the word "Hoopy" had come to mean anything related to hill culture. "Going down Hoopy to hunt," for instance, meant going to West Virginia.

The nurses at work started teasingly calling Stacey a Hoopy after her mother called the ward one day in 2003 and told Stacey to switch on one of the TVs in the recovery ward. There, on-screen, the nurses watched federal agents raid the farm of David Wayne Hull, an Imperial Wizard of the White Knights, the KKK's most violent paramilitary wing. Hull was a fellow Hillberry and Stacey's second cousin. A hospital aide who happened to be an African American man said Hull was a monster. Stacey told him Hull was her cousin. The aide apologized; he'd never thought people like that had any family, he told her. No, Stacey said, I'm sorry. Hull was sentenced to twelve years in federal prison for tampering with a witness, along with building, transporting, and detonating IEDs. Stacey wasn't surprised. Out hunting at his farm, she'd seen cut-out human targets for shooting practice, and a stack of wooden crosses waiting to be burned.

As an adult, Stacey had reclaimed being a Hoopy as a source of pride. It had been hard when she was younger. In high school, she was teased for being a poor country kid from Amity with the name Hillberry, synonymous with hillbilly. Stacey had attended Trinity High School in the city of Washington, which since childhood she had associated with wealth. After Pappy lost his job, Linda often took the girls along when she went to clean a thirty-two-room mansion in Washington. The mansion had a pool, where Stacey and Shelly were allowed to swim in the summer while their mother worked. In reality, the town's dwindling fortunes reflected those of the county: Washington was in the midst of an economic exodus, which has cut the town's population in half since the 1950s, from a high of 27,000 to 13,500 today. But Washington still meant money in Stacey's eyes, and when she reached high school, the city kids, as Stacey called them, had things like Nintendo and Jordache jeans, and Stacey felt ashamed of all she lacked. She sat in the back of the classroom and never raised her hand. The only extracurricular activity she participated in was rifle club. She was the team's best shot and was awarded MVP. Even rifle club embarrassed her, though, since Pappy couldn't afford to buy Stacey her own gun and she had to borrow one from the school.

Stacey was a senior in high school when she learned that college existed, and she told her mother she wanted to go, but, as Stacey recalled, Linda told her that poor kids from places like Amity didn't go to college. She'd be better served forgetting about it. This happened sometimes between them: Linda thinking that she was setting Stacey straight, helping to spare her daughter future disappointment by facing a humbling truth; Stacey feeling defeated, squashed. So she'd left home for beauty school and a life with her then boyfriend, Larry Haney.

She told no one she was leaving, and when she went back for her things, Pappy told her that Larry would always love his truck more than her, which made Stacey furious at the time but turned out, she thought, to be true.

To Stacey, home ownership was the next rung up the middle-class ladder. With Larry managing inventory at a nearby plastics plant and Stacey working as a nurse, they had enough money to buy a house with good water. When Stacey found the farm on McAdams Road, she loved the fact that it had once belonged to her great-grandfather. This happened often in Amity. Due to scant inventory and financial struggles, houses passed in and out of families. On McAdams, the quality of its water was the farm's best feature. She cherished the well, supplying water to her parents and sister, as well as to the Lower Ten Mile Presbyterian Church. The house, which cost $82,000, required a gut-job: a new roof and vinyl siding, along with work on the foundation. They also added a new kitchen, bathroom, and porch, salvaging what they could—"to keep the history," Stacey said.

She collected old things to fill the house where she planned to live forever: an antique sewing machine, her grandmother's Shaker rocker. Larry, like her, was meticulous about his surroundings. Together, they invested all they had in the house, installing a porcelain wood-burning stove in the kitchen that cost about two thousand dollars. They couldn't afford oil. They relied on the woodstove to warm most of the house. Around the stove, they installed a wooden mantel that Pappy made from a walnut tree on the farm and built a hearth with stone. She hand-plastered the parlor ceiling with careful swirls, stenciled ivy up the stairs and the animal tracks over Harley's walls, painted Paige's room with bunnies and tufts of grass, and hung pink valances decorated with John Deere tractors in her windows.

Beneath this veneer of rustic perfection, however, Larry and Stacey were struggling. At first, when Harley had colic, Larry would walk him for hours. But when the kids grew old enough to make messes—Paige leaving around her piles of Polly Pocket dolls—he grew impatient. Paige was afraid to ask him for anything, even a glass of water, in case he yelled at her. He preferred order and being outside washing his truck. By the time he left in 2007, Stacey was happy to see the back of him. Although in her mind she cast his departure as his fault, the product of his losing interest in the kids, she'd lost interest in the marriage too. She worked hard at convincing the kids that they were better-off without him, and Larry felt cast as a bad guy, pushed out of their lives. Harley and Paige saw him only occasionally when he took them for awkward dinners at the nearby tavern, Ye Olde Kopper Kettle, which had served as a stagecoach inn a century ago along the National Road.

Stacey met Chris Rush at the Kettle in 2009. She stopped in for a rare drink after working a catering gig to make extra money. She was self-conscious about the strong smell of the chicken and gravy she'd spilled down her white blouse. Chris, who frequented the Kettle for burgers and scratch-off lottery tickets sold out of a vending machine, saw her come into the bar and approached her. He knew who she was and was already infatuated. They talked about the kids, and he offered to take Harley on a turkey hunt. Turkey hunting is hard: the hunter has to imitate the female's call. But Chris was a master. Turkey season, however, was still months away, so Chris asked if she might be free one night for dinner. As a hunter, he couldn't resist her smelling of chicken, he liked teasing her later.

"That's a Hoopy mating call," she told me later, laughing.

Chris was much closer than Larry was to the ideal partner that Stacey hoped for. At thirty-four, Chris was still a bachelor and stiff and wary around strangers. After half a dozen Bud Lights, he loosened up, became funny and rambunctious, full of boyish hijinks, rapping fluent Lil Wayne or Snoop Dogg from the unlikely mouth of a burly Hoopy. Each loved the strong country identity the other possessed, and part of that involved maintaining an old-fashioned distance. Stacey was proud of being self-reliant and not calling Chris every time she blew a tire on the rutted road.

"There's a difference in Amity women than most women," she said. "We don't have to have a man in our lives." Stacey was perfectly happy about, or at least resigned to, chopping a winter's worth of firewood on her own, with the help of her family. As she saw it, that's what real frontierswomen did. The ringtone that Stacey picked for Harley and Chris—the tribute to Bo and Luke Duke—reflected her tastes. When Paige called, Stacey's phone whinnied. Chris held on to his bungalow bachelor pad in a nearby town known as Eighty Four, but he spent as much time as he could with Stacey in Amity, doing odd chores and watching Pirates and Steelers games.

Although Stacey and Chris saw being country as being different from the mainstream, the truth was that rural populism was trendy. On television, *Duck Dynasty*, hosted by the irascible duck hunter Phil Robertson, was the number-one show in America until Robertson's racist comments drove him off the air. *Duck Dynasty* and other reality shows, like *Honey Boo Boo* and *Buckwild*, portrayed crusty and outrageous characters who appealed to rural Americans as well as urban viewers. The broad jokes and small mishaps of country living seemed quaint, a throwback to a life that was disappearing. The disenfranchisement wasn't always economic—the Robertsons wore $150 Realtree camouflage boots and their pickups could cost more than a BMW—but it did signal a strong political pushback against the progressive values regarding race and sexuality that were ascendant during the Obama years. Soon, with the election of Donald Trump, urban Americans would learn that the pointed humor of these shows was popular not because it was exotic but because it was so widespread.

7 | "ONE HEAD & ONE HEART, & LIVE IN TRUE FRIENDSHIP & AMITY AS ONE PEOPLE"

On Sundays, Stacey filled milk jugs with water and drove them to the Lower Ten Mile Presbyterian Church, where her kids and Shelly's were the fifth generation of their family to be baptized. The church's well was contaminated with formaldehyde leached from the bodies of the former parishioners. In the graveyard, thin slabs of granite told a story about Amity over ten generations. For the past 250 years, its residents had once belonged to a community where people relied on one another, grumbling as they might about familial or communal obligations while chopping wood, or mowing, or butchering the season's hogs. These stories belied the myth of the individual frontiersman. No one could've made it here alone.

Among the parishioners buried in the graveyard was the Reverend Thaddeus Dod, his tombstone encrusted with lichen. A descendant of Puritans and an ardent Presbyterian, Dod arrived in 1777 out of Princeton. Suffering from rheumatism, he made six difficult trips over the Alleghenies from New Jersey, bringing his wife and an infant son, in order to found the church and minister to the embattled settlers. Most had arrived only four years earlier, in 1773, when a group of fifteen to twenty families came from New Jersey. They joined a handful of European settlers and five brothers named Bane at the Ten Mile Creek settlement, which would later become Amity and Prosperity.

Ten Mile wasn't undiscovered; it was a busy byway along Mingo Path, part of an ancient east–west route that would later become

America's federal highway, the National Road. Ten Mile Creek was also a dangerous place. The frontier was at war with Native inhabitants. In these forests, Shawnee and Delaware hunted for bear, buffalo, elk, turkey, and deer. There was a Delaware village about half a mile west of the settlement, Dod noted in his journal. It was called Anawanna.

Almost immediately after the settlers arrived in 1773, the Delaware attacked and drove them off the land. They soon returned to build log forts with gun sites and spiked wooden fences to guard against the Native American raids that would begin each year with the spring thaw.

The besieged community was in desperate need of spiritual guidance. Dod baptized babies and preached in forts about the need for personal salvation. He called for the renunciation of sin, and evoked hell's fiery travails in vivid color. Dod was a fervent advocate of the Great Awakening, the Protestant movement that swept through Europe and the colonies beginning in the 1740s. The need for salvation, with its promise of heaven, was immediate. Violent death surrounded them. The Great Awakening also contained a moral and spiritual imperative that justified settlers' claims on Native land. Expansion was God's will.

The conflict over frontier land also divided colonists from one another. This was part of the legacy of William Penn, the Quaker and pacifist who'd been given twenty-nine million acres of land by King Charles II in 1681. Penn saw this new world as a holy experiment to build a peaceable kingdom. As part of this divine contract, he believed that land had to be bought, rather than stolen, from Native Americans. For their part, the Native Americans didn't necessarily believe that individuals could own land. Nevertheless, Penn signed a land treaty with the Conestogas, which read that both parties "shall forever hereafter be as one Head & One Heart, & live in true Friendship & Amity as one People."

Tensions rose between the Quaker elite in Philadelphia and the land-hungry "back inhabitants" moving west. In December 1763, a group of frontiersmen, the Paxton Boys, slaughtered Conestoga men, women, and children, then marched east to Philadelphia to demand the right to land and representation, as well as retribution against Native Americans. When the Paxton Boys arrived at the city's edge, Benjamin Franklin listened to their grievances, eventually succeeding in sending them back to the frontier without violence in the streets of Philadelphia.

However, violence along the frontier proliferated. Despite Quaker disapproval, the back inhabitants kept pressing westward, cutting their initials into trees, establishing by "tomahawk rights" ownership over land that the powerful Six Nations believed they held in collective trust for future generations. John Penn, William's grandson and now the colonial governor, sought to contain the settlers. In February 1768, he issued a "most terrifying law," according to colonial records. Penn proclaimed that "if any Person or Persons, settled upon any Lands within the Boundaries of this Province, not purchased of the Indians by the Proprietaries thereof, shall neglect or refuse to remove themselves and Families . . . [they] shall suffer death without the Benefit of Clergy."

That winter, Penn sent colonial authorities out to illegal settlements to enforce the new law. But the squatters ignored the threats of death and refused to leave. That spring, when they kept seizing land, Tohonissagarrawa, chief of the Six Nations, complained to Penn: "Brother: It is not without grief that we see our Country settled by You without our knowledge or consent."

By the time Dod arrived at Ten Mile Creek almost a decade later, the law had changed, and settlers were finally allowed to own plots along the frontier. As they flowed westward in greater and greater numbers, skirmishes intensified. The Revolutionary War made things even worse between settlers and Native Americans; many of the latter hoped that the British might prove better neighbors than the violent colonials. King George III went so far as to promise Native peoples that

England would safeguard their claims to the land after the war, and many decided to fight on his behalf. The western frontier was one of the war's bloodiest theaters. One Native chief said that if his people had the means of broadcasting what the settlers had done to women and children, the settlers, rather than the Native Americans, would be called savages.

The Revolutionary War left the frontier in devastation. Many frontiersmen, poor to begin with, were already deeply in debt for the cost of building their homesteads. They'd served as soldiers both in the war and in an ongoing border dispute between Pennsylvania and neighboring Virginia that was finally settled in 1780. When they returned to their homes in Washington County, these veterans, already in hock, often found that their homesteads had been burned by Native Americans.

In response, the men from Washington County conducted a spate of reprisal killings. In 1782, David Williamson, soon to be elected sheriff of Washington County, led a band of men across the Ohio River, where, in a village established by Moravian Christian missionaries, they bludgeoned ninety-six Native converts to death, including thirty-nine children. Some of the militiamen opposed the massacre. Others, like Nathan Rollins, who'd lost a father and an uncle in Native American raids, led the attack. After taking a tomahawk to nineteen people, Rollins "sat down & cried," an observer wrote. Rollins "said it was no satisfaction for the loss of his father & uncle after all."

Against this blood-soaked background, Thaddeus Dod attempted to civilize the community at Ten Mile. He opened the Log Academy to teach Latin and the classics to boys. In addition to constructing the school and the church, the Dods also built an elegant log cabin, unique in that it had two stories and three fireplaces: one for cooking, one for heating, and yet a third in the basement. In 1785 they dug a communal well next to the cabin, which still sits there beneath a round wooden cover. The well provided the community water, and also security, since women and children didn't need to wander down to the creek alone, risking attack. But the well fulfilled a spiritual vision as well as a practical need. On September 7 of that year, Reverend Thaddeus Dod preached from the book of Isaiah 41:17: "When the poor and needy seek water, and there is none, and their tongue faileth for thirst, I the Lord will hear them."

When frontier veterans tried to rebuild their homesteads, they found that the salaries they'd been expecting for their military service were either never paid or paid in paper scrip rather than coin. The scrip arrived late, and when it did, it was practically devoid of value, plunging the frontier deeper into economic crisis.

Whiskey, instead, served as the most useful currency. Most farms had small stills, and the liquor could be used to pay for rent or labor. Whiskey could also be sent east over the Alleghenies to Philadelphia and New York. Transporting grain through the mountains was so unwieldy and expensive as to be hardly worth the effort. Whiskey, on the other hand, turned a tidy profit.

In 1791, under the auspices of Secretary of the Treasury Alexander Hamilton, the federal government imposed a Whiskey Tax intended to help repay the young republic's debts. Hamilton also hoped it would drive small rural producers out of business in the favor of larger ones. It was one of Hamilton's less laudable ideas, and the residents of Washington County reacted. When federal agents attempted to collect taxes on stills, the Whiskey Rebels tarred and feathered them and destroyed the stills of those who cooperated, until President Washington himself mustered nearly thirteen thousand troops and rode west.

Ill and ill-prepared for the winter weather, Washington was forced to turn back, while most of his men marched on, arriving in the town of Washington in an attempt to capture David Bradford, a leader of the Whiskey Rebellion. But Bradford had already escaped and was soon floating down the Mississippi. Washington's men did manage to capture some other leaders and march them to Philadelphia, where they were eventually pardoned. It was the only time in U.S. history that a sitting president led troops against his own citizens.

Each spring, this anti-federalist spirit flourishes in downtown Washington, where Whiskey Rebellion reenactors march beneath the uneasy gaze of George Washington, whose statue still perches atop the county courthouse. They march past vacant storefronts, a diner called Popcorn Willy, a statue of disheveled men standing by a parking lot that was erected as a tribute to the Whiskey Rebels, and the home of their leader, David Bradford, which sits across from a Suboxone clinic. The event used to culminate with a party hosted by Maker's Mark at the George Washington Hotel, where an inflatable bottle of whiskey dominated the lobby. Now it takes place at a Hilton Garden Inn.

The celebration is a gleeful way to reclaim a narrative of rebellion. In the past several years, a handful of artisanal distilleries have reopened in Washington. One, Mingo Creek Craft Distillers, produces Liberty Pole Spirits, named for the wooden staff that has been used since the days of the Roman Empire as an emblem of freedom from tyranny. When Washington's troops marched into town, these poles hung from the windows of buildings and homes. Today, in the distillery's tasting room, a portrait of Alexander Hamilton hangs upside down.

8 | DOUBTERS

In Amity, which lies along Appalachia's suburban edge, one might find a developer's McMansion next to an accomplished artist's farm. But the world Stacey cared about was smaller: a network of families known for their ties to the land and its history. In both Amity and Prosperity, this history centered around the old country churches. At Thanksgiving, the parishioners from Lower Ten Mile Presbyterian joined those from Amity United Methodist and Liberty United Methodist to share a turkey dinner. Stacey's mother, Linda, usually cooked the turkey. It was typically a joyful occasion, one that recalled a past when neighbors came together to help thresh wheat and barley on one another's farms.

In 2010, however, as news of Harley's recent diagnosis spread through Amity, Stacey felt awkward making her way around the volunteer fire hall. When she talked about the latest with Harley, some people remained silent. She suspected that people who'd always supported her—including her cousins the Hartleys—were avoiding her. No one challenged her directly, but that wasn't the way in Amity. She didn't need to be openly contradicted to feel the lack of support. As the story circulated, there were those who thought Stacey was acting out of hysteria, and others who suspected she was angling for a payday.

Her neighbors' opinions about Harley's health often had less to do with the boy's welfare and more to do with their positions on fracking. Few wanted to challenge the benefits. For the first time, the people of Amity stood to make money from the mineral wealth beneath their corn and wheat fields. With coal and oil, most of that money had left, filling corporate coffers and leaving only costs behind. With fracking, however, people finally were cashing in on what belonged to them in the form of bonus checks and royalties. There was also something innately American—befitting the libertarian ethos that individualism was the root of success—in the new oil and gas wealth that sprang from the ground. The United States is one of the only countries in the world where people can own separate rights to the surface and what's belowground. They can also own rights to the air above their heads. In Hoopy country, there's a saying: "In America you own heaven to hell."

These differences showed up in the Sunday collection plates. The larger landowners, who were making more money, mostly belonged to the Methodist churches, and not to Stacey's. The gas well checks allowed them the first chance in years to contribute more to their churches, but Stacey's church, with members living in town or on small plots of land, continued to confront hardships. One former Range employee explained the newly sown divisions to me like this: "We're going to give you a new road, but it's going to cost you this forty-five-year friendship and you can't pave over that."

To many of the larger landowners, Harley's story of arsenic poisoning also seemed far-fetched. Rick Baker didn't know what to make of the test results. It was true that arsenic was naturally occurring. The poison may be dangerous in drinking water, but it was already in the ground. It also wasn't used in drilling. So how could anyone be sure that Harley's arsenic poisoning had anything to do with fracking? Baker didn't live near a waste pond, but he did live only a few thousand feet from the compressor station. Around compressor stations, there were also health issues, which began with the simple act of building an industrial site—with dust laden with diesel particles—next to people's homes. When the compressors were up and running, according to one Pennsylvania study, 27 percent of participants who lived between 1,500 and 4,000 feet away reported throat irritation.

Other symptoms included dizziness, nausea, chronic bronchitis, and depression. Yet other than the fact that the compressor station could be noisy at night—much noisier initially than the company had prepared him for—Baker had none of the illnesses that people reported. He had no headaches, no nosebleeds; none of the Haneys' symptoms, and they lived about half a mile farther away from the compressor.

"It's the people who aren't benefiting from this who have nothing else to do but raise a stink," Tony Berardi, the land man, said. "Stacey's an anomaly because she does have skin in the game, but if she had fifty thousand acres and was making ten thousand dollars a month, I'm sure she'd feel differently." Harley's illness was also morally threatening. If he was in fact a guinea pig for industry while they were cashing life-changing checks, then it followed that the landowners were making that money at the cost of someone's health. Not a random stranger's, but that of Harley Haney, the great-great-grandson of Oliver Mankey and grandson of Linda and Larry Hillberry, members of the historical society, the volunteer fire department, and the altar guild. Nor was this experiment taking place sometime in the dusty history of resource extraction when no one knew any better. Whatever was happening to Harley was part of an industrial process that was just beginning and promised to cover more and more green hillsides.

Outside of church, both sides crossed paths at the chainsaw repair shop that Stacey's cousin Willard Mankey ran out of the old family business on Amity Ridge Road, which locals called 19. It was once a major thoroughfare not far from the National Road. Mankey Brothers used to be Amity's only car dealership. Until 1967, the Mankey Brothers hosted one of the town's most anticipated events: the annual arrival of the new-model Fords and Chevys. Before unveiling the cars, the Mankey Brothers hung gold curtains in the plate-glass windows and handed out Coca-Colas and rulers to kids. Then the interstate highway bypassed the town. The last car they sold was a 1967

Chevy. Willard made his living repairing chainsaws people already owned. There wasn't much of a market in Amity for anything new.

Then that changed: from 2007 to 2012, the gas boom brought fifteen thousand industry-related jobs to Pennsylvania. Alongside engineers and welders who arrived with expertise from places like Texas and Arkansas, the oil and gas companies brought with them a host of needs to fill. From motels to Laundromats to restaurants, the pass-on effects of industry lifted struggling businesses, including Willard's shop. Due to the boom, in addition to repairing chainsaws, he was finally selling things. Willard stocked the kind of toys grown-up boys liked, most of which the farmers of Amity never could have afforded before. Lately, his most popular item had become a portable sawmill, which cost five thousand dollars. The sawmill allowed farmers who loved to tinker on their land a way to make fences by cutting their own logs.

After Willard watched the first flush of gas-rush cash arrive, he witnessed a second. First landowners made money from leases; now they were selling right-of-ways for an underground web of pipelines. As the roughnecks who built the gas sites pulled out of town, a new slew of workers arrived: pipeliners. Building pipelines was big business, as well as a major controversy. Beneath Pennsylvania alone, there lay 77,000 miles of pipeline, enough to ring the earth three times. Sunoco Logistics had projects slated to generate nearly $4.2 billion in economic activity in Pennsylvania, support as many as 30,000 construction jobs, and generate nearly $62 million in new taxes to the commonwealth, according to a 2015 study by Econsult, a Philadelphia-based company. To lay these pipelines that would transport the primordial gas to urban markets, companies needed to dig trenches across farmers' land. Once again, farmers were compensated, and the more money that flowed into town, the deeper the divide grew between those getting large checks and those left out of the rush. The funny thing was, Willard stopped selling chainsaws again. Farmers had so much money they could afford to turn up their thermostats and burn oil.

Willard himself, having seen how sick Harley was, didn't doubt the veracity of his illness, but he also didn't want to cost himself the business of the larger landowners, like Stacey's neighbor Ray Day and her cousin Bill Hartley, who were highly respected in Amity and suddenly had money to spend in his store. Hartley, who ran a barbershop out of a trailer on his great-grandmother's farm, doubted Stacey's story. His son worked for Range Resources, as did many of the people he knew, and he just thought it sounded extreme. Hartley was hardset in his conservative politics. Above all, he adhered to the essential argument that landowners like him believed in and often repeated: over centuries, Amity and Prosperity had paid full well for the energy that city folk consumed, and now city folk who didn't own land and didn't stand to make any money off of fracking were jealous. As Hartley saw it, Stacey's story served as ready fodder for outsiders who opposed fracking. And anything that served as fodder for outsiders who thought they had the right to judge the lives of people about whom they knew nothing filled Bill Hartley with disgust.

Willard tried to stay out of it. "I'm in the middle of everything," he told me. "I make money off of farmers making money, so I'm okay with it," he said. "But with all that's happened to Stacey, she isn't." And nobody said anything bad about Harley directly, not once—"Nobody wanted to be smart-asses," he said. As Willard saw it, his first responsibility was to feed his family. His girlfriend and her two teenage daughters moved from the town of Washington to his home on Amity Ridge Road. At least three times a week, he had to haul water from Ruff Creek to fill his cistern for their showers. The city girls didn't understand its scarcity, and Willard preferred to haul more rather than to fight. With his newfound busyness, he saw less and less of Stacey and the kids. Willard's absence proved hardest on Paige, who'd seen her cousin as a father figure since her own father was largely out of the picture.

Behind these small domestic dramas, Stacey was deeply unsettled by the feeling that she was losing her place in the world. For so long, she'd prided herself on being a daughter of this soil. Now she feared that soil was turning against her.

This applied in particular to Stacey's most powerful neighbors. Among them were Ray and Jon Day, who, with their sisters, owned a three-hundred-acre cattle farm planted with orchard grass less than two miles from Stacey's. The Day Farm had been in the family for more than a century, and the Days were well-off even before the gas wells came. They were part of the local elite, which existed quietly in Amity and Prosperity. Some like the Days had earned comfortable pensions from full-time careers doing something other than farming. Every summer since their father passed away in 1980, they'd held an annual Beef Roast for 350 of their friends and neighbors. Stacey didn't know the Days very well, so she'd never been invited.

Ray and Jon Day also worked to preserve local history that recalled an earlier, more prosperous time. They collected Duncan Miller glass, which had been produced in Washington during the nineteenth century, before mechanization helped drive the factory out of business. Along with Stacey's dad and other people from Amity, they'd also restored the historic log cabin that once belonged to Thaddeus Dod. On nearly every Thursday morning over four and a half years, the men had taken the cabin apart, log by log, then rebuilt it. When Range Resources donated two thousand dollars to the historical society, Ray took it as a sign that the company intended to be a good neighbor.

He was less sure about Stacey. Although his sister worked as a nurse with Stacey at the hospital, and he knew Linda and Larry from the historical society, he didn't know Stacey well. In his opinion, if she were a true daughter of Amity, he'd see more of her at things like Amity's annual historical tour, alongside her parents. But he didn't. Stacey was aware of racking up community absences, and it made her self-conscious; it bothered her to be less active at church. But if she was working seven days a week, how was she supposed to be there?

"Sometimes when I'm in the thick of dealing with all of this, I can't deal with one more thing," she told me. "I've got to get the laundry done. I've got to get the food that we need for the house. I can't do the historical tour. Mam doesn't get it. I used to be able to do it all—take care of everything and go to the historical tour, and go to church on Sundays."

From a distance, Day didn't see Stacey's being a single mom working full-time and raising two kids as much of an excuse. Loyalty in Amity meant showing up for the community no matter what. He had even less faith in the Voyles. "They're not farmers," he said. They may have horses, but they didn't grow anything. What's more, they didn't join the Grange, a national organization founded in 1867 to promote new farming techniques and safeguard the welfare of farmers. Day had also heard the tales about the Voyles' litigiousness. Sob stories didn't go down well in Amity, where lots of people had it hard. Until the gas wells, Ray Day—who was sixty-three and wore the raw squint of hard work outside in all weather—had worked two full-time jobs. The first time I met him, when he gave me a tour of the farm, he chided me gently. "You haven't asked me what my profession is," he said. No one here could afford to farm full-time. For thirty-four years, until he retired, Ray taught science at Trinity Middle School, taking his place at the blackboard and looking out at the earnest faces of children whose parents he knew well. Over decades, much of Amity had passed through his classroom. Day had developed a knack for noticing a fatherless boy or one who might not be getting enough to eat. He'd hired these foundlings as farmhands to come help put up hay or do other small jobs, which also allowed him to offer a generous word, a meal, and enough money to help a family get through a rough patch. These days, however, Day couldn't afford to hire local boys in need. Due to regulations, the state required the Days to carry workers' compensation for everyone on the farm, and they couldn't pay for the insurance.

Instead, the Days turned to machines to run the farm. This pained them: they knew there was a need for local work. But smaller farms like theirs were being squeezed out by this kind of regulation that mandated expensive insurance. At the same time, the average age of local farmers climbed to fifty-six. Over the years, his experience of regulation and the excesses of unions, which he'd seen firsthand as a teacher, helped turn Day into a conservative Republican.

Like other farmers', Day's distrust of the federal government and of regulations was embodied in a dislike of the Environmental Protection Agency. As people in Amity saw it, the EPA didn't fix problems. They created them, by pointing out issues that required residents to pay for expensive alterations or face government fines. This helped to explain why the EPA was so unpopular. Here was a typical scenario, Day told me. When drilling started on his land, the dust from the access road was so bad that a neighbor kept complaining. The easiest solution would've been to pave the dirt road, but the EPA wouldn't let Range do it. "They'd have solved all the problems if they'd just black-topped it," Day said. It got so bad the man had to move, which exemplified the stupidity of paper pushers in faraway places making decisions for Washington County.

As Day saw it, the recent return of gas had been a boon. For years, their barn's roof "needed replaced," in the local parlance, and the fence that, by law, had to keep the cows out of his stream was falling down. Money from signing a mineral lease made these fixes and others possible. Although Ray and his brother Jon expected little when they signed with Range Resources, they'd been astounded when their first check arrived.

"It was more money than I made in the first twenty years of teaching combined," Ray told me. He preferred not to share the exact figure, as that would be crass. Regardless, he put all of it back into the property: replacing two roofs, buying a new hay baler, building his ninety-four-year-old mother a first-floor bathroom so she wouldn't have to climb the stairs and could remain in her home. Farmers like him didn't buy sports cars with their windfalls. They bought health insurance.

"We don't go to Florida," he told me, echoing his neighbor Rick Baker. He still spent his chilly mornings mucking cow stalls alongside Jason Clark, a former student now in his thirties and helping the Days in exchange for keeping his pigs in their barn. Clark was also making money off the gas boom. He had a small lease on his two acres of land. The few thousand dollars from Range had changed his life, he said, allowing him to buy better stock and breed stronger pigs.

The problem wasn't natural gas. It was excessive regulation. Every time Clark had to give a pig an antibiotic shot, the law now required that he have a veterinarian write a prescription. That was fifty dollars per farm call, plus the cost of the medication. What really burned Clark up, however, wasn't just the cost of the vet; it was the fact that if he wanted Oxy or any other opioid, he could just drive up the highway ten minutes to Washington, pop into the Med-Express, and say that his shoulder hurt him.

Clark had watched so many friends get hooked on painkillers, and then, when their scripts ran out, or to save money, move on to heroin, which was cheaper than the pain pills that doctors overprescribed. His pigs were under more regulation than humans, he felt, and that seemed wrong. Yet when outsiders came to his community, they wagged their fingers over fracking. Really? Pennsylvania had the third highest death rate from opioids in America. An average of eight or nine people died every day. Along with the ready availability of pills, it was the injuries born of heavy labor in places such as coal mines and farms, combined with the economic stress of poverty, that helped to drive the epidemic in small towns like Amity and Prosperity.

Still, Clark bristled at environmentalists and reporters who assumed they understood how corporations were taking advantage of rural Americans. The idea that people who lived on the front lines of Frackistan were somehow being duped by the shadowy forces of industry made him chuckle in anger. After Washington County had given

away its coal, oil, and gas for nothing, fracking was finally a chance
to get even. And the problem wasn't just the coastal elite, it was urban
people everywhere. "People who live in Pittsburgh or Philadelphia
are bottom-feeders who don't want to know where their meat or their
energy comes from," he told me. They could afford to leave people in
Amity and Prosperity alone.

9 | HANG 'EM HIGH

From the flood in the swamp

to frack of the mountain

this land down here is one big fountain

. . . And if you muddy my water, I will come after you

    —RISING APPALACHIA, "FILTHY DIRTY SOUTH"

N ot everyone wanted to be left alone. By the fall of 2010, a dozen Washington County farmers were gathering regularly with a handful of Pittsburgh activists and university professors. They met once a month in an empty bank building near the Meadows Racetrack. The meeting, called "Hang 'Em High," was organized by the local branch of the Izaak Walton League, an American conservationist society named for the avid English fisherman and author of *The Compleat Angler*, first published in 1653.

Its members saw themselves not as environmentalists—a term for political liberals advancing all kinds of agendas—but as conservationists who believed in the prudent use of resources. Many members were hunters and fishermen who, like Stacey's father, were also Vietnam veterans and former steelworkers and coal miners. To people unfamiliar with their pasts, these men might seem unlikely candidates to lead the local pushback against fracking, but they weren't.

Stacey, who hated big, rowdy gatherings, was willing to attend only because she trusted these old Vietnam vets. Like her father, they'd come home bearing the scars of a war they fiercely believed they'd fought for their country, only to lose their jobs in the collapse of America's steel and coal industries. Many still belonged to labor unions, and a history of distrusting corporations ran through their veins.

Even still, Hang 'Em High made Stacey uncomfortable: she feared being seen there. For so long, she'd believed that if she stayed out of the spotlight and didn't criticize the company publicly, Range would realize who she was: a concerned mother with kids sickened by exposure to industrial waste. She was a reasonable person, she thought. All she had to do was not embarrass the company, and eventually, Range would take responsibility. Yet weeks had passed since she'd delivered Harley's test results to Range's corporate offices, and although the company kept delivering water, she'd heard nothing. Her sense of personal disillusionment grew. So did her fear of collective harm. Run-down and racing between work, the farm animals, and doctors' appointments, she was driven by outrage and a feeling of ownership.

On one frigid night at the end of 2010, she climbed into the iron-cold Pontiac and drove thirty minutes north along Washington Road to the former Highmark bank building. She went to listen, not to speak. As nearly fifty people she didn't know swapped information they'd pulled off the Internet, she wondered about the accuracy of their sources. People were scared and they knew next to nothing. At some of these meetings, there was a sense of hysteria: people flocking to get aboard a bandwagon against fracking, which Stacey understood but wanted no part of. She also worried there might be industry spies among the strangers, and she didn't want anyone hearing her complain and then reporting back to Range.

She slid into her seat at Hang 'Em High in the dark. Before her, there was a blown-up photograph of a waste pond projected on the wall. Her gaze drifted to the little farm next door to the pond's void. She noticed a ranch house and a split-rail fence that encircled a horse paddock. Lower down the snaking road, there was a white farmhouse with a tin-roof lean-to.

That was her farm, Stacey murmured to a fellow nurse sitting beside her in the dark. Here, on-screen, was the pond she'd seen on Google

Earth. She could also see the surrounding canopy of trees more clearly. They were dark green as broccoli, except at the pond's southwestern edge, where several had turned red and yellow out of season. They appeared to be dying. Now that the image was enlarged, she could see in the dark gray waste what looked to be white misters. So that's what those white dots were on Google Earth: aerators.

The aerators spooked her. It looked from the swirls of white like there was some kind of spray coming out of them. If the chemicals from the water were spraying into the air, then she and the kids had a problem more daunting than water. If they were breathing poisoned air, replacing water wouldn't matter. She'd already suspected as much. There were the nosebleeds, and that winter, when the process of burning off gas, called flaring, began nearby, Stacey, Harley, and Paige felt like their headaches were worsening. Since testing the air was beyond the means of Stacey and her neighbors, she realized that she'd have to put the puzzle together by testing for what might be in their bodies.

That night, at Hang 'Em High, she began to ask the questions she'd long avoided. She feared what she'd find: if their bodies showed evidence of exposure to airborne toxins, they'd have to leave the farm. She moved around the crowded room asking if someone might know how to figure out the testing required for inhalants.

But that level of expertise was mostly absent at Hang 'Em High, which was often more of a generalized gripe session about the state of the world, and being left out of it. "We went to Vietnam to fight for the rights of people, and you come back and they're taking people's mineral rights," Ken Gaman, a retired coal miner and Vietnam veteran, grumbled. This rang true to Stacey. It was her father's kind of talk of fighting for a government that ended up selling you out. "We don't want to stop the drilling. We want to do it the right, American way," he added.

Their complex, sometimes contradictory history was present in the name Hang 'Em High. Ken Gaman had chosen the name because he thought it meant grabbing corporate interests by the short and curl-ies. He hadn't caught the obvious reference to lynching.

In certain respects, the retirees were cut in the mold of Teddy Roosevelt: they tried to further his mission to protect public land not for pristine wilderness but for the benefit of future generations. The principle of conservation has a longer history in Pennsylvania than almost anywhere else in America. The nineteenth-century movement arose out of the devastated landscape left by the timber industry. Philanthropists like Gifford Pinchot, the grandson of a lumber baron, campaigned to replant millions of trees by hand. Pinchot became the first chief of the U.S. Forestry Service as well as the governor of Pennsylvania. He also coined the term "conservation ethic," which balances the practical necessity of exploiting natural resources with the need to protect them.

From its beginnings, however, the conservation ethic was sharply curtailed by the coal industry. In Pennsylvania, when coal reigned supreme, from the Civil War to World War II, the industry was untouchable. Coal was exempted from most federal regulation, including the 1972 Clean Water Act and the 1974 Safe Drinking Water Act. (For the 2005 Energy Act, Vice President Dick Cheney successfully lobbied to exempt the fluids used in fracking from these same regulations. This was the "Halliburton loophole," which gave the industry much of the immunity from which coal had long benefited.) As multinational coal companies drove up their private profits, they socialized their costs, passing them off to locals in the form of health issues and environmental problems, along with joblessness when the companies went bankrupt and pulled out of small towns. When coal and steel were at their peak, the rivers of the rust belt were so toxic they caught fire. According to the U.S. Army Corps of Engineers, the Monongahela River was once more acidic than lemon juice. It couldn't support a single fish. In Western Pennsylvania, fishermen who were also conservationists were forced to give up the sport. The scale of the pollution alarmed them, although there was little they could do against the forces of industry.

"Only suicides, uninformed children, and the mentally deficient voluntarily dive into the lower Monongahela, the lower Allegheny or the upper Ohio," William Schulz Jr., a Pennsylvania conservationist, wrote in his 1953 *Conservation Law*.

Rachel Carson, the legendary environmentalist, grew up against the backdrop of this devastation. From her childhood window in Springdale, a river town north of Pittsburgh, she watched horses climbing a ramp into a glue factory along the Allegheny's bank. As an adult, Carson, who worked as a biologist for the U.S. Fish and Wildlife Service, embodied the shift from an earlier generation of conservation ethics to the beginning of the modern-day environmental movement. Like any conservationist, Carson believed in the human use of natural resources. She saw people and the natural world as interrelated, a principle she laid out in her 1962 book, *Silent Spring*. In it, she defined the way pollutants travel the food chain for the first time for a popular audience: if a mayfly consumed a harmful chemical like DDT, then a fish ate the fly and a human ate the fish, then DDT could pose a risk to humans.

This wasn't a radical idea; it was a reasonable one. And it had far-reaching effects. President Kennedy asked his Science Advisory Committee to investigate the implications of "Ms. Carson's book," and eight years later, President Nixon founded the EPA around the idea that "the environment must be perceived as a single, interrelated system." The chemical industry vehemently opposed *Silent Spring*, challenging its accuracy and Carson's biases. Carson weathered the battle while suffering from breast cancer, which almost no one knew about. She died in 1964.

Seven years later, Pennsylvania took the visionary step of adopting a constitutional amendment to its Bill of Rights, guaranteeing its citizens "the right to clean air and pure water." The amendment had overwhelming bipartisan support. Despite its lofty language, however, the Environmental Rights Amendment remained little more than a

gesture. During the seventies, the steel and coal industries of Western Pennsylvania were too powerful to have to pay much attention.

As the mills closed in the 1980s, a nascent green movement in
Pittsburgh mobilized around reviving the rivers for recreation as well
as for environmental health. Eventually the rust belt's rivers began
to grow cleaner. Yet there were ongoing problems. Acid mine drainage polluted fifteen thousand miles of rivers and streams. And waste
wasn't solely an industrial issue. Despite a federal mandate to cut the
amount of sewage flowing into the rivers by half by 2026, an estimated
nine billion gallons of raw sewage ran into rivers each year. One tell-
tale sign of human waste is corn. Hard for the body to digest, it often
comes through the system whole. Pittsburgh's streams were littered
with yellow kernels.

The pollution from fracking was harder to see and harder to clean
up. What if some of the chemicals used in fracking—the antifreeze and
fuels, the ancient radioactive materials, synthetics and astronomic levels of salt—combined to be more dangerous than people knew? From
the beginning, two of the biggest issues related to fracking concerned
water: where to get the millions of gallons required for a frack and
what to do with the liquid waste.

In Pennsylvania, the early efforts to dispose of this waste by hauling it to local sewage plants had proved disastrous. The local plants
didn't have the capacity to do anything but remove solids before dumping the water back into the river. Eventually, under pressure, the DEP
banned the practice. Instead, liquid waste was often mixed with sawdust and spread on farm fields, a method that enjoyed legal protection
under the label "beneficial use." Or it was trucked to deep wells in
Pennsylvania and Ohio, where it was injected into the earth. By 2014,
this practice had been demonstrated to cause earthquakes.

At Hang 'Em High, the retired miners and steelworkers of the
Izaak Walton League were learning to test the water flowing out from
old coal mines. The discharge coming from the abandoned mines

wasn't the ordinary mine drainage. It was high in a kind of salt called a bromide. When that salt mixed with the chlorine of treated drinking water, it formed a carcinogen.

Either this or something else was killing fish along the anglers' favorite rivers. The old-timers had taken to driving around tailing waste trucks as senior-citizen sleuths. There was one local waste hauler whose trucks they especially followed: Robert Allan Shipman. Shipman was Amity's former fire chief and the heir to a porta-potty fortune. He was also dumping industrial waste at night. Around Amity and Prosperity, Shipman's practices were no secret. Once, in the middle of the day, Beth Voyles spotted Shipman letting wastewater run into the creek down by her vet's office.

This enraged the men of Hang 'Em High, who traded intelligence about Shipman's escapades. They'd even gone so far as to tip off local authorities and were hearing rumors that Shipman was about to be indicted for environmental crimes. Stacey knew Shipman. Most of the men in her family had served alongside him as Amity's volunteer firemen. As she walked around Hang 'Em High, looking for someone to talk to about inhalants, she heard the old-timers grousing about Shipman and hoping he'd soon land in jail.

10 | BLOOD AND URINE

The medical tests that Stacey and the kids were to undergo at the beginning of 2011 required a lot of blood. Unlike most people in her position, Stacey, at least, had help figuring out what to test for. Stacey found Calvin Tillman through her growing contacts with a nationwide network of activists seeking more scientific facts regarding fracking. Tillman, the former mayor of Dish, Texas, taught Stacey about inhalants. Tillman's fellow citizens were not predisposed to distrust industry: they'd adopted the name Dish in exchange for free satellite TV. Yet the corporate interests of oil and gas were another matter, and Tillman had recently gone up against those interests to try to prove their operations were sickening his kids and his town and lost. It was nearly impossible, Tillman found, to make a causal link between exposure and illness.

Still, Tillman knew what to test for, so he sent Stacey a list that she gave to the head of the lab at Washington Hospital. He told her that assessing this kind of exposure required knowledge of the basics of toxicology, the branch of medicine that studied the harm that chemicals caused living organisms. Stacey, Harley, and Paige would be the organisms in question.

Stacey was still working out the inhalant testing when she received a call from Range asking her to come into the office. The results of her water tests were in. To discuss them, Stacey was scheduled to meet with two women, Laura Rusmisel and her boss, Carla Suszkowski, a regulatory and environmental director. Together, they often assessed water complaints from homeowners like Stacey and Beth. That day,

Beth received a similar call. Both families were to go into Range's offices on January 14, 2011. For moral support and also to serve as one another's witnesses, Beth and Stacey wanted to face Range together. But Carla Suszkowski preferred to meet with each family alone. Beth and John Voyles would take the first meeting. On the phone, Beth was already angry enough to spit fire, but she tried to be polite. She also assumed that if Rusmisel wanted to meet face-to-face, then Range was ready to admit something was wrong. She asked if she could bring something home-cooked for the employees, maybe sloppy joes or ham barbecue.

Stacey was hopeful too: If Range wasn't going to take responsibility for Harley's arsenic poisoning, why else would they call her in? Still, she didn't want to go alone, so she brought along Shelly's husband, Big Jim Pellen, a volunteer fireman who weighed more than three hundred pounds and was off work for an injury. Given his size, and a sullen brow that gave him an appearance of gruffness that vanished as soon as he spoke, Stacey and the kids called him Polar Bear. As long as he kept his mouth shut, his glower intimidated.

On a frosty midwinter morning, she and Jim loaded Harley into her car to drive to Southpointe. Off of I-79, one industry billboard read "While the energy debate continues, we'll keep powering America." By 2011, the fight over whether or not fracking was safe was putting pressure on the industry to prove that drilling wasn't harmful to water or to air. People like Stacey and Beth were threatening, in that their experiences challenged the industry's claims. To fight back, the gas companies advertised the benefits of what industry would bring to the region: jobs. Along I-79, another billboard featured a photograph of a translucent baby against a black background, asking, "Engineer? Welder?"

To Stacey, these signs were manipulative: people needed steady work. Some young people she knew were even taking jobs in oil and gas so that they could get health insurance. That was what the world had come to, she thought. People were so desperate for health insurance they were willing to take jobs that made others sick. She got off the highway and turned left at the exit, then pulled into the parking lot of a redbrick building with green glass windows. In the lobby, they met Bob Saflin, a senior land man at Range. He asked Harley how his guitar playing was going. Harley guessed Saflin heard he played guitar from his teacher, Rick Baker. Although Saflin was trying to be friendly, the question unnerved the boy. Harley took it as a threat: a means to let the fourteen-year-old know that he had been looked into, investigated.

On the way into the conference room, Stacey, Harley, and Jim ran into Beth and John Voyles on their way out. By the wildness in Beth's eyes and the set of her jaw, Stacey could see that Beth was livid. They're taking our water, she whispered at Stacey before they moved on down the hall. Stacey and her family were ushered into the conference room, where Laura Rusmisel and Carla Suszkowski waited. Stacey noticed that Rusmisel was pregnant and that Suszkowski had dyed her pixie haircut fire-engine red.

Together they told Stacey that in two sets of tests, on November 10 and 19 of 2010, the independent water testing company hired by Range had determined that her family's water wasn't affected by their operations. Rusmisel handed Stacey test results to confirm that her water was perfectly fine.

But Stacey believed that she had proof otherwise from the rapid arsenic tests she'd been performing on her own well. According to her results, the levels were low but there was arsenic in their water. Harley asked about his arsenic poisoning. Wasn't his illness evidence enough of contamination? The arsenic could've come from anywhere, the Range employees told him. Maybe he got it from woodshop.

Woodshop was only one semester, he replied. And he'd been out of school sick. Across the room, Harley studied one employee who had his boots up on the conference table. The man kept checking his phone. Harley saw this as a marker of privilege and disrespect. To him, the act signaled how little he mattered.

Stacey scanned the results. She'd asked Range specifically to test for ethylene glycol, the antifreeze she and Beth had been concerned about for months. Based on her late-night reading online, she knew the chemical was in frack fluid. She'd read on the Centers for Disease Control website that glycols leach into groundwater. They target the eyes, skin, liver, kidneys, and respiratory system, as well as the central nervous system. In her research, she'd learned that other animals are more sensitive to glycols than humans. A few drops might kill a goat but not a person. On the tests in front of her, glycols were missing. When she asked the women about glycols, they told her they hadn't found them, so they weren't on the test results.

Since their results indicated no contamination, the company had no obligation to provide water. Range Resources was going to remove the water buffalo. Laura Rusmisel had just handed Beth a letter saying much the same thing.

Stacey begged the two women to let her family keep the water buffalo, and, by the meeting's end, although the women didn't say yes, they didn't say no either. Two weeks later, on January 21, 2011, Dean's showed up next door to remove the water buffalo from Justa Breeze. The Haneys' water buffalo stayed put.

Stacey noted that in her dealings with the company, she should try to remain reasonable and keep her mouth shut in public. She assumed that she'd kept her water because she'd behaved better than Beth did in their meetings at Range's Southpointe headquarters. In private, however, she kept testing her water and asked Bob Fargo, the hydrologist she'd hired, to come back out for another round of testing in early February. She wanted him to test for glycols.

On February 23, 2011, Fargo called Stacey to tell her he'd found both diethylene glycol and triethylene glycol in her water. She grabbed a sheet of loose-leaf paper from her journal and took down what he said: *Extremely toxic causes severe abdominal pain.* Maybe arsenic was only part of the problem. Maybe antifreeze too had something to do with the toxic burden on Harley's body. Concerned, Bob Fargo alerted the DEP to the fact that he'd found glycols. The DEP, in turn, alerted Range. In the internal emails that ensued, Rusmisel prepared a list of chemicals used in the frack for the DEP and asked her boss, Suszkowski, if there were others. Suszkowski expressed concern about handing over such information to the state agency: "Is Vince asking for those data sheets? I am not sure I am comfortable with the ask. We can look at them. But we need to make darned sure that there is no arsenic or ethylene glycol shown in any of those chemicals because that is most likely what they are looking for."

During that difficult winter of 2011, Stacey knew only that Fargo's test results and Range's didn't match. She hoped that the inhalant panels, which would show if they'd been exposed to airborne carcinogens, would help shed light on what was happening to them.

On February 2, 2011, the day of the tests, she noted, *5 tubes of blood for all 3 of us . . . Hard to watch.* The twenty-four-hour urines were trickier: they required peeing from morning to night into an orange plastic jug. The half-lives of some of the contaminants were so brief, she'd have to pee almost immediately after exposure or the poison wouldn't show up in the tests.

Stacey was buoyed by the belief that she and the kids would soon be vindicated. By now a parade of special agents and various investigators from the Environmental Protection Agency was visiting her house regularly. Both civil and criminal investigators spent hours interviewing Stacey and the kids. Soon afterward, a public health inspector arrived from Philadelphia.

Lora Werner assessed chemical exposure risks for the Centers for Disease Control, and she'd heard about Stacey and Beth through fellow government employees. Werner worked at the CDC's Agency for Toxic Substances and Disease Registry (ATSDR), which, since the eighties, had been evaluating not just individuals like Stacey and Beth but entire communities. The agency was hobbled in its efforts to assess the oil and gas industry, however. Decades before the Halliburton loophole exempted fracking waste from most federal regulation, the fossil fuel industry was freed from the superfund legislation under which ATSDR functioned. Werner and her colleagues could investigate health risks related to drill sites only in very narrow terms. Werner was regional director; she was also from Philadelphia, which made her a stranger. But Werner, who came to this work from a background in environmental science, struck Stacey as especially committed and down-to-earth. Maybe because she was a woman, and also a fellow mom, her concern seemed deeper, more genuine, than that of some of the others traipsing through Stacey's house. Like Stacey, Werner wore little makeup and loved the outdoors, taking her two kids camping in national parks. A member of Werner's small team had also grown up in Washington County, which made Stacey comfortable with their sitting at her antique kitchen table for hours at a time.

Through Stacey's involvement with the EPA, a scientist named Richard Wilkin found her. Wilkin also worked for the EPA, in the scientific wing of the Office of Research and Development. As an environmental geochemist, he'd investigated everything from coal mining to fireworks, and now he was tasked with heading a two-year nationwide study to investigate fracking's impact on drinking water, he told Stacey on the phone. Mandated by Congress in 2010, this study, called "Hydraulic Fracturing for Oil and Gas: Impacts from the Hydraulic Fracturing Water Cycle on Drinking Water Resources," was going to be the largest of its kind, and Wilkin asked Stacey if she and her neighbors were willing to participate as one of only five test sites across the United States.

For Stacey, being chosen for the study bolstered her hopes. Maybe all that they'd been through wouldn't be for nothing. She and the kids just had to endure the mess up the hill a little while longer. She didn't know, however, that the EPA had already tangled with Range Resources in Texas over water contamination—and lost. In 2010, the EPA found fuel had leached in two water wells near Fort Worth, where Range was operating. In response, the federal government employed its rarely invoked "emergency powers" for the first and only time against a gas company, ordering Range to cease operations that put human health at risk. (The EPA would later invoke "emergency powers" in Flint, Michigan.)

Range challenged the legality of the EPA's actions and argued that the contaminants were naturally occurring. According to an internal email from an EPA attorney, Pennsylvania's former governor Ed Rendell intervened in the case by meeting with Lisa Jackson, the administrator of the EPA, to discuss a possible settlement. Rendell's former deputy chief of staff, Scott Roy, a registered lobbyist, had been hired as vice president of Government Relations.

The EPA dropped its charges, saying that the agency wanted to avoid a costly legal battle. In exchange, Range agreed to participate in the agency's two-year drinking water study. This participation never materialized.

One morning in February 2011, a month after Stacey's and Beth's meetings in the Range offices, a tanker truck filled with liquid waste flipped over on the ice and slid down the hill toward the trailer guarding the Yeager site. Inside the trailer, two security guards were changing shifts. Carl Warco, wiry and pushing fifty, had just finished working graveyard, from midnight to 8:00 a.m. One of the only women on-site, Breanne Buttermore, had just arrived to take over the day shift. Warco glanced out of the trailer window and saw the forty-ton tanker sliding toward them. He grabbed Breanne and dove out of the trailer as the truck slid past, missing them by feet.

The truck belonged to Highland Environmental Solutions, LLC. As the hazmat team arrived to clean up its diesel and frack fluid spill, Breanne ran down the hill and banged on Beth's door. She told Beth that Warco had saved her.

Warco knew Beth's daughter, Ashley; they rode Harley-Davidsons together in a large group on the weekends. On mornings when he was leaving work, he often waited at the base of the access road for her. He knew that Ashley'd drive by on her way to her job at the Meadows Racetrack, where she was drug testing racehorses, taking blood and urine samples. Now that Jodi was dead, she wasn't barrel racing very often. She was struggling to keep a steady job. She kept shifting from drug testing to grooming at Burke's, a stable in Washington, then back again. She wasn't much of a talker. But sometimes she'd stop to chat with Warco when she saw him on the road.

He tried to keep the conversations casual as he told her repeatedly not to let her family or the animals drink their water. He didn't tell her why. In the early hours after dawn, he'd walked the perimeter of the waste pond when no one was around and seen liquid seeping from its side. Whatever it was gave off a chemical vapor, which he could see rising from the ground. The Voyles' and Haneys' farms lay directly down the hill. Warco didn't know the Haneys, but he worried about the water that the Voyles and their animals were drinking. He also didn't want to lose his job, so he kept his head down and his admonitions vague.

A few weeks after the accident, Beth was rounding the bend as she drove home when she saw another Highland truck coming down the gravel road. A valve in the back was gushing liquid. Beth stopped to flag the driver. You got something open back there, buddy, she recalled saying. It was just a little bit of wastewater, he replied. "A little bit my ass," Beth said later. She drove home to call the authorities. The spill was never cleaned up, and later, tests would reveal the presence of the fuels, benzene, toluene, and acetone in the Yeagers' field. Beth had begun watching that hill with a hawk eye.

On Valentine's Day, Harley came down with some kind of flu, so Stacey drove him to Dr. Fox's office in downtown Washington and picked up the test results for the inhalant panels. Dr. Fox didn't know how to read them. Stacey didn't either. When she got home, she called the head of the lab at Washington Hospital to ask for help assessing the levels of two acids in particular, phenol and hippuric acid.

It wasn't so unusual to find them in people's bodies, but mostly among truck drivers or city-dwellers, not among farmers or those who lived out in the country. Phenol indicated exposure to benzene, a chemical compound found in cigarette smoke, crude oil, and gasoline. Long-term, she learned, it can cause blood-borne cancers, including leukemia. The hippuric acid in their bodies indicated that they'd been exposed to toluene, another compound related to gasoline that causes cancer. Benzene and toluene are volatile organic compounds predisposed to moving out of water and into air. Some, heavier than air, will travel downwind and downhill.

Stacey worried how these exposures would affect their future. Some had the potential to alter genes, and most created more acute problems in children due to their stature, the size of their lungs in relation to the rest of their bodies, and the fact that their nervous systems were still developing. She wandered around the house sniffing as Chris made his signature lasagna for Valentine's Day dinner. To save money, they stayed home and gave each other cards. Stacey loved hers. The outside was covered with white hearts. Inside, the printed card read *If I had my life to live over again, next time I'd find you sooner so I could love you longer.* Below, Chris scrawled, *You have made me so happy again and I hope it never stops.* It was easier for Chris to put down his feelings on paper than to speak them aloud.

That night Stacey was distracted. They haven't just ruined our water, she thought, they've poisoned our air. Unlike the water, which had been replaced by the water buffalo sitting in front of her house, there was no way to replace the air. They were going to have to leave. She wondered where they could go. Her parents had one extra room; Chris had another in the bungalow in Eighty Four. The town of

Eighty Four shared its name with the lumber company, but no one knew where the name came from—maybe a mile marker on the Baltimore & Ohio Railroad, maybe a post office that opened in 1884.

No one had enough room for a donkey, a horse, two goats, two cats, a dog, and six rabbits. The thought of dividing the kids from each other and from their animals was too much to bear. It was still winter, anyway. Maybe they'd be okay when the wind was blowing the chemicals away from their home. She'd keep the kids inside and the windows shut. She wrote, *Feel we are trapped btw the flare and the impoundment; can't even open the windows in our house.*

When she poked her head into a Hang 'Em High meeting one Saturday night in mid-March, a retired miner who belonged to the Izaak Walton League approached to ask if she'd be willing to tell her story publicly. In the coming weeks there was going to be a large meeting at the airport in Morgantown, West Virginia, where people were coming to learn about what it was like to live near fracking. Stacey said she'd think about it, by which she meant no. In addition to her fearing Range's retribution, public speaking made her uncomfortable. She hadn't been raised to call attention to herself, and hadn't spoken in front of a crowd since she'd played Betsy Ross in the third grade. She was also terrified that if she told her story in public, she might start crying and not be able to stop. The retired coal miner reassured her that the people in the audience would be like-minded locals, not industry folk. But, again, she was concerned that a spy from Range Resources could be in the audience, and it didn't seem worth the risk.

That evening, however, at Hang 'Em High, she learned more about the possible health impacts of the antifreeze in her water. Like DDT and other pesticides, glycols were endocrine disruptors: they had the capacity to harm fertility and hormonal development, especially in children. These problems, or others, might await Harley and Paige. What if her children couldn't have their own? What if they got cancer twenty years from now? Who would be around to pay for the health costs in two decades?

She decided that night that she had no other choice than to speak out. If Range were to punish her by removing the water buffalo, then that was a price she'd have to pay for warning others about the potential harm to their children.

On Sunday, March 13, 2011, still reeling from what she'd learned about glycols the night before, she was bent on making it to church with Paige and Harley in tow. With the divorce, Harley's illness, and the mowing, deworming, and chopping wood for the dragon, Stacey hadn't been supplying the church water, or attending at all, since Harley got sick. She knew that when she and her sister weren't there, the congregation often prayed for them. Pappy and Linda were always in their pew. After the 10:00 a.m. service, Stacey followed her parents home about half a mile down Amity Ridge Road. Pappy built bird feeders outside the house, which he sometimes electrified. Pappy didn't like starlings. They ate all his feed and scared away prettier songbirds, so he rigged up a current that ran through the bird feeder's perch, and a remote detonator, which he could press to blow the unwanted starlings sky-high. Avian IEDs. Inside the house, Pappy had built the stone hearth and screened porch, and paneled most rooms with salvaged wood. Linda had made the kitchen cabinet doors out of tin, into which she punched heart patterns. She made breakfast. Once Harley and Paige had eaten, Stacey sent them outside to play.

She had something to tell her parents, and it wasn't good. Bob Fargo, the hydrologist she'd hired, had found glycols in their drinking water. Antifreeze, basically. It could mess with the kids' genes, and make it hard for them to have children.

Standing at the stove, her mother stayed quiet and thought about Pappy. Since Vietnam, she'd always suspected that his exposure to Agent Orange might be playing a role in his ongoing health issues, and maybe also in his erratic behavior. And in fact, Larry Hillberry would soon be awarded $3,300 a month from the Department of Veterans Affairs in compensation. Yet exposure to Agent Orange was just one of the ways that Vietnam had altered Pappy. In sleep he raved about hovering black helicopters, and his daughters had been instructed never to wake him. He could be dangerous, and Stacey had grown up afraid of him. But that wasn't who Pappy was now. He'd do anything for his two daughters and their children. He growled that he wanted to barricade the gates up at the waste pond. Stacey knew he wasn't capable of anything like that, but she was touched by his desire to defend her, which in her childhood had felt so lacking to her. She wrote in her journal, *Crazy Ole Vietnam Vet.*

11 | AIRPORT

O n the evening of March 22, 2011, the night before Stacey was scheduled to speak at Morgantown Airport, Paige started vomiting. Stacey thought she might have to cancel and went to bed hoping that Paige would be well enough to get on the school bus in the morning. Paige woke still nauseous, so Stacey bundled her in plaid pajamas and drove south with her toward the Ruff Creek General Store. Newly stocked for gas well workers and coal miners, the once-somnolent shop now made take-out pizzas and burritos. Every tired worker wanted a warm meal. From Ruff Creek to Prosperity, general stores were doing better than they had since the mills and mines shut down. Stacey and Paige waited outside in the Ruff Creek parking lot for an Izaak Walton League member who was going to escort her the last thirty miles to make sure that she didn't get lost.

Following the old-timer's car, Stacey and Paige headed south along I-79 until they crossed into West Virginia. They hurtled past a mountain missing its peak. The snowy hillside flatlined. This was mountaintop removal.

When Stacey and Paige arrived at Morgantown Airport, the arrivals and departures lounge was already filled with farmers, politicians, and local conservationists—mostly gray-haired with bristle cuts. Stacey recognized some of them from the Izaak Walton League meetings, but she was too nervous to say hello. She and her daughter slid into two empty seats toward the front of the room. Paige, who was still wearing her pajamas under an oversized sweatshirt, laid her head on her mother's shoulder.

"I'm hungry," she murmured. Stacey shushed her. She'd tried to get Paige to eat something before they left, but the eleven-year-old had said she felt too sick. Stacey scanned down the agenda and stopped at the third item:

"Effects of Living Near Marcellus Pit Using Evaporative (Misting) Technology in Washington County, PA." Stacey Haney, Nurse.

There was her name. She was going to have to go through with the talk.

Already bored, Paige took the agenda from her mom's lap and doodled pictures of animals in the margins: Chuck the Chicken, Bob the Donkey, a pig named Pork.

When the spokesman called Stacey's name, she walked to the front of the lounge and gripped the lectern.

"I brought Kleenex and hopefully I won't cry," she began. "We live in the middle of five well sites. Right above us is a four-acre chemical impoundment fifteen hundred feet from our house.

"Since September 2009 my son has been sick but we didn't know what it was. He has had severe mouth ulcers, severe abdominal pain, lymph node swelling, nausea, and been not able to hardly move.

"In August, September, October of 2010, our animals started dying. My son's Grand Champion goat aborted two babies. Our neighbors lost a horse and puppies and we started putting two and two together and there might be a problem with our water. We called our family doctor and were tested for metals. I contacted the DEP. They came out and sampled for several constituents in frack water, but not diethylene and triethylene glycol, which are not supposed to be there. Both are on our test results. Range Resources has been providing us with water but they're not assuming responsibility.

"The whole time my son was sick I never thought in a million years this could be causing it. Never in a million years did we think this could be the problem. No one checked him for arsenic poisoning or toxic chemicals. Doctors have never seen this. I could kick myself for not figuring it out, but neither did the doctors.

"My neighbors and I signed leases three years ago. We didn't know this is what we would be dealing with. If I would've known what I know now I would've done all I could have done to get my neighbors to not sign leases too. They come, show you all these pretty pictures of beautiful land and little well caps. We asked good questions, but they lie, and now here we are.

"Did the chemicals get into the springs around our house? Have they seeped into the aquifer? Is there a leak in the pond at the top of the hill? We don't know. It's a puzzle and we're trying slowly to put pieces together.

"Last month, we discovered the benzene and toluene in us. It took us two months to figure out what inhalants we needed to be tested for. It's expensive but so far insurance covers it. Benzene and toluene, constituents of gasoline, are known to be carcinogenic and to cause birth defects. We get a bad odor from this impoundment. They came out and put something in it. Now the weather's nice and my kids are very much outside kids, do we go about our business? We're getting nosebleeds and headaches and last night, after working outside all day to tear down our old barn, my throat and eyes were burning.

"Basically, they've ruined our lives. They've ruined my home. We can't use our water. My home is worthless in terms of value. People wonder why we just don't leave. It's not that easy. I can't afford to rent a place to take both the animals and the kids. We're kind of in a financial bind. We're lucky they provide water, but we were there first. I don't want to give up our house."

"You did good, Mom. You only cried twice," Paige told Stacey when she sat down.

The purpose of the Morgantown meeting was really to discuss the fate of Dunkard Creek, the stream that formed the southern boundary of Washington County. Dunkard was a major fishing hole, and its abundance of fish was testimony to how local streams had rebounded from decades of coal mining. But in 2009, something had poisoned the water, killing everything that lived within it: an estimated 43,000 fish, 15,000 freshwater mussels, and 6,500 salamanders. At first, no one had known why the bloated bodies of muskies and mudpuppies rose from the creek as if stricken by plague. It turned out that the creek was suffering from an overgrowth of golden algae, a saltwater algae rarely found in fresh water. The golden algae killed fish by releasing a toxin that causes fish to bleed from the gills until they suffocate. But where the salt was coming from—that no one knew for sure. The men of the Izaak Walton League thought they had an answer: Amity's former fire chief Robert Allan Shipman's midnight dumping runs. He'd finally been indicted five days earlier on ninety-eight counts of environmental crimes. For several years, Shipman had been hauling waste for Consol Energy, and dumping that waste into abandoned coal mines also owned by the company, many of which flowed into Dunkard Creek. The state attorney general agreed. "You can't say he killed X number of fish," her spokesman said. "But did he play a role in compromising the quality of Dunkard Creek and other waterways in the area? No doubt about it."

At the meeting that day, the EPA was going to announce the deal it had struck with Consol Energy as reparation for the death of Dunkard Creek. When Jessica Greathouse, the EPA spokeswoman, took the podium after Stacey, she announced that Consol had agreed to pay a $5.5 million fine for violating the Clean Water Act. Consol also agreed to build a $200 million wastewater plant in West Virginia. But the company wasn't going to admit any role in killing Dunkard Creek, and Greathouse didn't mention Robert Allan Shipman or his recent indictment.

There were cries of outrage from the men in bib overalls standing in the back of the lounge. They knew what had happened at Dunkard. They'd lived it. A $5.5 million fine was little compared with the $7 million a year Shipman Sanitary made dumping, according to state estimates. And Consol wasn't even going to admit responsibility? The EPA spokeswoman hustled to sit down as the barrage of angry comments flew at her. (She has since left the federal government to work in the oil and gas industry.) But the outbursts kept coming. This was one more instance in which the federal government was colluding with companies to sell out Appalachia, one gray-haired Izaak Walton League member said.

"We're one of the most mineral-rich places in the country, but all of the money is going somewhere else!" he said.

As the meeting broke up in frustration, I introduced myself to Stacey and Paige and asked if I might come visit their home. The next day, I drove an hour southwest of Pittsburgh to Amity for the first time. Wending through narrow valleys, I watched the blanched patchwork of stubbled hilltops drop into brighter green valley bottoms. Higher up the hillsides, where the paler hues indicated less water, I noticed what looked like giant rolls of toilet paper.

These were water buffaloes, Stacey told me when I arrived at her farmhouse. Farmers here were accustomed to using them at homes that didn't have access to public water, or when coal mining undermined land, damaging springs. We climbed into her Pontiac and, within a mile, passed the five well sites and two compressor stations. We rode through Amity and on toward Prosperity. Along the seven miles of back roads, in addition to the well sites she pointed out, the earth was churned raw by ditches awaiting pipeline. From earth movers to gas rigs to water trucks, industry was everywhere. It wasn't just isolated sites that were at issue; industry required an overwhelming amount of infrastructure connecting them.

"They show you a pretty picture and they lie," Stacey said. When we returned to the farmhouse, she took me inside to meet Harley, who raised a hand in greeting from the recliner. He was skeletal and gray. He didn't dream of becoming a veterinarian anymore; seeing sick animals had proven more painful than he had imagined. He wanted to be an architect: to build the golden bathrooms he saw on *MTV Cribs*.

PART 2

BURDEN OF PROOF

Underneath us, Marcellus could heat the U.S. for the next thirty years. Our nation has a thirst for energy and that will continue, but how do we protect our resources, namely water. That's what a man needs for life.

—WERNER LOEHLEIN, A.K.A. KING NEPTUNE,
WATER MANAGEMENT SECTION CHIEF, U.S. ARMY
CORPS OF ENGINEERS, PITTSBURGH DISTRICT

What we've done is make a deal with the devil. Which is what it is.

—KATHRYN TEIGEN DEMASTER AND STEPHANIE A.
MALIN, "A DEVIL'S BARGAIN: RURAL ENVIRONMENTAL
INJUSTICES AND HYDRAULIC FRACTURING
ON PENNSYLVANIA'S FARMS"
(*JOURNAL OF RURAL STUDIES*, 2015)

12 | "MR. AND MRS. ATTICUS FINCH"

A successful Washington County attorney in his early forties, John Smith was a relentlessly friendly local son who'd already made good. He loved the law and its history, and was fashioning himself into the modern equivalent of an old country lawyer known for being fair. He could also be, on occasion, a fast-talking smart aleck. Raised in the middle-class suburbs of Pittsburgh as one of four children, Smith had spent the first ten years of his career as a corporate litigator in white-shoe firms in Pittsburgh, where he rose to partner. Now he lived and worked in Cecil Township, an affluent suburb of eleven thousand people halfway between Amity and Pittsburgh. Cecil was the corporate hub of the oil and gas boom, and Smith was the township's attorney. With the return of the fossil fuel industry, he and his law practice, Smith Butz, stood to do even better. The small firm was profiting tidily from negotiating leases for up to ten new clients a day.

Smith Butz was situated a mile from the Range Resources headquarters in Southpointe, the industrial park built, in part, on the grounds of a former mental institution. Southpointe bustled with a golf course, gyms, Hog Fathers BBQ, and Chinese and Mexican takeout joints, as well as Smoke, a cigar shop and lounge that served itinerant oil and gas executives coming from Texas, Louisiana, and Arkansas. Smith Butz sat just off of Technology Drive, on the second floor of the Bailey Center. Named for a nearby coal mine, the brick building was leased largely to companies involved in extracting carbon: Corsa Coal

Corp.; FlexSteel Pipeline Technologies, Inc.; ROC Service Company; and Gateway Engineers, Inc.

For a time John Smith had been number one in his class at Thomas M. Cooley, the law school in Lansing, Michigan, where he met his wife, Kendra. She'd recently joined the firm as the second Smith to be a named partner. Thomas Cooley may not have enjoyed a high rank among law schools, but no one challenged Smith's nimble mind or his diligence in poring over legal arcana relating to property rights or zoning for the small towns of Washington County he represented.

Smith also founded the Cecil Township Historical Society. He cherished Washington County's history, especially the early exploits of George Washington, who'd first traveled to southwestern Pennsylvania in 1753 on a mission for the British to protest French designs on the land and its rivers. At twenty-two, Washington was looking to make his fortune, but, as he wrote in his journal, his western exploits ended in humiliation when he was defeated by the French and Native Americans in 1754 and surrendered at Fort Necessity, fifty-eight miles east of what's now the city of Washington. As payment for his military service, George Washington was given a plot of land near the Smiths' home in Cecil. When Washington tried to lay claim to the land, however, squatters refused to leave. Washington was faced with a quandary: forcibly remove the frontiersmen, or take them before the newly formed Washington Court of Common Pleas.

"Here's a guy who's the biggest hero ever and these guys tell him to beat it," Smith said. "And what's more, he doesn't take arms against them. He follows the rule of law in Washington County and files suit against them." There were other versions of the story, in which Washington set fire to the settlement and drove out families, but Smith favored the one in which Washington hired a lawyer named Thomas Smith.

"He could've hired Jefferson," John Smith said, "but no, he went with the local guy." John liked to imagine that he and Thomas might be related, but his three children often reminded him they weren't. Smith was descended instead from German and Italian immigrants who'd arrived on the cusp of the twentieth century. Most of his family had worked in steel mills, and Smith was one of the first to go into white-collar work.

He was better versed than most local lawyers in the basics of natural gas drilling. He and Kendra had learned about conventional drilling over the years from a gruff-talking, hard-drinking client out of West Virginia who owned several dozen shallow wells.

Unlike oil, which is what operators call a "Eureka!" business, natural gas is a widget business, meaning profit doesn't come from a sudden geyser. Profit comes instead from slow and steady work at the margins, and involves keeping costs as low as possible. This can make it tempting to cut corners by choosing less expensive safety measures, or bidding out work to the cheapest subcontractors. Since the Smiths understood the basics of the business, they were ready in 2001 when land men with phone books in the back seats of their cars began lining up at the Washington County Courthouse to sign up plot after plot.

As Cecil's solicitor, Smith had a front-row seat to the local fights between the townships and the industry. Overwhelmed, local township supervisors were struggling to get a handle on the traffic, noise, dust, and cracked roads that came along with industry's arrival. No one was talking about drilling here in Cecil yet. Still, the township and two of its neighbors, Robinson and South Fayette, were already drafting ordinances to gain some control over trucks and noise before they arrived.

Smith looked to Fort Worth, Texas, as a model for how cities and towns could coexist with drillers. He believed that fracking could be a good thing, and wanted controls rather than an out-and-out ban on the practice, which the city of Pittsburgh had recently enacted. In 2010, the city had placed a moratorium on fracking, effectively ending it before it began. The effort was led by a Democratic city councilman and former steelworker named Doug Shields, a man not afraid to don a fedora, and his wife, Bridget, a sharp and committed fractivist, as opponents to drilling were coming to be known. They were aided by public outcry after it came to light that the Catholic Church, one of the city's largest landholders, had signed gas leases in fifteen cemeteries. It was Doug Shields who first called John and Kendra Smith "Mr. and Mrs. Atticus Finch" when they started to risk going up against the oil and gas industry.

In the spring of 2011, however, John Smith still thought that industry could benefit Washington County, where people had suffered since coal and steel vanished. Smith also believed that the rule of law could protect Pennsylvania; that agencies like the Department of Environmental Protection could adequately police drillers and that regulation could also protect local communities if townships drafted their rules effectively. Yet while negotiating leases on behalf of landowners, he'd also seen what was lacking in people's ability to protect their rights on the surface. Operators wanted the minimum possible distance between industrial infrastructure and people's homes and streams in order to maximize their ability to drill. Washington County's citizens, who'd been signing mineral leases for a century, were well versed in the exigencies of setbacks and rights-of-way. "As much as landowners wanted to maximize their profit from gas, they wanted to protect their property above all," Smith said. Putting to use his experience with advising landowners on negotiating their leases, Smith helped draft the first local ordinances to limit the broad latitude sought by drillers.

For the companies, these local ordinances ranged from irritating to troubling. In Pennsylvania, which is made up of more than 2,500 municipalities, local government was remarkably influential. Townships had the power to make things difficult for drillers. Small-town boards used their right to establish residential, commercial, and industrial zones to determine where drillers could work. They put in place rules about noise and truck traffic that attempted to control how industry behaved in their towns. This was a problem for the drilling companies. Not only did these local ordinances curb operations but they also introduced risk into their business model. Range Resources and its competitors had gone to great lengths and expense signing leases, only to face the prospect of not being able to drill freely due to little towns pushing back. In Washington County alone, there were sixty-six municipalities, each with its own government.

The epicenter of these local battles was Mount Pleasant, the town where Stacey's new friends the Hallowiches lived and where Range Resources had succeeded in leasing 95 percent of the land. By the spring of 2011, the fight between the town and the company had turned ugly, and Smith was right in the middle. Mount Pleasant hired him as special counsel to help the township draft its ordinance and push back against industry's efforts to limit local regulation. The company tried to appeal to those who stood to make money with an unusual letter-writing campaign. One mass mailing was addressed to a fictitious "Mr. and Mrs. Joe Schmo at 10 Cash-Strapped Lane." It urged residents to bring pressure on their local officials to allow companies wide latitude to drill where they needed to, or there'd be no gas, and "no gas means no royalties."

Although Smith supported drilling in principle and his firm stood to profit from brokering landowners' leases, the aggressive moves by Range Resources and others disturbed him. This kind of strong-arming struck Smith as, if not illegal, antidemocratic—it went against that frontier spirit still on display marching down Main Street in Washington each year.

One morning in the spring of 2011, not long after Stacey spoke out at Morgantown Airport, her colleague Deb Wilkerson, a fellow nurse in the recovery unit, came into Smith Butz for a consultation about a

lease. Wilkerson wanted to sign one, but she'd seen what had happened to Harley firsthand and she wanted to protect her kids. Not
signing also posed a risk: if all of her neighbors went along with the
drilling, then her land could be orphaned, but she could still be forced
to deal with the noise and health repercussions without any payment
or protections. It was Stacey who suggested that Wilkerson find a
lawyer; through word of mouth, she found Smith Butz.

On the day of her visit, Wilkerson waited for an associate on a
tufted leather couch hung with Pittsburgh Penguins rally towels. The
lobby was always decorated according to the sports season, with Penguins, Pirates, or Steelers gear, and on game days, Smith Butz staff
members often wore team jerseys, as was the local practice.

After Wilkerson reviewed her lease with an associate, she asked
him if he could help Stacey, explaining that Stacey was a fellow nurse
at the hospital. Her kids were sick and their animals were dying, Wilkerson said. The young associate asked her to wait and left the conference room. She watched through the glass windows as he disappeared
down the hall. A few minutes later, he returned and led Wilkerson
into John Smith's office, its windowsill lined with a decade's worth of
his kids' soccer photos; on the slate-blue wall was one of his mother-in-
law's watercolors, which read *No guts no glory*. From behind his desk,
Smith listened as Wilkerson recounted the mysterious animal deaths
on the two farms near Amity, a teenager's arsenic poisoning, and the
recent discovery of benzene and toluene in the family's bodies.

The story was terrible, if true, but this wasn't the kind of case that
he or his firm usually took on. He hadn't pursued a personal injury
lawsuit since he'd been in practice, and he wasn't eager to begin. Such
cases were expensive. They could take years to prosecute. Small firms
like theirs survived on billable hours paid regularly by their clients. In
personal injury cases, lawyers typically got paid only if they won and if
the defendant paid the judgment or settled. Although eventually they'd
stand to make as much as 40 percent of any judgment in Stacey's favor
and 25 percent of a judgment for her kids, they'd have to be able to hang

on for years while laying out large sums for scientific testing, and being paid nothing, even for expenses. This could bleed the firm dry. Still, Smith knew what it was to have a sick child. His daughter Ainsley, the youngest of his three, had also suffered a mysterious illness. At three years old, Ainsley couldn't keep down food. After surviving a dangerous misdiagnosis, she ended up having an emergency surgery for a twisted intestine. She almost didn't make it. Those had been the worst days of Smith's life, and he wanted to show good faith to whoever this woman Stacey Haney was. So he gave the nurse a business card for her friend.

The next day at the hospital, Stacey scrutinized the card. In the weeks following her talk at the airport, she'd started calling attorneys. They also called her. Since she'd gone public, her phone had begun to ring with reporters, plaintiff attorneys, and fractivists from New York and Texas. She stood at her burgundy kitchen counter taking down copious notes, but she shared only the parts of her story that she could document. She preferred to keep her circle small, venting only to her high school friend Jamie, along with Kelly, Shelly, and Chris, and to a lesser extent her mother, who often irritated Stacey more than she comforted her, saying the wrong things, as mothers tend to do.

Stacey considered the firm of Erin Brockovich, the famed jobless single mother turned environmental advocate. Brockovich had taken on Pacific Gas and Electric after their use of hexavalent chromium in a natural gas compressor station proved toxic to those living nearby. Brockovich wasn't an attorney, but she had her own advocacy firm in California. Stacey eventually decided she wanted to find help closer to home, with an attorney who'd drive out to the farm and see Harley sick and the drilling and the pipeline everywhere. She and Beth Voyles also made a pact to sign with the same attorney no matter what.

In the midst of worry for Harley, who wasn't getting better, Stacey considered next steps. When she called John Smith's office two weeks later, Smith took the call. He put her on speakerphone with another senior partner as she recounted Boots's aborting two babies and Harley's missing a year and a half of school.

Whether or not there was scientific merit or enough evidence to prove her case, John believed she was telling the truth. He asked if he could come out and meet her. Stacey agreed. Then he hung up the phone and went next door to see his wife, Kendra, whose office walls were decorated with a decade's worth of valentines. He reported what he'd heard and asked Kendra what she thought of Stacey's story: the sick child, the black water, the test results that showed there was benzene and toluene in their bodies.

Kendra asked John how far the family lived from the industrial site. John wasn't sure, but Stacey'd told him about fifteen hundred feet. That was too far for exposure, Kendra told him.

Kendra Smith wasn't from the area. A former finalist in the Miss New Jersey competition, she grew up about twenty minutes from Princeton. At forty-one years old, she was just over five feet tall and one hundred pounds. She lived on Coke and snack packs of Veggie Stix, and although she'd been a star soccer player in high school and college, she often couldn't be bothered to remember that her brain was housed inside a physical body. Despite her bid for Miss New Jersey, which was an attempt to win a scholarship, Smith paid no attention to her looks. Her mind was apparently the product of both of her parents: her father was an engineer, and her mother an artist who held a master's in mathematics from Columbia University. Kendra's mother raised her to "never be financially dependent on a man." Until she became a lawyer, her goal had been to become a prison warden.

For the first few years of her law career, before she moved west to marry John Smith, she did criminal defense work in New Jersey for people with alleged ties to organized crime. Now she defended Fortune 500 corporations against workers' claims of chemical exposure. Her job was to destroy plaintiffs' cases.

"I take people apart for a living, and it's not always pretty," she said. She'd come to work at her husband's firm only after she was offered partner at another Pittsburgh-based firm, and the terms turned out to be disappointing. Like her husband, Kendra wasn't interested in pursuing a personal injury suit. She wasn't afraid to lose, but she knew how brutal her tribe of corporate defense attorneys could be, and she didn't think that with her and John working full-time and shuttling between church, school, and soccer practice, her family of five needed any more complications. But she too thought of how powerless she'd felt when Ainsley was sick, and was willing to help investigate.

The following week, on the day that their meeting with Stacey was to take place, John was stuck with other business, so after lunch, Kendra drove out to Amity. This was unusual. John, the charming almost-local, was most often the one to meet with potential clients. Kendra, with her hard-nosed mien, was the one to stay up into the early morning gathering the evidence to win suits. The two had also never worked together on a case before.

She decided to take a young male associate, Chris Rogers, along with her for the drive. She knew that the area around Amity and Prosperity was rural and poor. Given that this was the borderland where Appalachia began, she'd wasn't sure what to expect.

Driving south on I-79 in her white Cadillac Escalade, she instructed Rogers in what to look for on a site visit. She was accustomed to visiting railroads, since she'd litigated many cases for the industry involving workers who claimed they'd been injured on the job. On a work site, violations could be as simple as an open flame. At someone's home, it might be harder to see the problems. She exited the highway at Lone Pine and passed a truck stop where young rig hands were smoking cigarettes and eating Subway sandwiches on new picnic tables in the parking lot. She drove up the steep hill of McAdams Road past signs that read RIG TRAFFIC 15 MILES PER HOUR. When she spotted the small white sign with black lettering on the left side, Smith was surprised. This was a pretty farmhouse with a tire swing and a trampoline below the porch where Stacey stood waiting for them.

Kendra Smith and the young associate walked past the tricycle and climbed the porch stairs trellised with trumpet vine to the kitchen door. On her way in, Kendra made careful note of physical detail, as was her practice. With skin the color of fish flesh and deep circles under her eyes, Stacey Haney looked tired. To Kendra, also a working mother, this wasn't out of the ordinary.

Stacey led them past the laundry room and into the kitchen, where the table sat piled with her papers. She offered them water, from bottles she'd bought at Walmart. Through the large open doorway, Kendra noticed a wan teenage boy slumped on the couch in his pajamas. She felt rude wandering into someone's TV room, so she greeted him from the table and watched as he lifted himself off the couch gingerly, one limb at a time like an eighty-year-old man. Without his mother's prompting, he shuffled into the kitchen to shake her hand.

He's been raised right, she thought. She hoped her eldest, Dakota, who was a year younger than Harley, would do the same. Up close, Harley looked wizened: his eyes were sunken, and his face was gray like his mother's. She wondered what could be wrong with the boy; it couldn't just be living near a well site. She hadn't yet seen the high green fence across the road, but from what she knew of its proximity, it still seemed too far away to sicken anyone here in the farmhouse.

Stacey opened a green three-ring binder and led Kendra through a timeline of Harley's illness over the past eighteen months, the elevated arsenic level in his urine, the results of the inhalant panels she'd spent two months working out with the head of the lab at the hospital. She pointed out what she'd learned to read on her own: the phenols and hippuric acid levels, which indicated exposure to benzene and toluene in all three of them.

Kendra was surprised by Stacey's acumen. The nurse had taught herself a lot. But even though it seemed like something was wrong with

Harley, Kendra still doubted the problem was related to the site next door. She flipped through the pages of water tests and noticed elevated levels of manganese, but little else. Some of the tests' standard aspects were missing. Kendra, who was fluent in such materials, wondered if the company had supplied only these partial results.

Kendra asked Stacey if there were more pages of the test results somewhere. No. Should there be? Stacey asked. Kendra inhaled deeply to see if she could detect the rotten-egg smell about which Stacey had spoken to her husband on the phone—along with headaches, lethargy, trouble remembering things, nausea, nosebleeds, diarrhea, and an odd metal taste in her mouth. Kendra told Stacey the frank truth: she couldn't smell a thing.

Her job, she explained, was to come at exposure cases like this from the other side. If she didn't find any evidence to suggest a problem, she was going to tell Stacey that right out. Stacey valued this forthrightness. She liked this diminutive, direct woman who wasn't perturbed by anything Stacey said or showed her.

Beth Voyles arrived, huffing through the kitchen door. Stacey'd wanted to meet the attorneys on her own first. She knew that Beth could be a lot to take, and she feared her velocity and her talk about poisoning and "arsenip" might undermine the credibility of their case.

Beth breathed heavily and was so flushed that Kendra wondered where she'd gotten badly sunburned so early in spring. At the kitchen table, armed with her own folder, Beth laid out similar medical complaints and explained to Kendra what had gone wrong with her water. In their basement, the Voyles had a system that allowed them to toggle between two sources: spring and well water. The spring water came out of the ground below the hill, and of the two, the Voyles preferred drinking spring.

For Kendra, an East Coaster who'd always lived on city water, the distinction between spring and well was a new one. Spring water tasted fresher and flowed faster, Beth said. When their well ran dry and their water flow lessened to that "sprinkering," Beth explained,

Range had supplied the same 5,100-gallon water buffalo they'd brought next door to the Haneys. The company sent Beth a letter conceding that the construction of the nearby waste pond might have diminished the flow of their springs. Yet they insisted the quality of the water was not affected. Even so, Range had paid to dig the Voyles a new well, but that too failed, Beth said, when tests came back saying it was full of *E. coli.* Then, after the January meeting at which Laura Rusmisel and Carla Suszkowski had told the families they had nothing to worry about and were going to remove Beth's water buffalo, Beth had ceased being solicitous. She felt taken.

Beth had no problem calling Range, the DEP, the Fish and Boat Commission, the U.S. Fish and Wildlife Service, the National Response Center, the twenty-four-hour hotline for the Environmental Protection Agency, the local newspapers in Washington, or any of the other numbers she'd posted on the side of her black refrigerator. If something smelled funny, or if the road was torn up, she picked up the phone, earning something of a reputation for being difficult. After Beth called so many times to complain, one Range employee labeled her internally as an "anti-industry activist."

Kendra listened to the two women for four hours. It was late afternoon by the time she and her associate got up from the table to leave. Stacey walked them to the door and watched as they backed out of her grassy driveway. Then she and Beth sat at the kitchen table to decide whether or not they wanted the Smiths to handle their case. Stacey was certain.

"I think they've been sent by God," she said.

Beth still had a question. "Those guys were so down-to-earth," she said. "If they're so down-to-earth, how good could they be as lawyers?"

Kendra wanted to drive past the site on their way back to the office. As the SUV climbed past Beth's house, Kendra spied the high green fence ringing the hilltop on the far side of the road. The blanched grass around the fence appeared yellow against the green hill, but dead grass could mean anything. Other than the gravel access road and the white trailer that served as a guard shack, there wasn't much to see. As she powered the Escalade forward, she noticed that the road grade of McAdams was sharper than she'd thought. Maybe she'd under-estimated the likelihood of exposure. She was accustomed to play-ing out such scenarios in her head. Now she reconsidered. If the hill sloped steeply enough, surface runoff might flow farther and faster than she'd estimated.

They drove on past the Yeagers' farm, where a yellow sign trimmed in blue read PENNSYLVANIA BEEF QUALITY ASSURANCE PRO-GRAM CERTIFIED PRODUCER. They drove on past the Lone Pine truck stop and entered I-79 heading north. Once the winding roads were behind them, Smith asked the young associate if he had an odd taste in his mouth. He didn't, but Smith did. For the next two days, the taste of metal lay like a film on her tongue. Whether or not she and John took the case, she decided that she'd never tell Stacey and Beth. It seemed prejudicial. Smith preferred to deal with her clients on demonstrable facts. Yet the trip stayed with her; it was changing her mind about signing Stacey and Beth as clients. If there really was something from industry sickening Harley, she figured that together, she and John stood a good chance of determining what it was.

On Mother's Day 2011, a few days after Kendra's visit, Stacey took the kids to the Cracker Barrel in nearby Washington for lunch with her mom and sister. Driving home, they crested the ridge by the Yeagers' farm and hit a putrid wall of stench coming from the waste pond. It was so thick, it felt like being struck in the face. Stacey drew stars around the event in her notebook: *Smell from impoundment terrible, worst we have ever smelled.*

The next day, Monday, when the kids came home from school, the stench was still bad. By that evening, all three had headaches and Paige's nose was bleeding. When they woke up on Tuesday, however,

Stacey thought the reek had dissipated. That afternoon, Stacey asked
Kelly to come over and help sort through papers before she handed
them to John and Kendra Smith. Although she felt sure that the husband and wife attorneys were the right choice, she hadn't officially retained them yet and she wanted to talk the situation through with
Kelly, her confidante on all matters. At 3:00 p.m., when she and Kelly
were going through her binder, Harley came in the door from the bus
stop. His eyes were burning, and so were his nose and throat. He lay
down on the living room carpet and went to sleep.

After an hour, Stacey tried to wake him to go to his guitar lesson
with Rick Baker, but he was still too drowsy. She managed to coax him
upstairs to his bed. Within minutes, Harley was asleep again. That
afternoon, Stacey took Kelly on the driving tour. Kelly'd heard so much
about what they were living with—and breathing—but she'd never seen
it. The two headed down the road toward Prosperity and the Anawanna
Hunting and Fishing Club, following the winding back roads to the
top of a hill where they could see much of the surrounding countryside. At the top of a rise, Stacey counted three new well pads to add to
the five she already knew surrounded her farmhouse.

When Stacey and Kelly returned, Harley was still asleep. They
took Paige up to Justa Breeze to ride horses at Beth and John's. In
the ring out behind the ranch house, Paige clucked at her favorite gelding, Take the Money and Run. She'd been riding Money since she was
two. Now almost twelve, she was old enough to saddle Money and take
him around the ring on her own. Stacey loved to watch her ride; she'd
always loved horses, and providing Paige access to them was part of
the way she strove to be a good mother. She wanted to buy Money for
Paige, and Beth was considering it. But how Stacey would pay for up-
keep she didn't know yet. Beth, Stacey, and Kelly leaned on the split-
rail fence watching Paige ride until the sun dropped behind a stand
of oaks. In shadow, the spring earth cooled fast and Kelly and Stacey
called to Paige to come in so they could head back down the hill.

After they left Beth's farm, Kelly asked Stacey what the terrible stink was, but Stacey smelled nothing. Troy Jordan, an EPA investigator, had explained to Stacey that one of the signs of worsening exposure to some substances, including hydrogen sulfide, was an inability to detect their presence anymore. The body's ability to smell the hydrogen sulfide was its first line of defense. When the body could no longer perform that function, people slipped into olfactory fatigue. In itself, this phenomenon wasn't a concern. But in the case of toxic inhalants, the fatigue rendered exposure all the more dangerous, since Stacey and the kids could no longer tell when they needed to leave. Back at Stacey's, Harley was still asleep. Kelly wanted to take Stacey and the kids home to her house, but Stacey didn't want to disturb Harley. Instead, she spent the night, as she often did, awake and trying to figure out where they could go as a family.

The next morning, after Harley had been sleeping for fifteen and a half hours, Stacey shook him awake to get ready for school. He was in no shape to learn anything, but she had to get him away from the heavy chemical haze that had settled over their farm. At the hospital, she approached Dr. Koliner, a pulmonologist who'd been helping Stacey interpret the elements of exposure in her family's lab results. When patients came into the ER with similar symptoms, the hospital staff now gave them a questionnaire asking about their proximity to oil and gas wells. Stacey told Dr. Koliner about Kelly's visit. The pulmonologist knew and trusted both women. Kelly had smelled something overpowering that Stacey and the kids couldn't even detect in the air, she said. When she'd gotten home that night she had a terrible headache. Stacey feared it was hydrogen sulfide, that bacterial rot she and Beth had learned about.

Get out of the house, he told her. The fact that she couldn't smell the hydrogen sulfide indicated the olfactory fatigue that the EPA had warned her about, he explained. You need to get the kids and you need to get out of there now.

That night, she took the kids to her parents' to spend a few days there while she figured out what to do. With Harley sleeping under the eaves in Shelly's old room, and Paige in a narrow cot, Stacey climbed in to her childhood bed. It was depressing to be back at forty-one in a bed she'd intended to flee for good at seventeen. The next day, on May 12, she called the Smiths and officially retained them. In her notebook, she jotted down their fee: *33% CONTINGENCY, 40% IF GOES TO TRIAL.*

Up at the site, the stench remained overpowering. On May 13, Range employees exchanged emails trying to determine the source of the trouble. Since the large pond up at the Yeagers' was a centralized impoundment, frack fluids from other sites in Washington County were trucked and stored there. The workers suspected that noxious liquid from one of those sites was causing the problem.

"The nastiness is definitely coming from the Carrol Baker," one worker wrote, calling the liquid "demon water." Unsure of what to do, he suggested they go ahead and frack with it.

On May 16, after four nights at Mam and Pappy's, Harley still wasn't feeling better. That morning Stacey took him to see Dr. Fox. For the third time in six weeks, Harley tested positive for strep. The pediatrician told Stacey that Harley could no longer take the risk of exposure. Keep him away from the house for thirty days, he told Stacey. Don't even let him ride past the impoundment and stay outside a ten-mile radius of the site. Amity was too close.

Stacey took Harley to stay with Chris in Eighty Four, while she and Paige kept sleeping at her parents' house in Amity. As she began to shuttle the kids between her boyfriend's, her parents', the doctors, school, and the animals, Stacey was essentially living out of her car and driving an extra four hours a day. She was spending, on average, two hundred dollars a month on gas. Most nights, Stacey dropped Harley at Chris's in Eighty Four, then drove back to her parents' in Amity to sleep alongside Paige. They felt like refugees. *I'm running myself ragged,* she scrawled in her journal, *but if it helps my kids regain their health then it's well worth it.* Harley, however, still wasn't getting better.

"Our house has become a two-hundred-and-eighty-thousand-dollar cat mansion," she told me. She went to the farm only to feed the animals and to do laundry so that she could avoid using her parents' meager water supply. She developed a system. She zipped up the driveway to park, grabbed the plastic laundry basket from the back seat, and hustled up the porch stairs, into the back door, and through the kitchen to the laundry room, where she piled a load into the washer, fended off and fed the three hungry house cats, poured bottled water into their dishes, and pulled on her rubber boots. Then she ran up to the barn, turned on the garden hose attached to the water buffalo to fill the baby pool that functioned as a goat trough, scooped feed into their feed buckets, continued up to the rabbit hutch to do the same, then the horse paddock, and last of all, she attended to Bob the Donkey before racing back down to the house, transferring the wet clothes to the dryer, and running back to the car. During her long drives, she called friends and the few experts she knew to puzzle out the latest symptoms and to try to manage the logistics for each day.

"People ask me why I don't just move out, but where would I go?" she asked me one night on the phone while she drove. This was the decisive question that people who didn't live in Amity would pose, often more affluent people who didn't understand what it meant not to be able to carry extra rent, or didn't feel the same ties to their land. "I can't afford another mortgage, and if I default on this place, we will lose it," she said.

Stacey knew they couldn't live in limbo forever, but for now, she was out of ideas. One day, she came straight from work to load up a few months' worth of belongings as quickly as possible and head back to her parents'.

Amity had received terrible news: Robert Allan Shipman, the former fire chief who'd committed all those environmental crimes, had suffered a stunning loss. His seventeen-year-old stepdaughter, Savannah Hennen, had killed herself several days earlier. Savannah Hennen was a popular blonde junior at West Greene High School, just over the border from Washington County. A devout teenager, she'd worked with her local chapter of Children's Bible Ministries. A year later, when Shipman would finally come before the court, Judge Farley Toothman would let him off with probation and a fine. The DEP had never enforced such laws before. His stepdaughter's suicide was punishment enough.

How could a girl like that shoot herself? Stacey wondered as she packed up the car. Yet these days around Amity, suicide was increasingly familiar. Along with the drilling boom, the plague of opioids was hitting Washington County ever harder. Some people said the out-of-town gas workers were bringing in drugs, and while that may have been true, Stacey knew the scourge of prescription painkillers had been worsening before the gas well workers had arrived. She worried for the future of Amity's kids. Growing up in the shadow of the steel bust had been difficult, but this new era seemed even worse. At least with the bust, they'd all been in it together. The boom, however, threatened to divide them, with kids like Savannah suddenly hitting it rich while a handful like Harley suffered.

Although she hoped they wouldn't be gone for long, Stacey took what she could, leaving everything soft—couches, pillows, Harley's recliner, anything she couldn't wash—out of fear that the foam and fabric could hold on to fumes. She'd finally admitted to herself that Febreze did nothing. It didn't really mask the stench; they just couldn't smell it anymore.

13 | MUTUAL DISTRUST

The days of offering visitors sloppy joes were over. When a new water inspector from the DEP pulled into Beth Voyles's driveway on a May day in 2011, Beth, clad in a T-shirt and culottes, stormed out of the house. She skipped the niceties and demanded to know what was going on with the stench drifting over her farm. Although Stacey had left a few days earlier, Beth wasn't going anywhere. There was simply too much to do for the horses and dogs, and they couldn't afford a move for all the two- and four-leggers. Her only recourse, as she saw it, was to pester the DEP until someone took action.

At the DEP, John Carson had been evaluating water for only several months, but he'd spent sixteen years monitoring air quality in eastern Pennsylvania. Carson welcomed this new job as a chance to come home. He'd grown up near Amity and graduated from Washington's Trinity High School as a member of the class of 1976. He'd gone to Penn State to earn a degree in plant science in 1981, then on to work at Radio Shack for a couple of years before buying a lawn care company. When that didn't work out, he went to work for the DEP in 1994.

Carson called himself "the eyes and ears of the Department"; he took his job of protecting people seriously. But fracking was new to him. Standing before Beth in person, he said little in response to her angry inquiry about what the hell was going on. He didn't tell her he'd been to the site the day before and smelled something "oily and salty." Instead, he stood in the driveway sniffing. Irate, Beth assumed that Carson wasn't doing his job. (On another occasion, when she'd complained, he'd showed up but refused to get out of his car. As he'd rolled down the window, she'd stood there fuming. He'd told Beth that he couldn't take a complaint without three different complainants.)

A few days later, on May 26, 2011, John Carson found a bigger problem: the frack pond seemed to be leaking. Walking along the man-made hillside between the waste pond and the gravel access road, he "caught," in his words, a Range Resources employee testing water in a manhole Carson had never seen before. Its rubber cover lay off to one side. The manhole, the Range employee explained to Carson, functioned as a leak detection system. In the hole, there was a length of perforated pipe. If the holes in the pipe were dripping liquid, the pond was probably leaking.

There seemed to be a flaw in the design. Although the pond had two liners to guard against a leak, the employee thought that this detection unit was placed into the ground beneath both. By the time anyone found a leak it would have already come in contact with the ground, and possibly groundwater. As Carson peered into the cloudy water leaking from the pipe, he suspected he'd stumbled onto trouble.

Think: he wrote in his notes, *leak detection under both liners.* Carson snapped pictures and took a GPS reading—north 40 degrees, 5 minutes, 24.4 seconds; west 80 degrees, 13 minutes, 41.7 seconds. He tested the water over the next months, and his results revealed high levels of contamination: the inorganic salts from the ancient seafloor that are often used as a marker of water contamination related to fracking were fifty times drinking water standards.

Frustrated by her escalating clashes with Carson, Beth called her new lawyers for the first time. She got John Smith on the phone and recounted how Carson had once told her he couldn't take a complaint without three different complainants. The Smiths knew that there was no such regulation. To them, it seemed like the DEP wasn't doing its job.

If that was the case, what legal recourse did they have? Kendra asked John. As an attorney for municipalities, he was better equipped than she in interrogating the mechanisms of government law. He thought their best bet was to file a writ of mandamus, a request that a court order a government agency to do its job. By filing the writ, Beth Voyles would be suing the DEP.

The Smiths filed the suit on May 23, 2011. A lawsuit like this would require time, and they stood to make nothing from it. In legal parlance, *Voyles v. DEP* wasn't recoverable. If the agency was found to be in the wrong, the state wouldn't pay the Voyles anything. But maybe the DEP would do a better job by them, as they were still living there. It didn't take long for the DEP to respond. Within days, Range Resources also asked to join the defense. On June 1, 2011, all parties would meet at the Commonwealth Court in the state capital of Harrisburg.

To build a case against the DEP and prove how the agency had failed to do its job, Kendra needed to piece together what had happened at the well site. Once she had such a timeline, she could evaluate whether or not she thought Stacey and Beth had enough of a case to go forward as plaintiffs. For a civil suit like this, the Smiths' burden of proof would be lower than for a criminal one. They wouldn't have to prove beyond reasonable doubt that Range's actions had poisoned the water and sickened their clients. They'd have to prove only a preponderance of evidence—that their evidence was more convincing than the other side's.

To gather the necessary evidence, her first task was to ask Range for a list of every chemical used at the site. Range Resources was the first company to claim that it openly disclosed all of the chemicals used in the fracking process. "It's the right thing to do morally and ethically," John Pinkerton, Range's then-CEO, had said a year earlier in 2010, "but it's also right for our shareholders." The disclosure, Kendra thought at first, would make it easier to learn what chemicals

Range was using. And since, by law, Range had to supply the DEP with maps of the site, the Smiths requested every single document the DEP had in its files for the Yeager site—permits, correspondence, plans, and schematics.

Kendra was accustomed to snowing herself in under stacks of paper, then digging out with meticulous rigor. She'd always been a numbers person, and her specialized cases involved nearly unheard-of disorders and conditions, from berylliosis caused by exposure to beryllium, an element used in aerospace engineering, to different types of histoplasmosis, a disease related to bird droppings.

It was a useful background for a plaintiff lawyer. While representing railroads, she learned from industrial hygienists and physicians to read charts and graphs of air, water, blood, urine, and other lab tests critical to her job. She'd learned how to read CT scans from one of the foremost experts in brain cancer, and studied with one of the toxicologists credited with establishing the causal link between benzene exposure and acute myeloginous leukemia. From these experts, she'd learned to follow a three-sentence mantra: "Don't jump to conclusions. Get every fact you can. Never assume."

From the start, John and Kendra presumed they would have to demonstrate that a leak, or a similar problem up at the site, had contaminated their clients' water. As they understood it, the definitive evidence lay in the simple fact that the very same chemicals in the industrial waste were now in their clients' wells and springs. Both the DEP and Range would counter that this definitive test was too simple. There were other contradictory factors for the court to consider: the way water moved underground, and the differing ratios of chemicals at each location.

The first schematics to arrive from the DEP were construction plans that Range and its subcontractors had submitted in order to obtain permits. Kendra studied a sketch of the waste pond. She wanted to know what happened if it leaked. She saw no kind of leak detection system on the drawing, which she knew was required by law. Finally, when she received more documents related to construction, she saw that Carla Suszkowski had signed off on a system for detecting leaks that seemed deeply flawed. Independently, she began to have the same misgivings as John Carson about its construction. The pond had two plastic liners. If the first layer failed, the second was supposed to catch the potentially toxic fluid before it reached groundwater. The leak detector would alert employees that there was a hole in the liner. The trouble was that the leak detector was installed beneath both liners. And since the pond was dug fifteen feet into the ground, any contamination could leach into the soil and reach groundwater before anyone knew that there was a problem.

Once word got out that the Smiths were taking the case, the firm was inundated with all kinds of anonymous fracking-related tips. Often, these involved rants and conspiracy theories from pissed-off farmers. On rare occasions, however, they proved useful. Kendra opened her email one day to discover that a photographer had sent her aerial images of the site. To the north sat the rectangular well pad, and to the southwest, there was the enormous, red-tinted frack pond, which dwarfed the roof of Beth's ranch house next door. But now she could see a smaller drill cuttings pit also, which she hadn't known existed. When she saw the pit, she grew even more concerned. Under regulations, drill cuttings pits didn't have to have any leak detection system at all.

She began to comb through the Department of Environmental Protection website for notices of violation. If the pond had leaked, there was likely a record of trouble at the site. Although the DEP's online resource, eFACTS, was laden with information, the system was impossible to navigate. Reading through violations listed by numerical statute, Kendra thought the system might be designed to be deliberately obfuscating, but she knew its failures were a matter of the DEP's being broke. Before this case, Kendra had taken for granted that the government systems put in place to protect people's health were functional. Trying to track down public facts for Stacey and Beth's case was showing her otherwise, beginning with the dysfunction of eFACTS. When the inspector general's evaluation of the DEP's problems came out in 2014, he would single out the system as a particular failure.

Hunched before her computer, Kendra clicked and scrolled through the largely inscrutable DEP database until she found a notice of a violation at the Yeager site dated to March 25, 2010. What it was, she couldn't tell, so she sent an associate into the Pittsburgh office of the DEP to photocopy every piece of paper in the public file. Among them, she found an inspection report revealing that the drill cuttings pit, filled with flowback, had leaked "from a tear in the liner."

Holy shit, Kendra thought, the pit had leaked more than a year ago, and, according to its notice of violation, the DEP already knew.

On June 1, 2011, John and Kendra drove to pick up the Voyles for the four-hour trip east to Harrisburg for the first hearing of the case against the DEP. Although it wasn't yet summer, the day was unseasonably warm. A sultry wind gusted up from the hollow where the Smiths turned to climb the hill to Justa Breeze in their white Escalade. They drove past Stacey's newly abandoned farm. She and her kids had been gone only two weeks and already its unmown grass grew long and glossy. Stacey and the kids weren't coming that day. Stacey didn't like or trust the DEP either, but she'd never had the heated run-ins that Beth did, and she preferred to stay out of it. As soon as Kendra and John pulled into the Voyles' driveway, seven boxers bounded up to the Smiths' SUV.

A sturdy figure emerged from the ranch house behind the BOXER HEAVEN sign. From the car, John Smith asked, only half in jest, if it was safe to get out. When Kendra introduced Beth to John, she noticed that Beth's cheeks were still violently splotchy and her breathing labored. But this was a warm day and Beth was working outside, so Kendra didn't think too much about it. Beth herded the dogs into the basement laundry room, where the cleft palate puppy remained in the freezer. She called to her husband, John, and the two climbed into the back seat of the SUV.

Beth was bright-eyed and excited to speak in court. The DEP and Range Resources would have to sit there and listen. However, as she, her husband, and the Smiths entered the courtroom, they spied the DEP attorneys laughing and talking with Range's attorneys and employees. Beth wondered how it was they already knew one another. For her, it was like watching the police cavort with the people they should be investigating. She spied one DEP higher-up hugging Carla Suszkowski, whom she recognized by her short red hair.

The Commonwealth Courthouse was only a few blocks away from the DEP's headquarters, where Rachel Carson's name was carved into the office building's stone lintel. That day, as the hearing wore on, it appeared to the Smiths that Carson's legacy ended at some distance. The DEP and the oil and gas industry seemed to be on the same side, and, sitting at one table on the far end of the courtroom, they weren't even trying to hide it. The Smiths had heard the disparaging nicknames for the state's collusion with industry, "Department of Energy Production," and "Don't Expect Protection." They knew the DEP had been forced into a tough role policing an industry exponentially more powerful and knowledgeable than itself, but still.

At the hearing that day, the Smiths were expecting to present evidence. That's why Beth and John were there: to give testimony. But the judge didn't want to hear from the Voyles. He didn't want to hear from Range Resources either. Instead of presenting the evidence she'd marshalled, Kendra was allowed only to give a rushed version of the Voyles' story as to why the DEP wasn't doing its job. The lack of due process alarmed Kendra. She thought to herself, That's a red flag and we're going to get screwed.

Then Michael Heilman, assistant council for the DEP's southwestern division, argued that the agency "had investigated every complaint made." An officer had gone out to the site and the Voyles' property on May 17, 18, 19, 20, 24, 26, 27, and 31. According to the DEP, he did not detect a bad smell "on any of those occasions."

The Smiths were incredulous, Kendra especially so. How could the DEP claim that there were no problems up at the Yeager site when she'd already seen evidence of a leak? When the hearing ended, Gail Myers, an attorney for the Department of Environmental Protection, approached the plaintiff's table. She handed Kendra a shiny black binder. Inside, Myers said, were the complete results of water tests that Range had given the DEP for both Stacey Haney's and Beth Voyles's properties. It was unusual to hand over documents in that manner, but this was early in the case, and things were still fairly friendly and informal.

Kendra began to flip through. Right away, she could see page numbers missing, so she turned to the end of the binder, where each test should have had an official page verifying that the results were accurate and complete. The verification pages were missing too. She didn't want to jump to conclusions about what the missing pages meant. This could be an oversight. Or the missing pages could indicate that someone was trying to hide evidence. On the ride home from Harrisburg, she looked more closely, and made a note to herself to call the DEP to ask for what wasn't there. There was another way to verify these results. She could see the name of the lab that had done the testing, Microbac Laboratories—a Pittsburgh-based company that began testing dairy milk in the sixties—on the letterhead. She could subpoena Microbac directly in her search for the missing pages.

14 | BUZZ

On the drive west from Harrisburg along the Pennsylvania Turnpike, an evil-looking clown leered down at passing drivers. The message below him on the billboard read "I still believe in global warming. Do you?" Then there was another: "Wind dies. Sun sets. You need reliable, affordable, clean coal electricity." Yet another featured a picture of Yoko Ono and the message "Would you take energy advice from the woman who broke up The Beatles?" Sign after sign pitted energy companies against environmentalists. The billboards were the handiwork of a corporate lobbyist named Rick Berman, who had launched the Biggreenradicals.com campaign, working on behalf of industry. His campaign positioned fractivists as a bunch of rich outsiders. In his world, hypocrites like Robert Redford, who flew private, and kooks like Yoko Ono didn't understand the give-and-take long established in Appalachia between extractive industries and the communities that relied on them for their livelihoods.

Beth was in the back seat of the Smiths' SUV when her phone rang: it was her neighbor Loren "Buzz" Kiskadden. He lived about half a mile down the road from her and from the Yeager site, at the base of the valley. Neighbors called the place the Bottoms, or Dogpatch, and on its twenty-six acres, the Kiskadden family had run a junkyard until 2006. An ex-car-thief and recovering heroin addict, Buzz had been the neighborhood bad boy, "always driving around on something," he told me later.

Buzz was clean now, but chain-smoking cigarettes.

"I'm trying to quit but I haven't yet," he said. "It used to be Marlboro but now it's a cheaper brand. Pyramids." He and his brothers were known to drive their junkyard's tow trucks around the town of Washington, removing any breakdowns left on the roadside. Instead of repairing them, they stripped them for parts.

Of all of Buzz's scrapes, his most notorious took place in 1995, when he'd led half a dozen police officers on a high-speed car chase over the county's roads and back to Dogpatch. When Buzz came to a stop, one policeman tried to wrestle him out of the car, but Buzz slid out of his grip and the officer went over the side of an embankment along with Buzz's vehicle. The officer wasn't seriously injured, and Buzz spent five years fighting the case until 2000, when he served six months in Washington County Jail. That era seemed over now. Thieving was a young man's game, and time, above all else, had rendered Buzz and his brothers largely harmless.

Since his release ten years earlier, he'd attended Mount Herman Baptist Church. He believed that God had straightened him out. "I kept praying about it," he told me later, "so it must have been God." Now fifty-four, he still lived at Dogpatch in a trailer he'd bought from his mother, Grace, who occupied a small house next door. For most of her life, she'd lived within a mile of her current home. She'd grown up as one of thirteen children living in the three-room house of a wheat and corn farmer who worked in the local glass factory, Hazel Atlas #2, during the 1950s, before mechanization drove the glass industry out of business.

At twenty-one, Grace had gotten married and bought the land on which she and her children now lived. Over the past forty-seven years, Grace's three sons and four daughters had helped her run the garage and chop shop, removed radiators and batteries, and salvaged scrap metal from old school buses, cars, and trucks. According to Grace, some vehicles had been there as long as fifty years, and they weren't going anywhere soon. The bottom had fallen out of the family business.

Along with a bakery delivery truck, the carcasses of pickups and school busses rusted on the banks of Banetown Creek. There was also a rarely used bulldozer, high lift, and backhoe.

"Car business is no different from mining or steel," Grace said. "It's gone downhill."

Beth knew the Kiskaddens well; they were neighbors and also family. Beth's half sister married Buzz's brother, but the marriage had soured and Beth took the Kiskaddens' side. Buzz was still close to Beth Voyles. "We been friends all our lives," Buzz said.

On the phone, Buzz told Beth that his water had gone bad. He'd gone to fill up the kiddie pool for Junior and gray gunk had come out of the hose. Junior was Seth, the five-year-old grandson of Buzz's girlfriend, Loretta Logsdon, and Buzz loved the boy. Seth, his sister, Jade, and his mother, Summer Runyon, stayed from time to time in Buzz's trailer, along with Loretta. The smell from the water was god-awful: rotten eggs and raw sewage. If the water was bad, what did that mean for Buzz's vegetable garden? Every summer, he fed himself and his neighbor Mr. Gray his prized tomatoes. He wasn't sure if those tomatoes were safe anymore.

Beth told him to call the DEP and Range and have both come out to test his water. Buzz was upset. He'd lived in that trailer for five years, and spent most of his time on its couch smoking cigarettes with the air conditioner on and the TV blasting.

"I've never had any problems with my water before," he said.

There was no way to prove whether or not this was true. Buzz, like Stacey and Beth, had never had his water tested before the drilling began. Without that pre-drill test to serve as a baseline, a company could argue that any chemicals in the water were already present. A pre-drill was essential in proving that oil and gas had contaminated the water. With a legacy of coal mining, which brought with it methane contamination, there were preexisting problems. And even if not, industry claims could introduce enough doubt into a case to defeat it.

Since Pennsylvania doesn't require monitoring private wells, there was no record of what was in Buzz's well—though it sat on a flood-plain next to a creek that sometimes overflowed its bank. In addition to the rusted-out car hulks that littered the creek banks, the fields were full of old tires, which Grace Kiskadden was trying to dispose of. "I don't want them. I'm trying to get rid of them. They're an eyesore," she said later.

Without water, Buzz wouldn't be able to stay on his land. Unlike Stacey and Beth, he couldn't afford to buy even limited amounts. He'd lost his job making pots and pans at the Dynamet factory, and his health had long been causing him trouble. Since his late thirties, he'd suffered from diabetes. He took pain medication every morning, along with six or seven other pills for arthritis in his knees, shoulder, and back; another for a heart condition; and yet another for gastric trouble.

When Beth got off the phone with Buzz, she repeated to the Smiths what Buzz had told her. As Beth shared Buzz's history, the Smiths could tell he'd make the worst kind of plaintiff. His health alone, as well as his history of addiction and crime, would undermine his credibility in court. Still, he seemed to have a legitimate griev-ance, and possibly his test results could help them establish a clearer pattern of harm for their clients. They agreed to speak to him.

The following day, June 2, 2011, Buzz Kiskadden called the DEP and Range, and then moved a few hundred yards up Banetown Road to live in a cinder-block room in his mother's basement. Grace had begun to worry that maybe her water or air had something bad in it too. The summer before, although she said she'd never had a head-ache in her life, she had a fainting spell. Although Grace and her son resembled each other, with their paper-pale skin, icy blue eyes, and thin white hair, the two were nothing alike. Grace didn't take medi-cation, not even aspirin. To treat ailments like colds, she relied on vinegar, honey, and dandelion tea. Soon, test results would reveal el-evated levels of benzene in her urine too.

On June 6, 2011, a DEP water inspector came out to Dogpatch to conduct water testing. Just standing over Buzz's well, he could see there were problems. It wasn't properly sealed and it sat on a flood-plain, so every time Bane Creek rose over its banks, the top of the well was submerged and anything could get inside.

15 | MISSING PAGES

After their trip to Harrisburg, Kendra began to search for the pages missing from the DEP's black binder. She called the DEP to follow up, and waited for results to come in under subpoena from Microbac Laboratories. Slowly, by reading company names off of permit applications and site plans, she and John uncovered the other parties working up at the site, which led to more subpoenas, and shipments of bankers' boxes began to pour into their office. The more evidence she and John gathered, the more clearly they began to understand what was happening at Yeager, as they called it, and how it was affecting their clients.

That summer of 2011, remediation reports arrived from the DEP that sketched a patchy narrative of a large-scale cleanup going on at the Yeager site. Range was paying subcontractors to dig out and remove 4,250,000 pounds of that hillside. Kendra knew that the government required this scale of remediation only when something had gone seriously wrong. Attached to the report, there were soil tests that seemed to indicate the ground was still contaminated with elements of BTEX and arsenic. Certain that she could build a larger case against Range, Kendra was going to switch sides for the first time in her career from corporate defense to plaintiff lawyer. The Smiths asked Stacey if she'd be willing to serve as the named plaintiff in the case. If it went forward, *Haney v. Range* would pit Stacey, Beth, Buzz, and their families against the company and others, alleging the company had harmed them in different ways. But exactly what ways the Smiths didn't know yet. Given its scope, the case was going to take thousands of hours of legal

and environmental research and a year to file in court. In the mean-
time, the Smiths would pursue two cases against the DEP: first, on
Beth's behalf, to make the state agency do its job; second, to get Buzz
clean water if his well turned out to be contaminated.

In addition to building the timeline of potential errors at the site,
Kendra began building one that detailed her clients' health problems.
Those water tests were essential: she needed to know what they'd been
drinking and bathing in. Kendra and John began issuing subpoenas.
As soon as they filed a case against Range, this information would
become part of discovery, the pretrial process through which each side
obtains evidence from the other. Kendra started with subcontractors
she thought knew little about the case. It was standard practice to
start with such outliers who might offer more information, since they
didn't know what to hold back or hide. Inside the arriving bankers'
boxes were stacks of printed-out emails, including waste manifests
and field notes from workers documenting repairs up at the site. The
surefire way to catalogue what had occurred was to follow these bills.
Almost every contractor that had been paid to fix something or to
truck waste submitted a manifest that detailed the work done.

To sort them, Kendra sat on the floor in her large office, which
overlooked a corporate parking lot. A miniature skyline of paper stacks
stretched from her desk to her cabinets topped with lamps with red
satin shades. Manila folders covered her brown leather club chairs
and piled up on the table where she kept a Day-Glo yellow vest and
amber protective glasses for site visits. She separated paper into two
initial piles: one that seemed meaningless and the other that might
hold clues to her cases against the DEP and Range Resources. As she
pieced together the narrative of the remediation, she realized that the
chronology didn't track properly. She knew that the pit had leaked
once in 2010, but the cleanup was taking place a year later. She went
back to the DEP website and discovered that the pit had leaked again
in the spring of 2011. Eventually, she would uncover multiple leaks in
the frack pond also. She realized that the problems related to the waste

pond at the Yeager site were neither secret nor isolated. She suspected she was uncovering a systematic problem of Range's: the impoundments were leaking, and so were the white temporary pipelines between them.

"We all know they leak," one pipeliner working for a company called Red Oak Water Transfer wrote to another one. Issues at the Yeager site, however, seemed to be especially bad. In another email, a pipeliner asked another for directions to "the absolute worst flow back pit you can think of." His colleague responded, "Definitely either the Carrol Baker or the Yeager for Range. I would head to the Yeager in Lone Pine."

In her deepening piles, she found contractors' notes about fixing numerous holes in the liners. On separate occasions, animals had fallen into both the large pond and the smaller pit. Two deer had to be fished out of the pond, and a fox out of the pit. According to the emails, the animals' thrashing tore the liner, making holes through which contamination could leak.

There were also multiple spills, including the February 8, 2011, overturning of the tanker truck on an icy road that nearly killed the two security guards and spilled waste. She could also see from internal emails that Carla Suszkowski, the director of regulatory affairs at Range, grew angry at Range employees who called the DEP directly to report spills.

That winter, the temporary pipelines kept freezing and cracking. Apparently, Pete Miller of Range Resources was annoyed with Red Oak Water Transfer for not catching three separate leaks. "Mr. Miller is VERY frustrated with us," Richard Hoffman, Red Oak's director of safety and compliance, wrote in an email to his employees. They had to be sure that no more flowback spilled onto the fields from their frozen pipes. "We need to walk the lines regularly, our field employees do not make the decision whether something is a leak or not, one drop is a spill."

In the trucking manifests, Kendra could see that the sludge that was supposed to be trucked to a landfill in Ohio was cocktailed with other waste up at Yeager instead. She could see on the receipts for each load that the site in Ohio was crossed out and instead someone had scrawled *Yeager*, by way of destination. Yeager was also so busy because of thousands of gallons of fracking fluids and mud being trucked in from other sites, and as far as she could see there was no permit allowing this.

Binder by binder, throughout 2011, the Smiths' timeline of mishaps grew so long it took over the windowless copy room at the firm, which John christened the Haney Library. Early that fall, Kendra was still awaiting the missing pages of the water tests from the DEP when a complete set arrived from Microbac. She found the missing pages damning. They included the test results from the leak detection zone under the manhole cover. Once Kendra inserted them into a larger picture of what was happening on the hillside, she believed she could prove the link between the site and her clients' water by tracing how the chemicals flowed downhill.

One of her advantages in parsing results was that Kendra could read raw data, not just the summary reports given to her clients. The difference between the two was that the raw data contained everything found in the water. It couldn't be manipulated like test reports could. The list was a dizzying array of compounds, many of which Kendra could have grouped loosely and moved on. But she was after precision, and precision demanded a careful breakdown. Studying the raw data, she found that Beth's and Stacey's water test results revealed small amounts of chloroform, propynol, methanol, ethylene glycol, and propylene glycol, as well as oil and grease. In addition, Stacey's also had the phenols that had showed up on her inhalant panel. All of these constituents were found in low levels, below the reporting limits, but clearly, Kendra saw, they were there in the water and they shouldn't have been.

In her stacks, Kendra found something even more troubling: multiple copies of the same test results printed differently. Some copies contained glycols; others didn't. On the test results given to Stacey and to the DEP, there was no evidence of glycols. Kendra suspected that someone had doctored these results.

In response to her discovery requests, Kendra also received Range's test results for the water Ron Yeager and his cattle drank. She could see that his water contained levels of salt high enough to indicate contamination back in 2010, but there was no evidence to suggest that Range had ever told him so. As far as she could tell, both he and his cows were still drinking it. Once again, she found multiple copies of tests from the same sample that listed different results. In one version, Kendra saw that the lab listed ethylene glycol at a level of 10.2 mg/L in the Yeagers' spring water. But then in the next version, the glycols disappeared. She examined the test methods to see what had happened. She discovered that the lab had doubled the reporting limit from 10 mg/L to 20 mg/L. Since the amount now fell beneath the new reporting limit, it wasn't listed. What a clever trick this seemed to be. To Kendra, it implied that the lab could be at fault too in changing protocols to hide contamination in the water.

Laura Rusmisel at Range Resources had sent these results to Ron Yeager, along with a letter explaining that the high level of salt in his water could be caused by the township's salting the road against ice, "since calcium chloride is a common road treatment salt and the spring sources which were sampled today are located near a roadway." So Kendra and John wrote to the supervisors of Amwell Township, which included Amity, asking about road salts. Amwell Township doesn't use road salt, the supervisors wrote back. They use cinders, which don't contain high levels of salt. Intentionally or not, Laura Rusmisel had created an imaginary source of contamination.

Kendra remembered driving past the Yeagers' farm, with the blue and yellow sign on the barn that read PENNSYLVANIA BEEF QUALITY ASSURANCE PROGRAM CERTIFIED PRODUCER. The program was designed to boost consumer confidence by ensuring that the state's beef and dairy cattle were maintained in a manner that was "safe and wholesome for consumers." Yet the program didn't monitor cattle for potential exposure to the new oil and gas operations. She worried that without knowing it, Yeager may have been giving his beef cattle contaminated water for six months, at least, before selling them for human consumption. And there was no way to begin to track where they had entered the food chain.

16 | RAINBOW WATER

Late that summer of 2011, Stacey heard from a friendly inspector at the EPA that Range was going to close down the giant waste pond, at least for a time. To Stacey, that meant she and the kids might soon be able to go home. One July night, Stacey decided to celebrate by hosting a venison roast, inviting her sister and some friends over to the farm. Around an open fire, they roasted a deer that Chris had killed the previous winter. After dinner, the kids set the burn pile alight until the flames rose fifty feet into the night sky. The fire was so high that Shelly's husband, Jim, a member of the Amity Fire Department, called around to reassure neighbors all was okay. Shelly sat in the yard telling stories about how she quit smoking by drinking half a gallon of cotton-candy-flavored vodka and finishing two packs of cigarettes before passing out in her chair. Now she claimed she'd never smoke again.

Next door at Justa Breeze, Ashley was having trouble sleeping. She dreamed of dead horses. After Jodi's death, she'd never wanted to grow so close to an animal again. But barrel racing was her profession, so she started training a new horse, Oakie. A registered quarter horse with an impeccable bloodline, Oakie was doing well with Ashley on the barrel racing circuit, and they'd started placing in races, earning a paycheck. At night when she couldn't sleep, she went out to the barn to be with Oakie and Dude, her big paint gelding, combing them and talking to them about Jodi. When they whickered back at her, she was certain they could understand.

One evening that July, Ashley took Dude out for his daily ride, leading the large horse across McAdams and past their neighbors the Garretts. The waste pond sat at the corner of the Garretts' land, but they weren't reporting any problems with their water. Mr. Garrett told Beth that if their water went bad, he'd just drink beer. Ashley pressed Dude's flank with her heels to guide him up the sharp slope and around the outside of the fence that ringed the waste pond.

Dude was a source of solace to Ashley. Patient and steady, he took good care of her, and she did the same for him. That day, when Dude lowered his head to drink from a stream, he suddenly reared up. Ashley tried to force him to cross the stream, but he wouldn't. He was still being trained, and had to learn to follow her direction. But he wouldn't budge. She got off to take a closer look and heard bubbling. She could see a spectrum in the water. She got back up on Dude, and they ran home full stride. Something oily was running through the grass. "Rainbow water," Ashley told her mom as soon as she got home. Beth, as usual, called Stacey.

That night, Stacey headed to Justa Breeze and climbed on the Voyles' four-wheeler. She and Beth drove up the ridge to where Ashley had spotted the stream's oily runoff. Beth shot pictures with her phone of the bubbling water, which was thick with an oily substance and foam that looked like soap. Stacey noticed that there wasn't just one trickle of runoff; there were dozens of little seeps coming up out of the ground. Someone had put hay bales in the stream to block the flow.

The next morning, Beth called the Fish and Wildlife Service as well as the DEP to report the rainbow water seeping out of the side of the hill. The DEP sent a water inspector over to test. When his results came back, they showed the presence of oil, grease, and MBAS, a soap used in the drilling process.

The DEP inspector also observed something unusual. Dean's Water trucks were idling by the side of the drill cuttings pit. Wondering what they could be doing, he took photographs. When Yantko saw the pictures, he knew what he was looking at, and he wasn't pleased. Not long before, Carla Suszkowski had called Yantko. The contaminated springs at Yeager weren't repairing themselves, so she wanted to flush the leaky waste pit with thirty thousand gallons of water. Flushing the pit might help clean the springs before the EPA arrived in two weeks to test the Yeagers' water as part of their national drinking water study. In response, Yantko told her that pouring water into the contaminated pit would just drive the pollutants deeper into the ground. He told her she'd have to ask for permission in writing.

Without doing so, Suszkowski ordered the flush. When Yantko saw the pictures of Dean's Water trucks pumping water into the leaky drill cuttings pit, he learned that Carla had disobeyed him. "This action was both intentional and reckless and may have actually resulted in additional contaminants entering the water—the Yeager spring water supply," he wrote to his supervisor. The flush violated the Clean Streams Law, a 1937 mandate that protected the waters of the commonwealth, along with four other laws. The waters of the commonwealth belonged to the commons: the state held them in trust on behalf of all Pennsylvania citizens.

When Rick Wilkin and his EPA team arrived as scheduled two weeks later, neither he nor his inspectors knew that Range had tried to flush the leaky pit and contaminated springs. In windbreakers and chinos, Wilkin's team paced around the Garretts' hillside. From a distance, they looked like a forensic team searching for something unpleasant in the dead grass. Performing the necessary testing for the nationwide drinking water study had proven difficult for the EPA. The government struggled to convince oil and gas companies to participate. And without the companies' permission, the EPA wasn't allowed onto their sites. The EPA had tried to visit the Yeager site a month earlier, but Carla Suszkowski had denied them entry. In an email to a fellow Range employee, she wrote, "Hugh, is there some reason that the guard is allowing the EPA person on site? They have no regulatory authority by which to enter our site. And we should not be allowing them on site."

Now, a month later, the investigators were still barred from entering. Reporting there that day, I watched them fan out over the surrounding hillside as John Voyles drove me up the muddy bank below the waste pond on the back of a four-wheeler to see what was happening with the rainbow water. The ground was sodden, and dozens of tiny rivulets sprang from the mud. A thick vapor rose like smoke from the water, and the air was choked with the odor of bleach.

Four months later, in November, Suszkowski updated her bosses. "We have flushed the reserve pit with approximately 30,000 gallons of water, but I fear this is nowhere near enough, based on the amount of time that the reserve pit may have been leaking," she wrote. She suggested that Range offer to dig the Yeagers a new well. "I think this would avoid the DEP issuing an order for us to replace the water supply." If the DEP did issue such an order, that would make the contamination public. Even if the DEP didn't make it public, she had concerns that replacing the water would have ramifications: "I suspect when we agree to replace the water supply others in the area will get wind of it and more legal action will ensue." Still, she thought the order was worth it to keep "an otherwise supportive landowner happy," she wrote. Her boss, Ray Walker, replied, "I agree. We should replace it . . . and pray for lots of rain!"

Buzz and his grandkids weren't feeling well, so Stacey decided to pay them a visit late that summer. One morning, she drove down to the Bottoms to see if she could help. Stacey, like others in Amity and Prosperity, had stayed away from the junkyard over the years. Buzz's car chase with the state troopers and other such stories were ready fodder in the small community.

She parked near the rusted-out bakery truck and a charred outbuilding, and mounted the concrete block that served as a porch to knock on the aluminum door. Buzz was sitting on the couch. When Stacey asked how he was doing, he told her that he and the kids were having trouble breathing and their stomachs were sour. The trailer reeked of cigarette smoke; an army of amber prescription bottles sat on a TV table. An oxygen tank leaned against the couch. In this room alone, there was evidence of many factors that could be sickening Buzz and his family. Stacey knew that, but she also knew what she and the kids had been through, and she was beyond being skeptical. And there was the water: gray and filled with sediment like hers. But Buzz had to keep cooking and washing with it when he wasn't staying in his mother's basement.

His physician, Dr. Christiansen, who worked at the orthopedic hospital along with Shelly, had been treating Buzz for an injured shoulder. When Buzz's tests came back as part of his presurgical workup, the results alarmed the physician. "His blood work came back really off the scale—arsenic, benzene, a lot of chemicals we'd never seen in anyone's blood and I had to look them up," he told me later. Knowing that Buzz couldn't afford water, Dr. Christiansen tried to get Range Resources to supply the family a water buffalo, but to no avail. Eventually, he prescribed Buzz a gym membership, which Range lawyers would bring up later during a deposition as evidence that Buzz couldn't be so sick if he could make it to the gym. Dr. Christiansen corrected them. He wanted Buzz to be able to shower with clean water. "I've prescribed gym memberships before," he told me, "but never with the hope of getting someone out of the house."

For the rest of the summer and into the early fall, Buzz used his water sparingly as he awaited test results. Finally, in September, a letter arrived from the DEP. His water was high in inorganic salts and also in methane, two elements that can be associated with drilling, but not necessarily so. "We strongly recommend that you maintain a vent on your water well," the DEP wrote to Kiskadden. Although there were problems with Buzz's water, the letter went on, these problems were "not the result of Range's actions at the Yeager site, or any other gas well related activities." The contaminants might be leaching from the old buses, boats, and cars heaped in his junkyard.

According to this letter, Range owed him nothing and neither did the DEP. (A state inspector told him to pour a half gallon of bleach into his well at least once a month to manage the rotten-egg smell.) Buzz Kiskadden understood that he wasn't going to get a water buffalo. Despite the poor quality of his water, he'd have to keep buying his own at Walmart, or go without. There was more to the letter that he didn't understand, so he called the Smiths, who were now representing him.

Studying the DEP's letter, Kendra could see that in addition to the methane and salts, there were other problems with Buzz's water. It contained several known constituents of frack fluid. The DEP admitted as much in the letter—"Very low concentrations of several organic compounds were reported in the DEP sampling: butyl alcohol, chloroform, and acetone." But the DEP decided, inexplicably to Kendra, that these three were actually absent and the results were lab error. To Kendra, this was too convenient an explanation. From reading the raw data, she couldn't understand how they'd write off the chemicals as lab error. (When she later deposed the head of the DEP's lab, Kendra found she was right: there was no lab error.) And she could find no scientific basis for the DEP's claim that the junkyard was poisoning the well.

Kendra told John that she was prepared to challenge the DEP's determination, which meant filing suit against the state once again. As with the suit they'd brought on Beth's behalf against the DEP for neglecting its job, the Smiths would have to pay the costs out of pocket, and if they did win, they wouldn't make any money. Yet theirs would be the first case in Pennsylvania history to contest that the DEP's findings were wrong and that oil and gas had contaminated someone's water. Bringing such a case against the DEP, let alone winning it, was going to kick off a shitstorm, she told John.

17 | "DEAR MR. PRESIDENT"

Stacey wasn't going to move home with the kids until she was certain the noxious pond was empty, so that summer of 2011, while she waited for word from the EPA, she kept Harley at Chris's in Eighty Four. She and Paige stayed with Mam and Pappy in Amity. Although Harley's arsenic levels dropped as he stayed away from the farm, hers remained elevated. She kept returning to feed and water the animals. Together, they white-knuckled through the new normal. Paige was fighting with her grandmother after too much time in close proximity and the stress over water was mounting at her parents' house. With Stacey, Mam, and Pappy showering once a day, as well as twelve-year-old Paige, the family had to make the trip to the Ruff Creek water station three or four times a week to fill the cistern. Stacey was rarely there, and Paige spent most summer days sulking in the cot, which the family called her nest.

It was impossible to tell where Harley's physical ailments ended and his psychological struggles began. Those in Amity who didn't know the Haneys well and doubted they were suffering from chemical exposure credited Stacey's divorce as the root of the trouble. Those who'd seen Harley suffering up close were convinced that his illnesses were related to exposure. They were also friends, neighbors, and family. Harley spent the June night of his fifteenth birthday in tears. He missed his home, his animals, Mam and Pappy, and Amity, and he wanted to have a birthday party at the farm. But given the risk of exposure, Stacey said no. She didn't want other kids on the farm until she was sure it was safe.

Instead, for the kids' joint twelfth and fifteenth birthday party that year, they ended up at the town park. Stacey called in a pizza order, but she missed most of the party. At seven o'clock that morning, she'd gotten a call from a Pittsburgh fractivist asking Stacey to write a personal letter to President Obama. Josh Fox, the director of the film *Gasland*, was supposed to meet the president and hand him Stacey's letter. She still harbored the belief that if she could speak to Obama directly as a mom, and in plain language, she could convince him to protect her kids, as well as the other families living at the country's rural margins and paying the price for this boom.

"Dear Mr. President," she began. She laid out their story and ended with where they were now: "As of 35 days ago, the amt of chemicals we were inhaling from the impoundment got [to] the point where it was unbearable. Under medical advice, we were instructed to leave our home . . . I understand the financial benefits of the process and our need for having our own natural resources but making people sick in the process is criminal! . . . A farmer [can't] even drive his tractor across a stream in PA, but hundreds of thousands of cancer-causing chemicals can be dumped right beside my home for my children to breathe every day . . . I feel like we are stuck in a bad dream. Please, please help us."

June was turning into a very long month. One night, she sped home from a twelve-hour shift to don black dress pants and a white blouse. In response to national concern over fracking, President Obama had ordered Steven Chu, the secretary of energy, to form a natural gas subcommittee to advise the federal government on how to make the process safer. That night, at Washington & Jefferson College, the panel was holding a public meeting to listen to Washington County residents.

The oil and gas companies bused in supporters. A week earlier, Tom Shepstone, a consultant who worked for *Energy in Depth*, a pro-industry blog, sent out an email offering bus transportation along with free hotel rooms, meals, and tickets to see the Pittsburgh Pirates. The baseball tickets were later rescinded when the email came to light, but Chris Tucker, an *Energy in Depth* spokesman, defended the effort, saying, "It's exactly what the opposition does for every single local township meeting anytime one's held anywhere across the entire mid-Atlantic region." He added, "Difference is, we're not busing people in for a local township meeting. This is a public forum sponsored by the U.S. Department of Energy. Our folks have the right to be there, and if we have any say in the matter, they will be."

The small auditorium was now crammed with nearly five hundred people, the majority oil and gas supporters. By the time Stacey arrived at 7:05 p.m., they'd filled the two-minute slots to address the panel with pro-industry testimony. She wasn't going to be able to speak after all. Then a professor she knew gave her his slot. While she waited four hours for her turn, a heckler at the back of the auditorium held up a dollar bill every time anyone took the microphone to talk about the problems related to fracking. Stacey went up to him and put a finger in his face.

It's like this, buddy, she said. My kids are sick and people are trying to talk. He stopped jeering. Around 11:00 p.m., Stacey was one of the last of the two-minute speakers to come down the auditorium aisle and duck her head toward the standing microphone.

"My children are the real people that are dealing with this toxic chemical exposure," she began, setting herself apart from the boosters who'd preceded her. "Our lives have been ruined because of this and there's no job, there is no amount of money that any revenue can generate, that can replace the last two years of my children's lives." After she finished, she looked up at the five tired faces of the panelists on the stage and hoped she'd reached at least one of them.

As the summer wore on, she was still helping to gather evidence for a case against Range. A few days before the 2011 Washington County Fair began, after stopping at the farm to feed the animals, Stacey drove up the hill to the Yeagers' farmhouse. By now, it seemed clear that the cattle farmers' drinking water was contaminated: Range had paid for Dean's Water to deliver a 5,100-gallon water buffalo in July, which everyone could see.

Though they didn't initially know it, Ron and Sharon Yeager had one essential element of evidence that neither Stacey nor Beth did: a pre-drill test that established the baseline quality of their water. By law, Range had to test their water, as it lay within what was called the zone of presumption.

Kendra knew that the DEP must have a copy of the test and went digging. When she found it, she alerted the Yeagers' lawyer that it existed and might help him procure clean water for his clients. She also wanted a copy but needed the Yeagers' permission for the DEP to release it. Stacey took it upon herself to stop by and see if she could help move things along.

That afternoon, when Stacey pulled up in front of the farmhouse, she found Sharon Yeager outside. Stacey asked Mrs. Yeager for the pre-drill, but Mrs. Yeager demurred. Every time they called their lawyer, it cost money, Stacey recalled Mrs. Yeager saying. They didn't want to get in the middle of it. Stacey lost her temper. *Get* in the middle of it, she said to Mrs. Yeager; they *were* the middle of it. Stacey told Mrs. Yeager that she'd lost the total value of her home, and she didn't know what was going to happen with her kids with all of these cancer-causing agents in their blood. If you don't send those results, she told Sharon Yeager through the car window, my attorney will subpoena you, and that will cost you more money. Stacey peeled away, her tires spitting gravel.

A few days later, Stacey managed to get the kids and their animals to the fairgrounds. That Saturday in August, Stacey and Shelly set up the animal hair salon at their camper. Stacey blew out Paige's goat, Crunch, then Harley's goat, Winston Churchill. (Shelly named Churchill on Harley's behalf, since he was too queasy to care.) It was hard to imagine it was only one year since he'd won Grand Champion

Showmanship with Boots, and since Cummins had died. Together, they walked down to the 9:00 a.m. SPAM contest for which Stacey and Paige had concocted a SPAM-infused cornbread they called SPAM Good Morning Muffins, salty with baking soda and a preservative tang.

Although Stacey had rescued a blue and white tin spatterware plate from the farmhouse, she had no doilies. A doily-free plate wouldn't win with the judges. "I couldn't find a doily anywhere," she said to Paige as they stood beneath the humid pavilion watching the judges move up and down on the dais.

"Mom, that's how we roll," Paige said.

"That's how we roll *now*," Stacey replied.

When the judges announced their results, Stacey was disappointed. It was the first time in three years that Paige didn't place. Stacey milled around the fairgrounds, hardly noticing the events she loved, including the pedal pull, in which a toddler wearing a pink FUTURE DAIRY PRINCESS T-shirt was straining against the pedals of a toy John Deere tractor. Stacey was distracted by the brightly colored banners hanging from the rafters of the show barn. The number of oil and gas sponsors was proliferating, including Rice Energy and EQT, as well as Range Resources. Dozens of employees volunteered at the fair. To the company, the outreach and direct contact with the community that the fair allowed were crucial. As Mike Mackin of Range told me later, "Where we live and work is Washington County—and what better way to set up shop and have people come to us with their questions." Range was also able to collect valuable information; the company had become close with members of the Fair Board. "They can tell you a lot about people," Mackin added, "and a lot about the things you're doing right and the things you're doing wrong, and how to correct them. That's something important to us—real honest feedback."

To Stacey, Range's presence seemed anything but honest. It struck her that the companies were trying to slap their name on someone else's way of life as a form of cheap advertising. She wandered into a 4-H hall, where Pappy's butternuts waited to be judged. There, among the arts and crafts, was a Patterson drilling rig built out of Legos. From it hung a blue ribbon.

Stacey was raising her kids to play by rules that no longer seemed to apply. But her hopelessness proved partially misplaced. Although Paige didn't place at the SPAM contest, she took first in goats and rabbits. Harley was a separate case. He drifted glowering around the fairgrounds. Forget college, he thought, forget the brief dream of becoming an architect. He was going to get out of Amity, to join the military like Pappy. He wanted to be anywhere but the fair, and it showed. Winston Churchill misbehaved and Harley took a humbling sixth. He held Range responsible for his lost love of the fair, of his life.

And it turned out they weren't returning home. Stacey and the kids tried to spend a few nights at the farm, but Harley was sick within hours. Fumes were still wafting down from the site, and soon they learned from the EPA that the pond wasn't going to be closed after all. Stacey decided they couldn't keep shifting from place to place every night. The best solution she could find to their housing dilemma was to try to sleep in a camper parked in her parents' driveway. It meant she'd see Chris even less, since Harley would no longer be sleeping at his house and she didn't want to leave the kids alone for the night. But she saw Chris so rarely anyway, and she had to put the kids first. Sticking together was the important thing, and living in a camper was the only way to make this possible. They wouldn't last a winter in their old blue and white Coachman, so Stacey traded it in and paid an additional $27,758.65, in monthly installments of $230.51, for a new camper. She used some of the money that she and Beth were just starting to receive each month in royalties from Range. For the first six months, when the well was at its most productive, Stacey received big checks, which ranged from almost $3,500 to just under $6,000. After taxes, that figure dropped by a third, but it was still substantial. She was trying to put away as much as she could for a down payment on a new house, if she ended up needing one. Buying the camper was part of her savings plan. It was much cheaper than renting a house. With the arrival of out-of-state workers, demand for housing outpaced supply and rents were climbing by as much as 12 percent a month. This had unseen costs for rural families: in the neighboring county, those who could no longer afford adequate housing were forced to hand their children over to foster care. Stacey was determined to keep her family intact, even if they were living in a camper, with Paige in a bunk and Harley on a pile of leopard-print cushions on the steel floor.

18 | INSURGENTS

The debate over fracking was more polarized than ever by the fall of 2011; it reached well beyond Pennsylvania and across the nation. In blue New York, activists were bidding to ban the practice. They based their arguments on water contamination and other hazards. Their position was grounded in the precautionary principle: if a product or practice could put public health at risk, even if such risks were not yet fully understood, better to avoid it.

To combat this argument, and its potential to turn communities against them, members of the oil and gas industry gathered in Houston, Texas, in October 2011. The conference, "Media and Stakeholder Relations: Hydraulic Fracturing Initiative 2011," was billed as a means to form "a united front" against false claims about harm and the threat of "intrusive regulation." Sharon Wilson, an environmental activist known as "TXsharon," decided to attend. She registered openly on behalf of Earthworks, a nonprofit with the stated mission to protect people from the negative effects of mineral extraction. Earthworks paid her registration fee. Wearing a nametag that read EARTHWORKS OIL AND GAS ACCOUNTABILITY PROJECT, she headed into the conference past men in black suits wearing earpieces. It was a far cry from the gatherings she was used to, which resembled Hang 'Em High, with frightened farmers clutching jars of cloudy water.

As she started recording, her thighs began to sweat. She was waiting for one of those besuited guys with an earpiece to tap her on the back, or worse. She was surprised when the first speaker began the day with a call to be kinder and gentler, in order to win public

opinion. By the time the second speaker rose, however, that concilia-
tory message was lost.

"Download the U.S. Army/Marine Corps Counterinsurgency Manual because we are dealing with an insurgency," Matt Carmichael,
manager of external affairs for Anadarko Petroleum, said. Although
she wanted to sneak out before she got busted, Wilson kept her seat
for another session, led by Matt Pitzarella, the Range Resources spokesman. Pitzarella was raised in Washington County. He'd attended California University in Pennsylvania. Balding, he kept his head shaved
and often balanced sunglasses atop his forehead. He spoke next.

"We have several former psy-ops folks that work for us at Range
because they're very comfortable in dealing with localized issues and
local governments," he said. "Psy-ops" refers to psychological operations,
a counterinsurgency tactic, which the Department of Defense defines
for use exclusively outside of the United States. According to Pitzarella,
Range was employing these methods in Pennsylvania. "Really all they
do is spend most of their time helping folks develop local ordinances
and things like that," he said. "But very much having that understanding of psy-ops in the army and the Middle East has applied very
helpfully here for us in Pennsylvania." One of the people he was
talking about was Jim Cannon, a U.S. Marine and now an army re-
servist with the 303rd Psychological Operations Company, who served
under the U.S. Army Special Operations Command (USASOC) as part
of Operation Iraqi Freedom. Cannon was now the local government
relations manager for Range Resources in Pennsylvania. When he
learned what Pitzarella had said, Cannon was irritated. Pitzarella's
remarks had put Cannon in an untenable position. He knew it would've
been illegal to conduct military psy-ops inside the United States, and
he was doing nothing of the kind. To be fair, the primary aim of psy-
ops doesn't involve killing; it's designed to win over a population. And
while it was true that Cannon's time in Iraq had prepared him to
stand up in front of five hundred angry people at a community meet-

ing and attempt to quiet their ire by conducting field PR, any other comparison was nonsense.

After Wilson released her recording to the press and Pitzarella's claims were made public, he tried to shuffle back from the idea that Range was waging a counterinsurgency. "That's not something I think that we would do," Pitzarella said. "You're not dealing with insurgents, you're dealing with regular people who live in towns and want to know what you're doing." But the idea that Range saw itself as battling insurgents in Washington County was now part of the public record.

For Wilson, Range Resources' talk of waging psychological warfare wasn't the most disturbing aspect of the conference. Worse was the sales pitch for a burgeoning industry called stakeholder intelligence. Aaron Goldwater, a software promoter, stood before the crowded conference and said: "A number of people today have—in my words . . . how I've heard it—talked about having a battle with stakeholders and a bit of a war with stakeholders. So, if you look at the people who are experts at it, which are the military, the one thing they do, is gather intelligence . . . How do you gather intelligence about your stakeholders?"

He was promoting mapping software, which tracked the networks that people like Wilson belonged to: family, friends, fellow activists. On-screen, a series of dots and lines stretching across a map traced the kind of information Goldwater's services at his company, Jurat Software, could provide. His was not the only mapping service available. FTI Consulting, a corporate research firm, offered a similar service. The firm's clients included many big oil companies. Spooked by industry's mapping networks of people like her, Sharon Wilson did some research. She found that FTI Consulting shared links with Big Tobacco. The FTI executive David Quast, for instance, was the former manager of media affairs at Altria, the parent company of Philip Morris USA; now he worked at *Energy in Depth*, the industry blog that took on opponents. *Energy in Depth* was funded in part by Range Resources.

After Wilson blogged about the conference and about an ongoing case of water contaminated with benzene in Texas, Range Resources tried to sue her for defamation. Wilson kept blogging. "I was very sassy although inside I was quaking a little bit," she told me. Being targeted by Range Resources elevated her to superstar status in the fractivist community.

"Thank you, Range Resources, for shooting yourselves in the foot," she said.

For the industry, these kinds of scraps went beyond bad PR. High-profile opposition from activists like Wilson and celebrities like Mark Ruffalo, as well as Robert Redford and Yoko Ono, posed a substantive threat. Having drilled for decades overseas in war zones and unstable places, the oil and gas industry was accustomed to managing political risk. Calculating uncertainties related to war and unrest was part of the business. One upside to working in the United States was that Big Oil foresaw more stable political relationships. Yet grassroots opposition to fracking threatened that. It had the potential to change public opinion, and in a democracy, changing public opinion had the power to change votes and laws.

19 | BURDEN OF PROOF

Kendra Smith's SUV was piled with bankers' boxes when soccer season began that fall. Each day, at the office, she set a stack of documents before her. When she didn't get through them all by 5:45 p.m., she threw the rest into another white box and tossed it into the back seat, then drove the kids to soccer practice. She was coaching three separate teams, and during practice, she tried to leave the documents in the car. Her son, Dakota, asked her why she always got so much homework, and her kids grew accustomed to looking over to the sidelines and seeing the top of their mom's dirty-blonde head staring down at her iPhone. She didn't notice that her hair was starting to gray.

As Kendra built *Haney v. Range*, she recognized the hardest part of the task before her: to make it clear that her clients had been harmed by chemical exposure. If she could establish that the chemicals up at the site were in her clients' bodies, then she should be able to prove that the two were definitively linked.

It wasn't going to be easy, for various reasons. First, she still didn't know all of the chemicals Range and its subcontractors had used. Although Range told its shareholders that it listed every constituent on FracFocus, an online registry, that information was not at all comprehensive. With twenty years' experience as a civil defense attorney, she knew how to introduce doubt into a case, how to make it hard for the other side to meet its burden of proof. This time she was the other side: up against a powerful industry rather than representing one.

It wasn't simply about marshaling the evidence. In a case this complex, winning or losing would also be based on who told the better story, on who could convince a listening judge or jury that the facts supported their claims by as slim a margin as 51–49. The Smiths' victory hinged upon their ability to turn all this evidence into a clear narrative. With the litany of unfamiliar chemicals, conflicting accounts, and plaintiffs who included children, the case could be hard to comprehend. As Kendra explained to me one afternoon in the conference room, "Translating that evidence for the court is a job and a half."

She broke it down to a matter of cause and effect. Most of the exposure cases she handled were work-related. In these cases, both sides knew a hazardous product was on-site and that the chance for exposure existed. Usually, her job was to go out and see what kind of factors limited that exposure, including the amount of time the worker was around that chemical and any protections that limited contact. She laid it out like this:

"You go out to Stacey Haney's house, and even if we say that fracking doesn't cause problems, you ask are there any other factors that could harm their health: spills, leaks, releases, air exposure. Yes. I've found evidence of all of the above. Then you look at what are the blocks [impediments] between the family and the chemicals? Air? Nothing. Safeguards in the ponds? Nope. There's been no testing of liners and there's evidence of leaks. Now you look at terrain, could it be a further block to exposure? Do we have any evidence that it's reached a source? Yes. Through no fault of their own, their neighbors' drinking water was contaminated.

"Now you have air and skin exposure. They're bathing in it, and ingestion because they're drinking it.

"One. You've confirmed there's exposure.

"Two. Then you've confirmed the routes of exposure. Normally you've got one route, we've got three.

"Three. Now you've got a bunch of toxic chemicals, and you've got to ask if combining them multiplies their effect. Take asbestos and smoking. Combine both and your likelihood of getting cancer goes up

twenty times. You couldn't single out one, you had to look at them together, but they needed to know what to look for.

"The real problem is that we don't know all the chemicals."

Kendra's line of thinking wasn't always so easy to follow. Sometimes,
when deep in the data, she spoke in a kind of chemical-laden legalese,
and at such a brisk clip that a listener risked being left far behind. As
her bright interlocutor, John helped translate Kendra's complex arguments, so that a judge, or someday a jury, could follow. He also used
his wife's findings to prepare questions for upcoming depositions.

Each evening by eight, the Smiths got the kids home to their pale
brick colonial on a cul-de-sac, and settled them down to do homework
at their respective desks in the living room. Then Kendra went back
to work on the deck that John had built for her. The Smiths had been
married twenty years and spent nineteen in their house. John knew
his wife loved nothing more than being outside. "Her happy place is
the beach," he said. So he and his brothers built her a porch with sky-
lights, ceiling fans, a wooden floor, a TV, and a red sectional sofa. The
porch opened onto their large backyard, which contained the trappings of an active upper-middle-class suburban life: a gazebo, a large
soccer net, a swimming pool, a vegetable garden, and a trellis woven
with grapevines that John's great-grandparents brought from Italy
nearly a century earlier.

In their backyard, she traded her pantsuit for a pair of baggy soccer shorts and watched the kids fire soccer balls into the large white
net, calling technical advice from the porch to Dakota, twelve; Sienna,
nine; and her youngest daughter, Ainsley, who at seven had recovered
from her illness and already demonstrated the drive and athletic talent
Kendra possessed. The yard was edged with hydrangea bushes Kendra
had once tended diligently, and that had lately gone unpruned. Now
she sat on the porch's red sectional reading most nights until two in
the morning. Waking at six, she was averaging four hours of sleep a
night. From her days at law school, she knew how to perform on lack
of sleep. She and John had shot through three years of law school in

two and two and a half, respectively. Simultaneously, Kendra had served on the law review and worked as a research assistant for one of her professors. In law school, however, she didn't have to contend with motherhood. Dakota, Sienna, and Ainsley required as much attention as she could give them. She made a bargain with herself and with John: as long as the kids didn't feel neglected, she could give every last ounce of herself to her work. Everything else was off the agenda, including events like a coworker's baby shower. Kendra said, by way of a gentle no, that she just couldn't expend those hours. Of all the limited resources Kendra was facing in building her case—the incomplete files she was receiving in discovery, the bureaucratic runarounds with the state at the DEP—the sharpest restraints she faced were related to time. "When people talk about work/life balance, I've never understood why they use the word 'balance,'" she told me.

The Smiths weren't building one case now; they were constructing three. Each had its own stacks of paper: the Voyles' case against the DEP, on her desk; Buzz Kiskadden's appeal for clean water, on Kendra's office floor; the sprawling case for Stacey and the seven others, in the copy-room-cum–Haney Library.

Kendra's methods irked the other side. What she took as thoroughness, they considered a form of overkill that bordered on vendetta. To gather information during discovery, attorneys from one side draft questions known as interrogatories for the other side to answer. A typical number of questions hovers around ten. In her discovery requests, Kendra was averaging hundreds per defendant. She wasn't asking only the big players such as Range Resources and the Department of Environmental Protection for such answers. Now she was working off a list of as many as seventeen different parties who bore some responsibility, she argued, for what went awry up at Yeager. And she wasn't only seeing accidents; she suspected she was looking at fraud.

She discovered very different versions of test results of the exact same water samples. Both came from Beth Voyles's house. One version belonged to Atlas, a company sampling water that past summer alongside the EPA. The other came from Test America, the lab working for Range. She could see major divergences. The first and most obvious was that on the Atlas test, she could see high levels of nitrates, which can cause respiratory problems and increase the risk of thyroid cancer, along with small amounts of other chemicals, radioactive material, and sand. Nitrates have multiple sources, including manure. They could also be associated with drilling. Yet all of the contaminants were missing from the results that Test America gave to the Voyles and to the Department of Environmental Protection.

As the plaintiff suit grew, so did the number of defendants implicated in the litigation, which drew in several of Pittsburgh's top corporate defense firms. "Hell, we're employing half of Pittsburgh," John joked.

After decades of working alongside their opponents, Kendra and John knew them well. But now these colleagues were adversaries, and the Smiths were facing more aggression from the other side than they'd experienced in their careers. Kendra surmised that one defense attorney working for Range Resources, Ken Komoroski, seemed to have a particular problem with her. Kendra said that during a deposition, Komoroski lunged across the table at her. John wasn't there to see it. He was coaching Dakota at basketball that day. When asked, Komoroski denied any such action. "I have never acted in a way that is unprofessional and that includes towards appellant's counsel here, Kendra Smith and John Smith," he wrote in an email. "To be clear, I never lunged, nor could have been perceived to have lunged at Attorney Smith, nor any other counsel in my years of practice." Yet Kendra recalled other instances she felt were unprofessional, such as when Komoroski called out during a deposition the fact that she played Division One soccer in college, saying something about how this wasn't a soccer game.

These kinds of personal comments seemed to Kendra to be a hamfisted attempt at intimidation, an effort to put her on notice that the other side was looking into her background. They didn't frighten her.

"I kind of laughed," she told me. "If that's the best this guy's got, then he's in trouble." Playing soccer for a punishing college coach had taught her a form of mental toughness that she valued. "You walk a fine line as a female in this position," she said. "There's a certain amount of it you have to take before you reach out for help without looking like you're playing the female card." That mental toughness was one reason why she had both of her daughters play soccer now. Everyone made mistakes on the field, but making a mistake didn't let your team down. You let your team down when you made a mistake and refused to get over it. You don't let anyone get in your head, she told her two daughters. You're the only one allowed in your head.

Finally, the antipathy rose to such a pitch that Kendra went to the judge, who decided to sit in on depositions. Kendra suspected these attorneys were acting out because they knew she had the goods. She'd represented railroads and alleged organized criminals from New Jersey, and it didn't get much tougher than that.

20 | POLICING THE STATE

While Kendra clashed with opposing lawyers, John found himself engaged in a fresh battle against the state. In 2011, Pennsylvania's new Republican governor, Tom Corbett, was bidding to change its Oil and Gas Act in favor of Act 13, a new law that the state and fossil fuel industry largely drafted together. Although Corbett had received $1.17 million in campaign donations from the industry, his interest was more than political. It was ideological: he opposed environmental regulation. Upon entering office, he'd ordered a state environmental website scrubbed of any mention of climate change.

Despite the unprecedented profits associated with fracking, Pennsylvania charged oil and gas operators next to nothing in taxes or fees for the right to drill. As part of the new give-and-take under Act 13, industry would pay an impact fee to local governments, a flat fee per well. In exchange, companies would be able to bypass old arrangements that required approval from small municipalities. If a driller wanted to dig a frack pond next to a school, say, or in a church parking lot, under the new law, the town would have no right to say no, as long as the pond was at least three hundred feet away. In practical terms, if the new law went into effect, a frack pond could sit five times closer to someone's house than the one uphill from Stacey.

John Smith's concerns about the new law went beyond health and environmental issues. It could spell financial ruin for the small communities he'd been helping to protect by drafting local ordinances. This new law would negate every one of them, and if a town decided to challenge the industry by taking a company to court and lost, the town would have to pay the company's legal fees. As a solicitor, Smith knew what that meant. His client Robinson Township, for instance, had an annual operating budget of four hundred thousand dollars. If Robinson tried to challenge an oil and gas company that hired corporate lawyers billing at four hundred or five hundred dollars an hour, then a ten-day trial could easily bankrupt the small town.

The proposed law had other problematic aspects, including one that foes called the physician gag rule: it stipulated that doctors sign a nondisclosure agreement in order to learn what chemicals might have sickened their patients. Under the gag rule, a doctor wouldn't be able to tell other doctors or even his or her patients the toxic contents found in their bodies. To Smith, this constituted a clear violation of the Hippocratic Oath.

Just as chilling to Smith was a privacy clause: if a neighbor's private water source was contaminated by drilling, and he settled with the oil and gas company, the people living next door had no right to know, as long as they relied on private wells instead of public water. In a case like Stacey's, if Ron Yeager settled privately with Range, he wouldn't have to say a word.

Smith wasn't the only one who saw problems with the new law. The fight against Act 13 didn't just pit left-leaning environmentalists against conservative Republicans. Two of Washington County's conservative Republicans led the dissent. Throughout 2011, Dave Ball from Peters Township and Brian Coppola from Robinson Township traveled to Harrisburg along with a Democratic ally, Andy Schrader, to speak out against Act 13. In Washington County, Peters was as rich as Robinson was poor; Peters's budget amounted to more than $23 million a year, more than fifty times that of Robinson's. One afternoon, Ball and Coppola met me at the Southpointe Country Club to discuss their objections to the law.

"I'm not opposed to industry," Dave Ball said. "But by the same token, I will absolutely defend people's constitutional rights." This proposed law was a violation of people's right to private property, Ball said. These rights were enshrined in Article I of the Pennsylvania Constitution, including the right to protect one's property from harm.

For forty years, Ball had worked for U.S. Steel in eight countries, including Venezuela, India, and Thailand. What he'd seen of extractive industries in remote and impoverished places cast a frightening foreshadow. "I've seen places immensely rich in resources that are incredibly poor, just like in Appalachia," he said. To him, the problem was less about the resource and more about the system that sprang up around its extraction: government corruption. "Gas is new, sexy, mobile, agile, and cash heavy," Ball said. All of these factors gave the industry overwhelming political power in both Pennsylvania and Washington, D.C. As he saw it, this gas boom was eroding public welfare in the form of political payouts like the million-plus dollars that went into the governor's campaign coffers.

Ball's fellow fighter Brian Coppola had other concerns. Working in real estate development, he too believed that allowing companies to "drill everywhere" would destroy property values. Of course people had a right to do what they wanted to on their private property, but they didn't have the right to inflict harm on others. There was an ancient Latin maxim for this: *Sic utere tuo ut alienum non laedas*— "Use your own so as not to injure your neighbor."

Coppola saw another problem approaching. By 2011, smaller wildcat companies were bidding to be bought up by larger ones. Super majors like ExxonMobil and Chevron were entering shale plays. The Marcellus, in particular, offered the promise of vast returns. But the upside was limited by transportation concerns. Unlike oil, shale gas couldn't be trucked. It had to travel by pipeline. For the smaller operators, whoever could prove they could get the gas to market would be most attractive to buyers. Each company was building its own infrastructure, much of it redundant, to prove it could get gas to Philadelphia, New

York, and other major markets as quickly as possible. Coppola's township, Robinson, was at the center of this construction glut.

"Right now these companies are entrenching themselves," Coppola said. "The argument is that they're creating jobs, but they're destroying our long-term wealth, which is based in property. People who can afford to will leave, and that will gut our tax base." Western Pennsylvania had been through this before. It was part of the oil, gas, and coal cycles of boom and bust. An extractive industry came to a place, bringing with it money and overbuilding, and then it went away, taking jobs and leaving behind a legacy of failing infrastructure and abandoned homes in places like Prosperity.

Despite such dissent, on February 14, 2012, Governor Corbett signed Act 13 into law. His critics called it his sweetheart gift to industry. That day in Robinson, the township held a meeting. The council members decided to ask John Smith to lead a legal challenge against the law. Smith was willing to try, but not as some kind of protest suit or political gesture. "You don't fight them with shouts, you fight them with facts, and we have the facts," Smith told me at the time. Working with Stacey, Beth, and Buzz had taught him some of the problems fracking could breed, as well as the state's inability to stop or fix them. He no longer believed that the state possessed the power and the will to protect its citizens. "In the past, everyone assumed that it was safe and I was one of them," he said. "We thought that the DEP and EPA were doing their jobs. They weren't."

Like Kendra, John wasn't interested in the ideological battle between left and right around fracking; he wanted to protect the rights of the little towns that were his clients. He believed the idea of the public good applied to Republicans and Democrats alike, and that companies were violating that principle. However, unless there were grounds to declare the law unconstitutional—and he didn't see them at first—he wasn't going to take on the case.

Frankly, he didn't want to lose, and he didn't want to risk setting a bad precedent. Furthermore, they had only ninety days to find and write some kind of challenge. And the cost for the townships was prohibitive. Robinson's budget was hardly the war chest needed to take on oil and gas goliaths, not to mention the state. But Robinson wasn't alone. Soon other townships contacted Smith, until there were seven in all, including Mount Pleasant, where Range Resources had drilled the first Marcellus well.

At his desk down the hall from his wife's office, Smith combed through the proposed law, looking for flaws to attack. Finally, he found something. Under the state constitution, spot zoning was illegal. You couldn't just carve out a little industrial island in the middle of a residential neighborhood, yet that's what the new law gave the state the power to do.

As a small-town lawyer, Smith knew the ins and outs of zoning better than anyone. Zoning was "a police power," an arcane term that meant the government had not only a right but also a responsibility to protect its citizens from harm. And zoning—between commercial, residential, and industrial spaces—allowed little townships in Pennsylvania to decide where things like adult bookshops and gas stations and cement factories were allowed to set up shop.

This was the kind of argument few outside attorneys or law professors would think to make. Smith also knew how his conservative clients thought and felt about their property rights. The judges were also likely to be conservative. If Smith could cast his argument in terms of the state government overreaching into its citizens' God-given rights, he might get some traction in court.

For industry, this new law was as much about managing risk as anything else. Matt Pitzarella of Range Resources called it "predictability." Having one uniform legal code across Pennsylvania, especially if that code was a permissive one, made it easier for drilling companies to operate. Both the companies and the state argued that natural gas was playing a role in economic recovery and that these little local battles impeded that recovery. In order to solve the problem, under Act 13, state law would trump local law every time.

"To give predictability to oil and gas, you have to take it away from every other Pennsylvania citizen," Smith argued. People who'd bought their homes or chosen school districts based on health, safety, and property values faced the prospect of losing everything if the township could no longer protect them through zoning.

The Smiths were becoming the most formidable attorneys to oppose industry in Pennsylvania. They were also unusual. They weren't looking for a national platform to advance a blanket argument against fracking; they were sticking close to the particular statutes and incidents related to their cases. For Kendra, that meant following the pathways of chemical exposure; for John, that meant adhering to the provisions in Pennsylvania law that protected people's constitutional and property rights.

To bolster their challenge to Act 13, Smith went looking for partners. He started locally with Jon Kamin, one of the best land-use lawyers in Pittsburgh. Kamin, who called himself "a mercenary," was used to taking on controversial clients. Among them were billboard companies and Blush, a Pittsburgh strip club—enterprises that communities typically didn't want. But he was also the township lawyer in South Fayette, which wanted to join the fight against Act 13, so Kamin met with Smith.

You're out of your fucking mind, Kamin told Smith when he first heard his argument. But when he listened to the substance, he changed his mind. Maybe Smith could prove that taking the right to zone away from communities was unconstitutional. In any case, the challenge was audacious, and Kamin liked that. So Kamin signed on, and Smith sought out other local allies. To contest the physician gag rule, he joined forces with a doctor named Mehernosh Khan, who was already concerned that this new law might affect how he could treat patients.

Ostensibly, the gag rule allowed companies to share information with doctors while keeping their proprietary ingredients secret from the public. But Smith thought the gag rule was really a matter of making it impossible for doctors to testify on behalf of their patients in court.

The greatest divide Smith needed to bridge lay in the centuries-old split between Eastern and Western Pennsylvania. He now had enough of the scrappy western part of the state on his side, but what about the snobby east? In Bucks County, a wealthy eastern part of the state, Smith found Jordan Yeager (who bore no relation to the cattle farmers in Amity). A civil rights attorney who'd served as legal counsel for the Pennsylvania Democratic Party, Yeager had experience in municipal law and in environmental issues. Yeager was already planning to challenge the law. He also believed that Act 13 violated the constitution, but for different reasons.

For the past forty years, according to Article 1, Section 27, an obscure amendment to the state constitution, Pennsylvania had guaranteed its citizens the right to clean air and pure water and to the commonly held assets of public natural resources. Pennsylvania was one of only three states in the nation to enshrine such environmental rights in its Bill of Rights. (The others were Montana and Rhode Island.) Jordan Yeager wanted to use the amendment to argue for the Public Trust Doctrine: that regardless of land ownership, there are some resources that the state holds in trust for public use.

The idea dated back to the Roman Empire. According to a mandate adopted by Justinian, who governed from A.D. 527 to 565, the sea, shoreline, air, and rivers belonged to everyone as part of the commons: *Salus populi suprema lex esto*. The welfare of the people is the supreme law. Since the Environmental Rights Amendment passed into law in 1971, it had remained largely untested. Although no one was certain whether it had teeth, Jordan Yeager believed that it could form the basis of a constitutional challenge.

To Smith, this seemed like a liberal long shot, which he feared wouldn't play well to the largely conservative bench of the Common-wealth Court of Appeals. (The word "commonwealth" comes from "com-monweal," an archaic term for "public good.") But Jordan Yeager had similar doubts about Smith's claims about zoning. If the state said fracking was safe and legal, what could local governments actually do? Despite their skepticism about each other's arguments, they agreed to team up. Smith realized that the legal challenge was going to be expen-sive, even at the reduced rate of one hundred dollars per hour he charged townships. (For other clients, Smith billed out at $250 an hour.) If he lost, he'd have spent taxpayer money on a lost cause that local sup-porters of industry were already calling frivolous. Elizabeth Cowden, a pro-drilling supervisor in Cecil, suggested that if Smith lost, he might have to pay back the township for anything he spent on the case. He gathered the partners at his firm and asked if Smith Butz could take the case on for free. His partners agreed. They estimated it would cost fifty thousand to one hundred thousand dollars; it would actually end up costing close to one million.

With the new Oil and Gas Act slated to go into effect in April, Smith and his team moved to block the law. They were going to ask a judge for an emergency injunction by arguing that once the new law was in place, you couldn't "undrill" a well. Smith wanted the judge to hear firsthand what it was like to live next door to a waste pond, so he asked Stacey if she'd be willing to speak in front of a hearing in Harrisburg. No longer afraid of angering Range Resources, Stacey said yes. It was only a matter of time before she officially sued them. As soon as the Smiths finished writing their complaint in *Haney v. Range* and sub-mitted it in the Washington County Courthouse, the plaintiff case would be public. Stacey wasn't sure what the local notoriety of suing a big company would cost her family socially in Amity, but she didn't care anymore.

"Ultimately what we want is for this not to happen to other people," she told me. She was still a nervous wreck, however, on April 10, 2012, when she met the Smiths in a Harrisburg courtroom. "I'm always scared I'm going to say the wrong thing," she told me. That morning, the judge called all the attorneys into his chambers, while Stacey and others waited in the courtroom. Behind closed doors, both sides laid out their arguments. On one side of the judge's table sat John and Kendra, along with Jon Kamin and Jordan Yeager, arguing to protect the constitutional rights of Pennsylvania citizens. On the other, Pennsylvania's attorney general sat alongside attorneys for the oil and gas industry, arguing together to allow the law to go into effect within days. The optics were bad, the Smiths thought, and soon, when the DEP joined the case to support the new law alongside oil and gas, it would look even worse.

Stacey never had to speak. After an hour of listening to heated arguments in his chambers, the judge excused everyone and said he'd make a decision that day. The Smiths were driving back from Harrisburg when they got a call from their office. The court had granted the emergency injunction. The Smiths couldn't believe it. It took judicial guts to block a powerful industry, as well as the governor himself. As he cheered, John had trouble keeping the car on the road. Although the case was far from over, their victory that day halted the drilling and validated their arguments in the eyes of those who'd said they had no chance of winning.

21 | WHAT MONEY DOES

Stacey and the kids had learned to avoid the camper's aluminum walls while they were sleeping. On freezing nights, if they rolled over, they stuck to its sides. In general, despite having to squat in the camper in Mam and Pappy's driveway, they felt their lives were getting better as 2012 began. Away from the site, Harley was beginning to improve and Stacey's hypervigilance eased. Despite working overtime to pay for the camper, the mortgage, and ongoing medical co-pays, Stacey had the mental space to return to what she loved. She could hunt again with the kids during deer season and spend time with Chris on weekends.

Stacey went back to the Lower Ten Mile Presbyterian Church on Sunday mornings, which gave her a sense of being part of the community again, and a better person in trying to get right with God. Since this mess began, Stacey had prayed more than ever before, speaking to God on a daily basis, asking for help in just getting through the day. But she was also angry, asking, in exasperation, why God was putting her and the kids through these trials. Harley had similar questions. When he was first diagnosed with arsenic poisoning, he had asked Stacey why God would choose them—*him*—to suffer these illnesses. Stacey told Harley that their family had been selected to serve a greater purpose because they were strong enough to bear it. God wanted to warn people of what these chemicals could do to children, she told Harley. And it wasn't like they were babies, so they'd survive. What's more, God knew that Stacey wouldn't sit back and keep her mouth shut. In this vision, she cast herself as chosen by the Lord. He was testing her and she had to prove she was up to the task.

The Lord sent her strange signs. At a gun bash held as a fundraiser for a nearby fire department, Stacey had recently won a crossbow, which she was struggling to learn how to use. One afternoon, as community service, she and her sister drove into the town of Washington to help clean out the house of a stranger who'd died. That day she was wearing a long-underwear shirt that read in cursive *Bowhunting is beautiful*. She opened a dresser drawer in the stranger's house and found an old pad of paper. On it, in ghostly writing, someone had scrawled a note that read *Bow-hunting is cruel*. She wondered what divine message she was supposed to glean from the note. The experience troubled her, and she tried to ignore her gnawing fear that God was punishing her in favor of positive thinking.

Toward the end of November, on one especially uplifting afternoon after Harley had gone three days without needing the antinausea medication Zofran, she dropped him off at basketball practice. He didn't play for long. Although he'd once been a rising star, he was self-conscious and out of shape. Harley was sitting on the bench so much, he told Stacey, that it wasn't worth it. "Mom, I could be working," he told her. Harley was already working at the local mall, at a store called Zumiez, a skate shop that sold tween T-shirts and Vans. At the time, Harley was trying on another identity—skate rat—to render his loner lifestyle a little more palatable, and Stacey wanted to support that even if it made no financial sense. Working part-time, he made fifty to a hundred dollars a week, and it cost Stacey almost an extra hundred dollars a month to put gas in his car. But she thought it was worth it to have him talking to other teenagers while running the cash register or stocking shelves. He was also cutting grass after school and on weekends for his cousin Mike, who needed help mowing church cemeteries. With his own son grown, Mike wanted Harley to take over the business. Harley agreed. Maybe mowing lawns was a more viable

future than serving in the military. Sick all the time, he didn't think
he could pass the necessary physical exam, and after the state's failure to protect his family, he no longer trusted the government. Why
would he sign up to fight for a country that had sacrificed him to corporate greed?

When Harley came to Stacey with the idea about running Mike's
mowing business, she knew that meant more work for all of them.
"How are we going to take that over?" Stacey said, but she wanted
to encourage Harley, and maybe mowing was his future, so she spent
seven thousand dollars on a mower, borrowing some from her mom.
Getting Harley out of the house had been the right move, Stacey
thought. Other than a cough, he was feeling better and actually felt
like eating. Stacey could turn her attention toward finding them a
new home.

On Google Maps, she and the kids had figured out how to measure
distances so that she could determine how far a prospective home was
from the gas wells and compressor stations she could see on-screen.
She was committed to keeping them at least a mile from any kind of
drilling infrastructure. But there were limits. "In Texas, they've found
that the chemicals go five miles before they dissipate," she told me.
"I don't think we can get five miles from a compressor station." Finding a new home around Amity proved difficult. Property was in high
demand due to the influx of gas well workers into an area where people
rarely moved and families occupied properties for generations. "I can't
believe it, but there's nothing," she said. "Everyone is holding on to
property because they think they have a fortune in this gas well shit."
She'd made a flyer to stuff in mailboxes that read "Local family desperate to build or buy." She and Chris's mom drove around Washington
County hanging the flyers in supermarkets and Laundromats, even
going door-to-door to hand them out.

Her best bet, in the short term, was finding a house that belonged
to the coal company, which owned much of Prosperity. Stacey was looking to rent one of these abandoned farms. She saw the irony: moving

the kids into a home damaged by a previous generation of extraction. They'd be living with a water buffalo no matter what.

Money was also a problem. Stacey still owed the bank $140,000 for the farm and continued to pay a $1,200 mortgage payment each month. She asked John Smith for help, but when he went back and forth with the bank over selling the farm, an agent told him that the bank couldn't issue a mortgage to a buyer due to potential contamination. Stacey was also afraid of saddling another family with health risks from exposure. She resolved to hang on to the house as long as she could, even though it was empty and the thought of leaving her home abandoned tugged at her.

The worst part was leaving the animals unprotected. She'd managed to find temporary homes for most, including Bob the Donkey, the Casanova of McAdams Road. For a while, Beth and John Voyles tried to keep him, but he risked injuring Doll with his advances, so Stacey'd found him a place at the farm of one of her fellow nurses. She'd kept Bob to ward off coyotes, as donkeys do. With Bob gone, Stacey worried more about what might befall those left behind.

One day that past December, Stacey had gotten a phone call from Lora Werner, the Philadelphia health professional working for the CDC. Werner told her that Stacey's favorite federal agent, Troy Jordan, was leaving the EPA.

Troy Jordan went to work with Chesapeake [Energy], Stacey wrote in her journal that night. *Will be moving to Ohio. I'm shocked, but just one more example of what money does to people.* Although she felt betrayed, she also understood; Jordan had to support his family. The pattern of swinging through the revolving door from regulation to private industry was more common than she knew. In Pennsylvania, from 2007 to 2016, tracing the arc of the gas rush, thirty-seven people had moved between the public sector and private industry. Public institutions couldn't retain skilled people because they couldn't afford them. The best people tended to go work for industry. Scott Roy, who had served three separate Pennsylvania governors in Harrisburg before going to work for Range in Southpointe, epitomized this lucrative migration from public to private.

One day in December, Stacey was on her way to an appointment at her endocrinologist's when Beth called to say that she and John had been up until 4:00 a.m. fighting off a pack of wild dogs that kept running the horses. A German shepherd, a Dalmatian, and a dingo-looking dog among them, they were likely abandoned pets.

After Beth and John managed to chase the dogs off, Stacey could only imagine where they'd gone. She climbed into the Pontiac and drove to her abandoned farm. When she got out of the car and waded through the winter wheat toward the barn, she heard silence rather than the familiar bleating of Paige's goat, Floppy. Then she saw a smear of blood in the pale grass and the mangled body of Chuck the Chicken. She looked for the duck but didn't see him as she continued to the goat shed in dread. Floppy's pen looked like a crime scene; there was blood bumped across the wooden walls, along with bloody paw prints. Floppy's body lay in red hay.

Stacey turned and ran outside to track down their old horse, Duchess. She found her in the hayfield, wounded and unable to walk. She called Shelly and her husband, Jim, to come help so she could still make it to the doctor on time. Stacey went to the endocrinologist only once every six months, and it was likely that if she contracted some kind of cancer from exposure, the first place it would appear would be in her glands.

When Shelly and Jim drove over to help, Stacey got into the car and sped toward her doctor's office. She sent me this text:

we had a mess today wild dogs killed Floppy last night and Duchess until she couldn't walk we had to put her down they killed Chuck the chicken and we think they took the duck it was horrible

A few nights later, after working overtime, she went to Chris's house in Eighty Four. Desperate to crawl into bed, she entered the bedroom and slipped off her scrubs. She reached for a T-shirt to sleep in—she soaked one through with sweat every night. She was so broke, she couldn't afford new bras, and tried to make the four she had last, despite their broken clasps. Chris squeezed into the cramped room behind her. He was nervous as hell as he dropped to one knee, his fingers clutching a ring set with a top-cut square diamond that he had picked out himself.

"Are you sure?" she asked him, and they laughed.

Despite the bright moment of the engagement, the wild dogs ruined Christmas and marked the beginning of a downward spiral that continued into the new year. Stacey watched in dismay as Harley sickened once again. He felt nauseous every morning. Reluctantly, she went to the medicine cabinet and retrieved the Zofran. The doctor had also prescribed Cymbalta, an antidepressant, for Harley's deepening sense of despair. Stacey and Harley were having a hard time. She'd found bongs and a scale in his room, and then he got caught high at school. When she went to pick him up, she lost it in the car. She was terrified that Range was looking for evidence to use against them in court and that Harley had just handed it to them. She called Shelly and told her that something really bad had happened. Her golden boy was gone, and she feared that Harley's pot-smoking was evidence of newly antisocial behavior, but Harley swore it wasn't. His stomach felt terrible, he told her, and he was still spectrally thin. Smoking pot was a way to make himself hungry enough to swallow food, and to find a way to relax. Stacey wasn't so sure. She started drug-testing Harley at home.

The two of them grasped for any external solution to fix Harley. Since he felt he had no friends, they decided he should change schools that fall for eleventh grade. Stacey signed him up as a homeless student at Bentworth High School in a small, rural school district nearby. Being a student in the homeless program embarrassed Harley, and although it was true they'd lost their home, he felt the teachers treated him differently. Also, most of his classmates had been in school with one another for a decade, and he hated being new. Feeling frustrated and alone, Harley increasingly turned to Shelly and Jim for consolation. In their run-down home, with two wild boys of their own, they were more tolerant of mistakes. Harley texted his aunt, *I hate myself, this is all my fault.* Shelly didn't tell Stacey, fearing she'd worry her sister that Harley might be so full of self-loathing he'd hurt himself. Shelly was sure Harley would be okay. So she tried to ease the friction between mother and son by listening to her teenage nephew. She knew how bad the gas wells had been, but she wished her sister would ease up a bit. Her rants about Range weren't helping Harley.

Harley rebelled in smaller ways too. One day, while Paige was riding in a horse show, Take the Money and Run bucked, and Paige ended up in the hospital with a concussion. Stacey got a text in the emergency room that Harley was getting his ears pierced. Before she saw him, she wrote in her journal, *I told him it better not be those damn gauges or I will chew his ear lobes off with my teeth.* They were gauges, but small ones.

Stacey kept shuttling Harley to doctors, trying to puzzle out what could be sickening him still. On her own, she'd gone to see toxicologists at UPMC in Pittsburgh, a large hospital conglomerate and the region's biggest employer. But now that the Smiths were involved, she no longer had to bear the burden of his illness alone. Kendra Smith, as a fellow mother and an assiduous investigator, was focused on helping Stacey figure out what was going on with Harley. But after Kendra called UPMC to follow up on Stacey's appointment and introduced herself as Stacey's attorney, a UPMC representative told her that getting involved in the case, or trying to make a causal link of any kind, could cost them their funding.

We're going to have to take this out of state, Kendra told John. Finding specialists outside of Pennsylvania wasn't cheap. As the cost of the case mounted, so did the financial burden the firm bore. In addition to their unpaid hours, they hired a temp just to handle the photocopying, and their copy costs ran to thousands of dollars. There were also expert fees for engineers, industrial hygienists, analytical chemists, toxicologists, and hydrogeologists. For an engineer trained in well pad construction to look at three pieces of paper could cost as much as ten thousand dollars. In these fees alone, Kendra and John were watching their bills rise toward two hundred thousand dollars.

To be sure, the Smiths stood to make millions of dollars if *Haney v. Range* eventually settled on the right terms or a jury found in their favor. Kendra and John kept on going, even after a partner left their firm because the pro bono work on Act 13, along with their two cases against the DEP and their preparation for *Haney v. Range*, was taking so much of their time and cutting into the firm's revenue.

Personally, the Smiths were able to manage. Having paid off their school loans and mortgage years earlier, John and Kendra had never run on a deficit in the course of their twenty-year marriage, and they weren't going to start now. Other than tuition for three kids at Catholic school, they cut back on costs, including going out to dinner. The Smiths' caseload doubled. They worked into the night and on weekends to make sure they were billing enough hours to paying clients. Together, they managed to earn between four and five hundred thousand dollars a year. For Kendra, most of these hours involved defending railroads. In addition to working more hours than she and John ever had, Kendra had the intellectual challenge of switching sides in her mind every day. Of all her cases, and all her clients, Harley's ailments churned in her mind.

There were two kinds of doctors who could help her answer her questions: epidemiologists and toxicologists. Kendra didn't spend much time seeking out the former. Although their job involves determining possible environmental factors making people ill, epidemiologists can rarely establish a direct causal link between illness and a particular exposure. Toxicologists use clinical techniques on bodily fluids and tissue samples to identify chemicals in the body. Their results are more reliable and legally dispositive. So Kendra went looking for knowledgeable toxicologists, and eventually found one in Texas. Still, very few had any experience analyzing health problems related to fracking waste ponds. In addition to the potential exposures to glycols and elements of BTEX, there were issues with bacteria. Yet the possibilities of exposure were too new, and no one was studying them yet. When bacterial studies did begin to appear, they didn't investigate pathogens that could harm humans. They focused instead on what grew deep beneath the surface in a highly salty environment with almost no oxygen.

To determine what was ailing Harley, Dr. Michael Pezzone, Harley's gastroenterologist, wanted to perform an endoscopy. The Smiths had also found Charles Werntz, an occupational health physician and professor at West Virginia University. Dr. Werntz was seeing similar problems in gas well workers who came to him from across the border in West Virginia. He suggested that a bacteria or a virus from the waste pond might have lodged in Harley's gut. There wasn't enough literature out there to support such a claim, however. If a human pathogen from the waste pond had caused Harley's illness, then his would be the first documented case.

Even if a pathogen was the culprit, no one knew which strains of bacteria to test for. So Stacey went looking for experts. She started with John Stoltz, a microbiologist from Duquesne University she'd spoken to over the years, and he called colleagues who put together a list of seven different types of bacteria that might be in the pond. This was nothing more than an educated guess, and Kendra didn't hold much hope for the tests, but she went about finding a lab that would be able to perform them. With the help of Stacey's colleagues at Washington Hospital, she discovered one in Pittsburgh that could test Harley's specimens.

On February 20, the day of the endoscopy, a courier waited nearby to carry the specimens by hand to the lab an hour away. Since Stacey worked at the hospital, she was allowed to remain in the nurses' lounge while waiting for Harley to come out of the operating room. As she waited, Stacey grew furious at herself. Why hadn't she gotten Harley an endoscopy a year ago? Why hadn't she gotten one for herself and for Paige too? She'd assumed that their illnesses were tied directly to exposure—that simply being around the chemicals in the air and water was making them sick. She'd also feared the possibility of genetic mutation or cancer in the future. On Kendra's advice, she'd taken out an insurance policy against cancer treatment, for which she paid $33.80 a month for her and the kids. However, she hadn't considered the kind of mysterious chronic illness that Harley seemed to present. Dr. Pezzone, the gastroenterologist, came into the lounge to find Stacey.

Harley had a gastric ulcer and several gastric and duodenal erosions, the doctor told her. Stacey was surprised. As a nurse, she was used to dealing with people with ulcers, mostly elderly people who either struggled with alcoholism or took too much anti-inflammatory medication.

With all of the possibility of unknown ailments, Stacey decided to get her tubes tied. Two weeks later, as she drove to her tubal ligation at Washington Hospital, she stopped to get donuts for her fellow nurses. The procedure went fine, she wrote in her journal. *If it wasn't for all this mess, I probably would've tried to have more kids, since Chris doesn't have any. It's just too much of a risk with all the chemicals that are in me.*

Later, when she came across a peer-reviewed health study that established a correlation between birth defects and babies born within a half-mile radius of a well site, she felt that she'd done the right thing. The lingering effects of the exposure were hard to predict. Paige, who was athletic, kept getting injured with small things like stress fractures or broken bones in her foot. These weren't major injuries, but they took forever to get better. "After the gas wells, we just don't heal right," Stacey said. She often struggled at work with the other nurses' perfumes, which had never bothered her in the past. Her complaints created odd frictions, which made an already difficult job all the more challenging. Kelly, protective of Stacey, listened for any fellow nurses who might be speaking against Stacey or gossiping about Harley, but no one did. If any of her colleagues doubted what Stacey was going through, they kept it to themselves.

The following month, the EPA came out again to test water at her abandoned farm. Stacey took off work to spend most of the day with the inspectors. It was a longer period of time than she'd spent at the farm in more than a year. The metal taste in her mouth, headache, dizziness—all of her symptoms returned, and the next day, she passed out on a gurney at work. Her arsenic level had spiked. She called Dr. Fox, who thought it likely arsine gas was still in the house.

That made sense to Stacey. She could follow the basic mechanics of exposure. Harley's ongoing illness was harder to understand. Now that his ulcer had been diagnosed and treated, he should be faring better. But he wasn't. When the results of the tissue samples in his gut came back, they confused her too. Ulcers are most often caused by a bacterium called *H. pylori*, which Stacey was just learning about. But Harley tested negative for *H. pylori* and positive for the presence of two forms of streptococcus and another bacterium called neisseria, which Stacey had never heard of.

On May 25, 2012, the Smiths filed *Haney v. Range*. At 182 pages, it was the longest complaint either had written, and the first they'd written together. It named as defendants Range Resources, along with sixteen other parties, including two labs and two individuals, Carla Suszkowski of Range Resources and Scott Rusmisel of Gateway Engineers. Rusmisel had designed much of the site, and his wife, Laura, worked with Suszkowski at Range. Among the violations, the Smiths' case charged negligence, conspiracy, and fraud.

In their filing, the Smiths argued that, for at least two years, Range had known about serious problems at the Yeager site: groundwater on the Yeager farm had become contaminated before flowing downhill to the Voyles, Haneys, and Kiskaddens. They alleged that even though Range Resources knew the pit had been leaking, Carla Suszkowski, and possibly others, colluded with two supposedly independent water testing laboratories, Test America and Microbac, to hide test results from Stacey, Beth, and Buzz, as well as the DEP. This, they argued, involved both conspiracy and fraud.

The complaint noted that Test America had created a computer program called "Total Access" that allowed users like Carla Suszkowski to take off or change unwanted test results. In an email related to the case, a Test America employee named Barbara Hall had written to her colleagues:

> Just got off the phone with Carla Suszkowski of Range—we walked through Total Access and she couldn't say enough good things about it. Once I walked her through the reg limit comparisons, explained how she can customize the columns, and especially how long the data was accessible to them, she said she was wild about it. I think it is a great selling point for us . . . She is very vocal in the producer community and I think she may tout this tool to our benefit.

What Hall called "customize," the complaint called fraud.

Microbac, the other water testing company contracted by Range, had also altered test results, according to the suit. Laura Rusmisel of Range, the complaint specified, had tried to get Microbac to use the symbol "ND," or non-detect, to indicate that glycols weren't there, which, the Smiths alleged, was a lie. The head of the lab demurred. So Rusmisel and Microbac struck a different deal: if there was a low level of contamination in the water, instead of using an absolute value, the lab would employ a less-than symbol, which was legal. To the untrained reader, including John Carson of the DEP, as he testified under oath, a less-than symbol on a water test implied the chemical wasn't there. But Kendra could see this wasn't necessarily so. She had collected at least twelve different copies of results that Microbac had printed out and she could clearly see where, on the results that Range gave to Stacey and to the DEP, the glycols were missing. This kind of laboratory fraud, the Smiths said, wasn't new. The EPA called it "pencil whipping." Alongside this and other conspiracy and fraud theories, the suit alleged a series of environmental crimes that violated the Pennsylvania Clean Streams Law, the Solid Waste Management Act, and the Hazardous Sites Cleanup Act, as well as the Oil and Gas Act.

With exhibits, the case file came to 1,734 pages. To back her assertions, Kendra attached an exhibit for every allegation, which was highly unusual. "When you present an argument, you'd better be pretty right," Kendra said. Knowing they were going up against formidable foes with a history of aggressive measures, the Smiths took extra precautions. Range Resources had a record of suing those who spoke out against them—including families and activists—for defamation. The Smiths wanted to be sure, after all that Stacey and the kids, along with Beth and Buzz, had been through, that they weren't putting them at further risk of retaliation.

As soon as the Smiths had filed the case in May, Matt Pitzarella of Range Resources issued a statement to the *Pittsburgh Post-Gazette*. "This isn't about health and safety," he wrote; "it's unfortunately about a lawyer hoping to pad his pockets, while frightening a lot of people along the way."

Stacey was distracted from the back-and-forth. In May she and the kids finally moved out of the camper and into the former Amity post office, a white house trimmed in dark green that was just across the street from Mam and Pappy's. Some kindly neighbors were willing to rent it to Stacey and Chris until the neighbors found a buyer. The old post office was perfect for now, but Stacey didn't want to buy it and couldn't afford to anyway. She didn't want to live in the middle of town where there was no room for animals. One warm afternoon, Stacey cleaned the cobwebs out of the basement, feeling that the move was bittersweet. Soon they'd have to leave again, but the small farm she was looking for wasn't materializing. All those flyers were yielding nothing.

Moving into the old post office didn't seem to help Harley. In June, he spent his sixteenth birthday in the bathroom, doubled over in pain. Demoralized and frightened, he called Stacey in. Stacey wrote in her journal: *Harley's 16th birthday*—He had a large amount of black stool in the commode . . . I don't know if his ulcer won't heal. I don't know if it's the Cymbalta. I don't know what to think. The poor kid. Hasn't had a good birthday the past few years. So much for his 16th.

Paige, however, was thrilled by the move out of the camper. She had her own space; and although Stacey couldn't pay for much, she bought pink paint to decorate Paige's room. In celebration, Paige dragged her nest across the road to their new home. She was starting to do better in school again. Like Harley's, her grades, which had once been As, had dropped precipitously as they shuttled between different houses, but now they were climbing, mostly because Stacey was making her put the time in.

One evening, Paige lay on the braided rag rug in their new living room and sketched an English-class project on a piece of poster board. She drew farm animals with Xs for eyes. Next to the pond they were drinking from, she'd drawn barrels of poison, then wrote in black marker: "Fracking is an unsafe procedure and should not be permitted."

The old post office was only about half a mile from Shelly's farmhouse. Between them lay Rinky Dinks Roadhouse, where Stacey and Shelly used to take the kids for burgers and curly fries. A twenty-foot cowboy stood lit up outside the weathered false front of an old-timey saloon. Children were now banned from Rinky Dinks due to the changed atmosphere. Gas well workers or pipeliners up from the Gulf came there to drink and sometimes to fight. They overran the place, and Shelly called them "gasholes."

With their arrival in rural Pennsylvania, crime rates had spiked: DUIs, theft, sexual assault, and disorderly conduct, which usually meant bar fights, doubled from 2008 to 2011. "We had quite a few numbers of pipeliners and fracking people, and they brought drugs and drug culture with them. Every other license plate was Texas, Oklahoma, Colorado, New Mexico," Blair Zimmerman, the former mayor of Waynesburg, told me. "They brought in prostitution, and that was unheard of."

Rather than walking down the road to Rinky Dinks, Stacey and Shelly drove the kids eight miles to Rudnick's instead, taking along stacks of quarters so that the kids could play pool. One night, while he was standing near the pool table, Harley overheard two kids bragging about robbing a farmhouse near Amity. He loped back to Stacey right away. Stacey put her burger down. She knew the kids weren't talking about her house. She'd been over there earlier in the day and everything was okay. Next time, however, it might not be.

The drug scourge affected not only out-of-towners but local kids as well, particularly young men. To scrounge a few dollars, they broke into houses and stole any kind of metal they could sell. Now that the farm was empty of both people and animals, it was a perfect target.

Sometimes, without the kids, Stacey still went to Rinky Dinks. One July evening in 2012, she ran into Toby Rice there. Rice was the CEO of Rice Energy, the rival oil and gas operator to Range Resources around Amity and Prosperity. Although the two companies competed to sign local leases, they also cooperated by swapping them when one needed a particular plot to be able to drill. Rice also looked the part of a wildcatter. Thickset in work pants with shaggy hair poking out from beneath a hat, he didn't appear to be who he was: the twenty-nine-year-old son of a hedge fund manager from the affluent suburbs of Boston.

After arriving in southwestern Pennsylvania in 2007, Toby had built Rice Energy from four employees, including his fiancée, to several hundred. Among locals, Rice's reputation varied. Some people sized him up as a trust-fund kid playing at country boy, but Stacey liked him. He seemed down-to-earth. He was the head of the company, and he still came to places like Rinky Dinks sometimes and rode on hoverboards around Southpointe with his employees. He also knew Harley was sick, and empathized. Stacey thought he saw her side of things. At Rice Energy, Toby tried to avoid using waste ponds. The company did own and operate one in Pennsylvania, but attempted to store most of its waste in steel tanks. At the bar, Rice told her that her kids' photos hung on his wall from buying their animals at the fair in past years. Later, when asked, he didn't remember the details of their conversation. But Stacey wrote that night in her journal that Toby had said he looked at Harley's picture every day and thought of them, and that Harley had a "black mark" on him because of the public fight with Range.

Makes me so mad, especially at the fair, she wrote. Here was one more way in which Range had ruined their lives, she thought, making her already-shy son the object of rumors and doubt. Stacey wrote that she was heartened when Toby Rice promised to buy Paige's and Harley's animals at the fair this year. (Despite their displacement, she'd managed to keep two pigs in a coworker's barn.) That would show Range.

The next month at the fair, true to his word, Rice bid on and bought Paige's pig. Paige credited the pig socks she'd worn to the show every year since she was eight. Stacey was grateful to Rice and counted his purchase a small victory. There was infighting at the 2012 fair, however: the cash infusion from gas leases meant families could invest more in their children's animals, and as the stakes increased, parental competition predictably worsened. After Stacey's friend Linda Winklevoss's daughter's pig won Grand Champion, someone slipped an anonymous letter under the door at the fair office saying that the pig was on steroids, which Linda Winklevoss swore it wasn't. *The competition has gotten out of control,* Stacey wrote.

On the day that Rice bought Paige's pig, Beth Voyles called Stacey to let her know that another of their horses was dead. This time it was Ashley's four-year-old Oakie. In order to train Oakie, Ashley had overcome her reluctance to getting so close to another horse. She'd struggled with her fear of loss, and conquered it so she could get Oakie to be her best at running barrels. Ashley'd just finished breaking her in. Two days earlier, Ashley'd ridden her at a barrel race in West Virginia, and she won by half a second, which was a lot. Within forty-eight hours, Oakie couldn't stand up. As Oakie flailed in the hay, Ashley lay down and put her body between the horse's head and the floor of the barn, trying to cushion Oakie's skull as it beat against the ground. Dr. Cheney came out to give Oakie an IV, but within an hour, the horse died. The vet couldn't figure it out. Beth was beginning to worry about her daughter's mental health. In the past two years, she'd lost Cummins, Jodi, the puppies, and now Oakie. In her grief, Ashley had gotten another tattoo. She had a photograph of one of Oakie's eyes and had the image tattooed on the back of her neck.

Stacey found it hard to believe that the Voyles still lived next door to the site, but Beth refused to move. "Where can we go that we're sure to be safe?" Beth asked me. Well sites and compressor stations were springing up everywhere. What if they moved only to find themselves in the same situation? Instead, she tried to spend most of her days away from the farm, loading up the seven dogs and driving them to a park in Washington. Beth's wheezing worsened, along with the dizziness and violent splotches of rash on her skin. Still Beth sat tight, keeping a sharp eye on the comings and goings of trucks, talking on the phone, and scouring the papers to follow the developments in her and Buzz's lawsuits against the DEP.

During the summer of 2012, the Smiths' fight with the state over Act 13, the new Oil and Gas Act, was also in the news. On July 26, 2012, the Commonwealth Court, a state court of appeals, handed down a split decision that struck down much of Act 13 as unconstitutional. The Smiths' victory was stunning, yet it came with caveats. On some issues, including the physician gag rule, the court found in favor of the state. The court also upheld another provision that limited the disclosure of health hazards. If a landowner had a case of poisoned water, neither he nor the state nor the oil and gas company had any obligation to let neighbors who used private wells know about the contamination, or any compensation deal.

Later, Stacey came to understand that this provision applied directly to her predicament. She learned through Beth that the Yeagers had struck a private deal with Range, under which the company paid the couple a hundred thousand dollars for the loss of their water, along with a lifetime supply of trucked-in city water to fill their buffalos. According to Beth, who attended Ron Yeager's deposition, he testified under oath that they also paid him $27,000 each time the fluid in the pond was used to frack at another site. Although the DEP was aware of the contamination, the state never issued a notice of violation. So there was no public record of what had happened. The state wouldn't list the Yeager site among its cases of water contaminated by gas drilling, thereby keeping the problem off the books and undisclosed to neighbors. Under the new provisions of Act 13, this was legal.

These losses, however, paled against the Smiths' monumental win. John's argument that local governments had a duty to protect their citizens had carried the day. The scale of his achievement startled him. Little towns had vanquished the much more powerful state. At the same time, as he had expected, the environmental rights argument that Pennsylvania's citizens had the right to clean water and clean air went almost nowhere with the largely conservative court.

Right away, the state of Pennsylvania and the DEP appealed the decision, and the Pennsylvania Supreme Court agreed to hear the case. The supreme court was led by Chief Justice Ronald Castille, a conservative Republican. The prospect of arguing against the state before him was daunting.

The Smiths celebrated their win, and Stacey did too. Good news was rare enough, and every time public opinion swayed in her favor, she took solace in it, and also pride. She starred the day's entry in her journal.

ACT 13 RULED UNCONSTITUTIONAL, she wrote. *The state judges ruled it unconstitutional! Thank God. It's a good day for the state of Pennsylvania.*

22 | RUIN IS THE DESTINATION TOWARD WHICH ALL MEN RUSH

The summer of 2012 was a Batman summer as well as an election season. *The Dark Knight Rises*, starring Christian Bale, was out in theaters. The film featured Pittsburgh as Gotham in decay, cracked water pipes issuing steam above the blasted macadam of abandoned sidewalks. The postindustrial landscape, its crumbling infrastructure, was intended to be a sign of our times. The breakdown of the physical world reflected a collapse of the social order. The collective no longer mattered: it was every man, woman, and child for himself, and even Batman was beyond caring.

Around Amity, citizens expressed their displeasure at the local and national state of affairs, staking their various claims by posting road signs in front of their homes. Along a five-mile stretch of Amity Ridge Road, these road signs dueled. They began at the highway exit, where someone had planted a flock of black and red signs that read STOP THE WAR ON COAL, FIRE OBAMA. Less than a mile on, someone else had procured a backlit road sign, the kind you might find at a drive-thru, that read RANGE IS NOT A GOOD NEIGHBOR. RANGE & DRILLING = NO WATER! RANGE SAYS PROVE IT. Another read only THE WATER WASN'T BAD BEFORE.

Finally, just before Dean's Laundromat, another backlit sign read:

OBAMA-BIDEN

RIDDLER-JOKER

GOD BLESS AMERICA

One summer afternoon, two miles farther down Amity Ridge Road, Shelly sat on the porch of her two-hundred-year-old farmhouse. In her lap, she held an orphaned baby raccoon, the fifth raccoon pup she'd raised since the ten-thousand-gallon water trucks started hurtling up and down the road on their way to well sites. For the past several years, she'd taken to walking the roads to search among roadkill for survivors. This fifth one, whom she'd named Ripepi after her favorite doctor at the orthopedic hospital, she'd spotted from her car as she rounded a sharp bend. She hadn't gotten out, just opened her door and scooped up the baby from the pulp of its siblings and mother.

That summer, Shelly had won a major victory for the town of Amity. She called it "hitting the lottery." She'd been fighting to bring the town a public water source, and now, as we talked on her porch, we watched one of the little yellow trucks laying a water line along Amity Ridge Road. For the first time in two hundred years, the town was getting public water.

Her campaign had begun one Sunday in church two years earlier, when a fellow parishioner turned around in his pew. Wayne Miller drove trucks for the oil and gas industry. He wanted the local water company to run a line to his house, but the company told him he needed more people—nine customers per mile—to make it financially viable. Miller thought of the Presbyterians, their well rotten with formaldehyde. He also knew that neighbors like Shelly had very poor water or none at all.

Tell me what needs done, Shelly said. She spent much of the next two years walking up and down the nine-mile stretch of Amity Ridge Road that marked the edges of the village. Heading up the right side of the road, she'd knocked on the doors of eighty houses, then crossed the dotted yellow line to the left side and knocked on seventy more on her way home. Only two people wouldn't sign the petition for city water.

Pleased with herself and thinking she was finished, she turned the names in to the local water authority, but the town needed money: a seven-and-a-half-million-dollar grant from Pennvest, a state agency that offered low-interest loans for building public water systems. The loan required signatures from twenty-five businesses in that nine-mile stretch. This, she thought, was impossible. There simply weren't enough businesses in Amity. But she knocked on doors again anyway. When Shelly got her mind on something, she didn't let it go.

What she found surprised her: many people were running small businesses out of their homes, including a horse boarding stable, a photo studio, her mother's Avon makeup shop, a masseuse, and some-one selling candles. It turned out there were twenty-five businesses hidden along Amity Ridge Road. The town got the grant, and now the water was coming through. Delighted by the victory, she was still frus-trated by the injustice of having to fight for the right to water in the year 2012.

"What a shame to have to sit in a meeting and argue with people over trying to buy a natural resource that multimillion-dollar indus-tries are ruining," she told me. "I'm watching the fifth generation in my family struggle for water every time I watch my kids haul it from Ruff Creek pump station and dump it into a hand-dug well that runs off of a spring that comes from the great Marcellus land that we have in Pennsylvania."

Despite her efforts, Shelly wasn't getting the new water. She didn't have enough money for the one-time tap-in fee, which cost seven hun-dred dollars at first and would rise to fourteen hundred after the first six months. The rummage-sale Jacuzzi would remain in her living room as a laundry basket, she said. Her two boys, now teenagers, had long since learned to wash their own clothes. Her husband, Jim, was on disability, home from his road crew job at the Pennsylvania De-partment of Transportation, sitting around doing little because of a back injury, his eyes glassy from painkillers. Shelly was growing tired of him, and tired of being the only one working a job and holding their house together. When she'd bought it, no one had lived on the second floor in thirty years, and Shelly spent the first seven on a mattress on the first floor with J.P. and Judd, two turtles, and a nocturnal hedgehog.

Shelly also collected fossils and kept one the size of a honeydew melon: a 350-million-year-old chunk of tree from a genus known as *Lepidodendron*, which flourished during the time of the giant dragonflies. Under pressure and over time, these trees became coal. That fossil was about all Shelly owned when it came to minerals, and she didn't care. She'd never been concerned about grinding her way into middle-class life and acquiring possessions. On the wall of her kitchen, she hung a sign that read *Jesus turned water into wine, I made it into liquor.* She'd always been one to worry more about others than herself.

The arrival of a city water supply solved only part of Amity's problem. In the summer's heat, a drought had begun, which compounded the problem of excessive water withdrawals. All over Washington County, and beyond, many of the region's streams were at flow levels 50 percent lower than normal. The lack of rain played a role; so did water trucks dropping hoses into the creeks to suck out the four million gallons of water it took to frack a well. Anyone driving around Amity and Prosperity could watch fresh water disappear from two local reservoirs that a former real estate developer turned fracking mogul had bought in 2005. It was legal for drillers to use water they owned. It was also legal for them to drop hoses into the commonwealth streams. Or almost legal. In theory, there was a formula that regulated how much water could come out of a stream, but there was no one to enforce that regulation, so the water kept on disappearing.

"We don't know how much is in the bank and we keep giving away," Rose Reilly, a biologist for the Army Corps of Engineers, told me later. For thirty years, she'd watched an upward tick in the quality of the region's water. Yet with the return of industry, both quality and quantity were diminishing. In this way, coal mining had quite a lot in common with fracking: both were done by powerful industries successful in fending off regulation that could cut into profit. "We started mining coal in the 1700s and 1800s," she said. "It took us a hundred years to regulate it. I don't expect this industry to be any faster. Until then, it's a free-for-all." Reilly was talking about the waters of the commonwealth, held in trust for all citizens. Through a combination of ineptitude and inattention, the state was opening its vaults and cheering a run on the bank.

Economists describe the Tragedy of the Commons like this: cattle herders sharing a pasture will inevitably place the needs of their cows above the needs of others', adding cow after cow and taking more than their share of the common grass. The "free rider" takes advantage of the commons, and consumes it until it's gone. This, the argument goes, is human nature, which sets individual gain over collective good. Traditionally, the Tragedy of the Commons has supported the case for individual property rights: since it's impossible for people to act together to protect commonly held assets, we might as well carve up those assets and leave individuals to look after their own. But what if the commons did not need to end in tragedy? What if people were able to work out effective practices of sharing the commons and transmit those traditions to their descendants? Elinor Ostrom, a professor of political science at Indiana University, argued that the solution to the Tragedy of the Commons for the twenty-first century lies in common sense. Sharing had succeeded in the past and could succeed in the future. Ostrom was awarded the 2009 Nobel Prize in Economics for this work. She died in 2012.

Historically, in Amity, the solution to governing the commonly held asset of water was to share it. Draw from the Dods' well until it runs dry. Take turns using the volunteer fire truck to fill cisterns from the creek. Send Stacey and Shelly next door to the neighbors with empty milk jugs. Yet this notion of sharing couldn't be extended to extractive industries. Coal, oil, and gas companies weren't regular neighbors taking sips from a shared straw: they were industrial guzzlers. This is where, in theory, government regulation could enter in. But this wasn't so easy. First, the cash-strapped state government couldn't afford to properly monitor water levels in the commonwealth's streams.

Second, the revolving door between industry and those who were supposed to police it weakened the ability to enforce laws. Third, many
Western Pennsylvanians saw regulation as the enemy—one more instance of an invasive federal government poking its nose in where it
didn't belong.

This wasn't just the case in Amity and Prosperity. It was also the
thinking among many residents of Rachel Carson's hometown of
Springdale, Pennsylvania, about an hour and a half away. On the first
day of spring, I drove up to Springdale to walk in the woods Carson
first wrote about when she was eleven. I wanted to hear how people in
Springdale understood the celebrated environmentalist's legacy. I
knew that they lived in the shadow of a coal-fired power plant, and
that Springdale was selling its water to oil and gas companies to sat-
isfy the tremendous thirst created by fracking. I wondered how Carson's
memory survived alongside the give-and-take of profiting from the
gas rush.

I went for a brief walk in the remaining scrap of her woods, then
went to meet with Dave Finley, president of the Springdale Borough
Council. "In Western Pennsylvania, fresh water is the greatest resource we have," he said. Rachel Carson, a local hero, was right to call
for the protection of water and its quality, but not at the price of government interference, he felt.

"Rachel Carson's work led to the environmental movement," Finley continued. "She was a trendsetter before her time, but I don't
think she envisioned the federal government getting involved. If she
knew how much of the gross national product went into paper shuf-
flers in D.C., she'd pass out." Washington, D.C., had a bad name in
these small towns, he added, and a much worse reputation than extractive industries did. Finley was right that Carson didn't explicitly
call for federal regulation of the environment. Her argument was much
more tightly focused than that, explaining how synthetic chemicals
entered the food chain in order to demonstrate the principle of interre-
lation. Yet according to the EPA website, *Silent Spring* did help lead to

the formation of the agency in 1970. "The influence of her book has brought together over 14,000 scientists, lawyers, managers, and other employees across the country to fight the good fight for 'environmental protection,'" the EPA website used to read, though this section has since been removed.

"We've had gold rushes before," Finley went on. "We've had the steel gold rush. We've had the coal gold rush. The last twenty percent of what they leave behind, someone else has to clean up. It happened with coal and steel, and it will happen with Marcellus. It sounds like a big sad tale of woe, but it isn't."

23 | REMOTE PEOPLE

Despite the leaks and spills Kendra uncovered, she didn't focus her disappointment on Range Resources. By 2012, the company's stock price had climbed by twenty dollars to seventy dollars a share, and, as natural gas increasingly replaced coal in fueling power plants, the price was poised to sour higher. Range was a billion-dollar public company: it was duty-bound to serve the interests of its shareholders, to tout quarterly profits on phone calls with stock analysts and not mention glitches like leaking ponds. Kendra understood. What she couldn't fathom was the state of Pennsylvania's role in this saga. The DEP kept making mistakes. One concerned an air study that the state had conducted at several sites, including Yeager. In it, the DEP concluded that there were no significant problems. But when Kendra requested the raw data, she discovered serious errors in the calculations that, as she redid the math, revealed astronomic levels of a gas called methyl mercaptan, which was hazardous in its own right and often found with hydrogen sulfide. When she pointed out the faulty math to a DEP technician, he admitted his mistakes and confirmed the accuracy of Kendra's numbers. There were ongoing concerns related to both air and water. As she studied the tests the DEP performed for homeowners who complained that oil and gas may have contaminated their water, she found them to be sorely lacking—"a joke," as she put it.

By the fall of 2012, she thought she'd uncovered a larger pattern, in which the DEP was giving people results so limited as to be intentionally misleading. The issue revolved in particular around potentially hazardous metals. When a DEP water inspector went out to someone's home to test water, he submitted his samples to the lab to be tested. When the results were ready, he typed a code into the computer to access them. But what came back to him was incomplete. There was a gap between what the DEP was testing for and what it reported to homeowners. In its lab, the DEP was testing for twenty-four different metals, yet it was reporting results for only eight. Copper, nickel, zinc, chromium, boron, titanium, cobalt, and lithium—all could be harmful and relevant to drilling contamination. However, if any of these were in someone's water, they were missing from the test results homeowners saw.

If the DEP were a company, Kendra, in her world of corporate law, would charge that it was committing fraud. But this was a state agency, and at first she wasn't quite sure what to do. She decided she had no recourse other than to kick up a controversy. She wrote a public letter accusing the DEP of withholding critical results from citizens and sent it to Michael Krancer, then secretary of the department. Secretary Krancer made no secret of his position on oil and gas. He saw it as his job as DEP secretary to facilitate drilling. "At the end of the day, my job is to make sure gas is done and gas is done right," he said upon his appointment. After resigning in 2013, he returned to private practice as an oil and gas attorney, with Range as one of his clients.

In November 2012, when *The New York Times* reported Kendra's discovery that the DEP withheld data on poisons near a gas site, the story broke nationwide. The DEP denied the charges immediately. Kevin Sunday, the DEP spokesman, called Kendra's claims an "outrageous contention." The agency released a statement saying that the letter was "an effort by a plaintiff's attorney to mislead and manipulate news coverage in an effort to litigate his cases in the press instead of the courtroom." According to the DEP, the test methods were standard and similar to those used in other states. Matt Pitzarella of Range Resources, who was openly calling the Smiths ambulance chasers, echoed those comments. "They have absolutely no case whatsoever and they know it, which is why they've resorted to taking their argument to the media," he said. "We will continue to fiercely defend our operations and our reputation."

The Court of Common Pleas at the Washington Courthouse is an imposing stone building with a demilune colonnade. A statue of George Washington still stands on its dome, looking over the city and warily waiting for the annual march of Whiskey reenactors. Like much of Washington, the courthouse, originally a log cabin, has seen more prosperous days. A parking space for ASAP Bail Bonds is reserved permanently out front.

On January 29, 2013, when *Haney v. Range* landed in a courtroom for the first time, Kendra, in her black pantsuit and curled hair, stared down at least a dozen corporate defense attorneys representing Range Resources, along with Halliburton, which had supplied some of the chemicals up at the site, and fifteen other parties. That day, several of the defendants were arguing that they should be let out of the case.

From the back of the courtroom, its walls painted red against dark wooden benches resembling church pews, a casual observer might have thought that the tiny woman pitted against the phalanx of besuited men was in trouble. She wasn't.

Kendra also wasn't the only woman at the front of the courtroom. That day, the Washington County president judge Debbie O'Dell Seneca was hearing the arguments. At sixty, O'Dell Seneca was the first female justice in Washington County; she'd already been sitting on the bench for twenty-two years. Kendra knew that the judge had a history trying asbestos cases, which meant she'd be familiar with the basics of exposure. This made Kendra's job of telling a comprehensible story about complicated science a bit easier. Kendra didn't have to make her case that day, however; instead, she had to argue to O'Dell Seneca why these defendants bore responsibility to her clients and shouldn't be dropped from the case.

The defendants' argument centered on the interpretation of strict liability. Halliburton's attorney argued that Stacey, Beth, Buzz, and their families weren't the intended end users of their products. Under the terms of strict liability, the company bore no responsibility to them because they were bystanders. Under Pennsylvania law, if a defective tractor blade flew up and chopped off the head of the farmer driving the tractor, then the blade company could be held liable. Yet if that same blade flew up and chopped off the head of a neighbor, the blade company bore no responsibility, since the neighbor wasn't the intended end user of their product. The attorney for Red Oak Water Transfer, the pipeline company being sued for negligence, argued along similar lines. It didn't matter if their temporary pipelines had frozen and cracked, leaking chemicals into the fields uphill from homes. The leaks didn't occur on the plaintiffs' properties, and the Smiths hadn't cited any cases in their brief in which a pipeline company bore a responsibility to "remote people."

The attorney for Test America, the independent laboratory that allowed Range Resources to edit the results of water tests through their Total Access system, made a similar case. The Haneys, Voyles, and Kiskaddens weren't paying them, so the families weren't their clients. Range Resources was their client, and the company had the right to do what it wanted with the results Test America supplied.

Kendra, unsurprisingly, argued the opposite. Bystanders or no, her clients had been harmed by these companies. The companies had a duty. They breached it and caused injury. The harm had already begun, she argued: "Part of the skin thickening, the blistering of the nostrils, the throat, and that coupled with the toxins that have been found in their bodies, benzene, toluene and arsenic have resulted in these future diseases . . . It's not a matter of if; it's a matter of when for them in terms of what's in their body."

The same rules applied to the water-testing laboratories that had presented themselves as independent. Their employees had met with her clients; they'd visited their homes. They had a duty to present full results. They couldn't simply claim a lack of responsibility now. Kendra argued, "'It's not our problem. We washed our hands of it because we just report whatever our client wants us to report and it's on them what they do with it,' is in essence giving someone a gun and bullets and laying it in front of them with a bottle of whiskey, saying, 'It's not our problem. Do with it what you want.'"

Whiskey, bullets, and a gun. When the words reached Beth and Stacey, sitting toward the rear of the courtroom, the two women looked at each other. To hear their side argued aloud was a salve, proof that they actually existed, and Kendra was more of a bulldog than they'd dared to hope.

"As small as Kendra is, with her words she is so mighty," Beth said. In the mostly empty gallery, Stacey and Beth sat a row apart. A stranger wouldn't have associated one with the other. Stacey, her arms folded uneasily, was self-conscious about being the subject of the heated discussion unfolding at the front of the courtroom. Beth was the opposite. She seemed to relish every moment of scrawling copious notes in her new notebook. Beth's old notebook had been stolen several weeks earlier. Her half sister, Lori, an ex-con who'd served time in prison on charges related to drugs and prostitution, had come to the Voyles' for a New Year's Eve party and left with a Dean's Water jug filled with pennies, some brand-new cooking pots Beth got for Christmas, and the notebook. She'd called Beth to tell her so.

Lori told Beth that she gave Beth's notes to Range. It was too odd. Could it be true? Lori was always looking for money. Could she have found some other interested party to buy the notes? It was far-fetched—to an outsider, implausible—but in the unexpected events in Amity, and in particular around Beth Voyles, it was impossible to rule out. Later, while she was being deposed by a Range attorney, Beth asked him if Range had her notes. He told her no.

———

Among all the daily disappointments for Stacey and Beth, finding the Smiths was the one good thing that had happened to them. As the winter of 2013 wore on, each woman placed more of her hopes in the Smiths than ever. Stacey'd given up on the state's ability to protect them. The DEP was useless; they'd failed to do anything to stop Range from ruining their water and air and driving Stacey and the kids off of the farm. Stacey was losing faith in the federal government also. That parade of EPA investigators who'd shuffled through her home seemed to have marched right out of the picture. Their investigations were proving not only endless but also inconclusive.

I just don't understand what it is with the EPA, she wrote in her journal. *They are supposed to be protecting us.* Even kindhearted Lora Werner, the health inspector from Philadelphia, was growing frustrated with the agency's pace. She apologized to Stacey that everything took so long, which Stacey appreciated. Yet it didn't change her mind that the federal government was either ineffectual or deliberately dragging its feet.

For the past year, Kendra had also grown more and more skeptical about the EPA's involvement. After the pond had been found to leak, the state mandated that Range install ground-well monitors up at the site. When the results came in, they indicated the presence of ethylene glycol at a depth of up to eighty-two feet. To Kendra, contaminants at that depth suggested that fracking fluids had reached the groundwater. But the EPA wasn't planning to test her clients' water either for ethylene or for propylene glycol, even though it had already been found at low levels in the Haneys' and Voyles' water.

"Can you tell me why that particular glycol is not being tested for?" she'd written in March 2012 to Rick Wilkin, who was leading the EPA study. "In testing done by Range, propylene glycol was found in both the Voyles' and Haney's drinking water sources."

"Propylene glycol is not being tested for—we are working on more reliable methods for propylene glycol and ethylene glycol," Wilkin replied.

To Kendra, this seemed like a dodge, a way for the EPA to deliberately avoid finding problems in the water. In fact, the EPA had been searching for more reliable methods to test for low levels of glycols, and one agency scientist had recently found them. The oil and gas industry, however, according to sources familiar with the testing, was fighting approval for the new methods, so the agency was stuck relying on tests it didn't fully trust. Still, the federal government was their last hope, so Kendra allowed Wilkin's team to return, with the following caveat: "It remains our hope and that of all our clients that the EPA's motives for this second round of testing are science based and not politically driven as our clients have already been abandoned by the state agency entrusted to help otherwise powerless people."

Her dealings with the EPA remained fraught. Finally, in March 2013, Rick Wilkin contacted Kendra. His team was ready to give the Haneys, Voyles, and Kiskaddens their results. Yet he wanted to do so over the phone, not in writing, as Kendra had asked him to do. So the Smiths set up three different conference calls in their offices, one for Stacey, one for Beth, and one for Buzz. During each, Kendra drilled questions into the speakerphone. On the other end of the line, there were members of several governmental agencies, and she thought this was their chance to get answers to technical questions.

The EPA's answers were mixed. Beth, Stacey, and Buzz had chemical compounds in their water that could indicate the presence of diesel fuel but didn't definitively do so. And these issues were bad enough that none of them should drink it. But the government agents weren't willing to link these problems to drilling. Nor would they put them into writing, unless the Smiths petitioned the EPA, and that could take years. Over the phone, Kendra found herself pleading for them to do so, which caught her by surprise, since pleading wasn't her style. If the federal government sent a letter outlining the trouble with

Buzz's water, she could take it to the state of Pennsylvania and try to get him a new supply.

Without such a letter, she could do nothing at all. The health inspector Lora Werner suggested that Kendra appeal to the federal government. How long would that take? Kendra asked. A year and a half, Werner replied. That would put the case into 2015, and Kendra assumed—wrongly, it would turn out—that the case would be long over by then. A few minutes after the conference call ended, their speakerphone rang. According to Kendra and John, it was one of the health inspectors calling from his cell to say once again and emphatically that Buzz shouldn't drink his water. Later, however, when I contacted him directly, the inspector said he'd never made the call.

24 | IGNORANT MOTHERFUCKERS

Kendra liked to perch on the rock wall in her backyard and study the magenta blossoms on her weigela shrubs. The blossoms didn't yell or come at her across a conference table. On a mid-August afternoon in 2013, she was sitting on the wall when her phone rang: Buzz Kiskadden was calling. Buzz liked Kendra; he trusted her plainspoken approach. Stacey and Beth turned to John as their messenger, since he was easier to reach and Kendra often had her head in a binder of blood-test results, but Buzz called Kendra when he had something to say.

He had cancer in his blood and a tumor the size of a softball, he told her.

Although he didn't use the word, Kendra knew that cancer in the blood meant leukemia. She, like everyone else, also knew that he was a chronic, pack-a-day smoker, and a former heroin addict. And still, Kendra thought. August was becoming a rough month for her clients.

Ten days earlier, Stacey had driven back to the farm with Pappy to retrieve circuit breakers. She and the kids were moving again, this time into a cousin's home on Mankey Lane, which she and Chris were renting. The two-bedroom house was cramped and it needed work, but there was room for the animals and they'd managed to stay within Amity limits. Within a few months, they'd converted Chris's proceeds from selling his bungalow to a down payment. Even in the new house, she cooked with bottled water, just in case.

To keep the move as cheap as possible, Stacey was salvaging everything she could from the old place. Although a new circuit breaker would run less than twenty dollars, she was going to squeeze every last penny she could out of what she'd had to leave behind.

That morning, she took her pistol and a respirator along. When she and Pappy arrived, she noticed the grass outside had been smashed flat. With humans gone, she assumed that deer had taken to bedding down in the yard. Then she spied a pile of ashes. At first, they looked like snow out of season, and Stacey couldn't figure out where they had come from. When she reached the porch, she found part of the living room's wood-burning stove. The front door to the farmhouse had been kicked open. She and Pappy stood still for a moment, to make sure there weren't sounds coming from inside, and then pushed open the splintered frame and walked into the kitchen.

The place had been ransacked; anything metal had vanished. The stove, the refrigerator, the dishwasher were gone. Stacey and Pappy moved slowly through the living room, where the couch and the recliner had been flipped over and their remaining possessions, old kids' Christmas TV shows on VCR tapes, were strewn over the shag carpet.

In the first-floor bathroom, where Stacey had tried to mask the water's stink with potpourri, the plumbing had been pulled out of the wall. So had the copper piping that ran up the dining room wall by the stairs that Stacey had once lovingly stenciled with ivy.

The house felt gutted in an animal sense, its arteries and veins ripped out. Stacey climbed the stairs to look into her bathroom, which was also missing its fixtures. Oddly enough, the only other thing missing was her nail polish collection. Later, she learned that the acetone in nail polish remover could be used to manufacture methamphetamine. In Paige's room, the pink John Deere valances still moldered in the window, and in Harley's, the bear, moose, and white-tailed deer tracks remained intact on the wall.

When she and Pappy headed down into the basement, they discovered that the thieves had severed the oil lines and bled the oil all over the basement's cement floor. They'd busted out the basement window, and there was broken glass everywhere. She was grateful that Pappy, a man in whom suffering had bred a powerful quiet, was with her.

In Amity and Prosperity, the scrap metal market worked much as it did all over the world. When the price of metal spiked, people hauled whatever scrap they had in their yard to sell it. A glance at the Kiskaddens' junkyard could tell you where the metal market stood. If prices were high, the mangled heaps were gone, and the gulley was suddenly pristine.

But Stacey's wood-burning stove wasn't scrap. Worth at least a couple of thousand dollars, it was one of the few items of value she'd hoped to take to the new place on Mankey Lane. The robbery sickened her—the unsettling nature of strung-out strangers pawing through the last of her things. Then the loss after loss after loss of it. Although she did her best to think about moving forward, Stacey could feel the separate rages stacking within her.

I want someone to burn this house down, she thought to herself. She feared that when she called the bank to inform them about the break-in, the bank would charge her extra insurance against the added risk. She was right. The bank required an extra five thousand dollars a year in forced insurance. She was going to be paying sixteen hundred dollars a month to hang on to a wrecked dream, and that figure would soon increase to two thousand dollars when she started missing mortgage payments. With their crowbars, the thieves had struck home the simple fact that the farm was finished. For good. Maybe it was time to face it. She wondered if she could convince the bank to condemn the house. It was hard to imagine herself even thinking that way, but better to let it go and save money on the mortgage. "It's like a bad dream you can't get out of," she told me. She was going to have to find another job, or pick up even more hours on call at the hospital.

She'd still managed to buy the kids goats for the 2013 fair and board them at a cousin's. At seventeen, Harley would soon age out of 4-H, and Stacey wanted to keep him engaged for as long as possible. Now he was going back to Trinity, but this time as a cyber student, taking his classes online three hours a day. Cyber schooling was a growing trend in Pennsylvania, as elsewhere, with two out of every hundred public school students enrolled. Cyber school is designed for kids who struggle in regular public schools for various reasons: work, sports, anxiety, or other illnesses. Anyone could tell it wasn't enough to engage, much less challenge, a smart kid. But Harley had lost his enthusiasm to learn.

"School's a waste of time," he told me. "I like cyber school. I can do four classes, three hours a day, whenever I want." To Harley, the idea of college had become a joke. He didn't care about graduating from high school either, but Stacey was going to force him to get his diploma. He kept contracting strep throat, and Stacey wondered whether the strep bacteria in his throat and the strains of strep bacteria found in his ulcer were related. His immune system seemed to have been compromised. And his spirit was clearly ailing. "I don't have any friends," Harley said, and that made Stacey feel terrible. The bond between them was still strained. Stacey kept testing his urine at random.

These drug tests were now a matter of public record—as were many of his other vulnerabilities. Harley thought often of the uncomfortable deposition he'd given the previous summer. Sitting in front of a dozen defense attorneys, Harley had held his tongue, as he'd been raised to do. Yet he simmered with rage. When the attorney for Range asked him what had happened to his goats, Harley replied, "My Grand Champion fair goat, Boots, miscarriaged two Grand Champion babies, around Thanksgiving . . . And then, on Christmas Day she was starting to get more sick and worse, so we brought her into the house, and she died that night. She was having seizures." Harley went on to tell them about his mouth ulcers, nausea, headaches, and other symptoms. "At first they thought I had acid reflux, but they sort of ruled that out, because they were treating me for acid reflux and it wasn't getting any better." The attorney asked, "Did anyone ever tell you that the mouth ulcers were caused by the gas drilling operations near your home?" "Yes," Harley said. "Dr. Fox had thought that they were affiliated with the gas drilling." The attorney moved on to ask Harley questions about his father, Larry, the person Harley most hated to discuss.

"How did you feel when your parents separated?" the attorney asked.

"I was upset."

"What do you mean by 'upset'?" the attorney pressed.

"Are your parents divorced?" Harley snapped.

"I'm here to ask you questions," the attorney said.

"I don't know."

"Well you said you were upset. Tell me how it made you feel. Tell me what you felt like."

Harley could hardly keep in his seat.

"I was sad."

Later, the Range attorney asked Harley why he hadn't moved in with his father when they were forced to leave the farm. "Just didn't want to live in town," Harley said. "I love being in the country, love having no neighbors, backyard, peace and quiet." Harley didn't say that Larry had virtually abandoned them. The Range attorney ran down a list of Harley's symptoms, including black lines that appeared in the grooves of Harley's teeth. He asked Harley why no one had taken a picture to document them. "I'm just a kid. There was no reason for me to document that," Harley said. He knew that the attorney was implying that those lines had never existed. When asked, Harley told the attorney right out that Stacey drug-tested him, "Just to be safe, to make sure I'm not doing anything bad."

"Is your mother still urine sampling you?" the attorney asked.

"Yes."

"With what frequency?"

"Probably every couple of months, I guess. I don't really act up, so there's no need to do it all the time. She knows where I'm at."

Harley didn't mind talking about the testing. He wanted everyone at Range to know how bad things were—that they had cancer insurance and that he could hardly hunt anymore. "I wouldn't trust the deer from over there anyway," he said—they could be drinking contaminated water. Harley had seen one covered in purple tumors in the woods, and when he shot another and sliced it open, he saw that "its organs were bad," he said. But the Range attorney kept asking about Harley's feelings and the fact that he'd been in therapy with his mom to "build trust." Why was that necessary? Harley wasn't sure what they were driving at, but he suspected that the attorney was trying to make him look crazy, or just unwell, as if something other than the gas wells had caused his problems. And Harley was likely right: defense strategy often involves discrediting the witness, especially if the witness is a troubled teenage boy.

Harley replied, "Just so we could talk with each other and be more open about things, because I was being quiet through it all, because when my dad left and walked out, then it's just like you build your own little shell and put up your own little wall and you don't want to talk to anyone."

"I would've cussed them out if I had a chance," he told me later. "I was pissed the whole time. Everything they asked me just got on my nerves." What agitated him most was that he thought the attorney treated him like he was making things up. "That Range guy was a dick," he said. "He didn't believe me. He'd give me the look like he thought you were lying." Nothing bothered Harley more than being doubted, especially by Range Resources. Harley took most of his upset inside him and fed his resentments in silence.

Stacey knew that Harley's anger didn't serve him, but she didn't know what to do. For him, the physical and emotional turmoil had become one. "In seventh and eighth grade, being an outcast, when I got out of the loop then, that was the start of it," he told me. "Going down the hallway made me feel anxious and like I didn't belong there, and I feel like that still to this day," he added. He just didn't know how to fix it. So he'd gone back into counseling with Chuck Porch, the therapist Stacey had found for him during the divorce. Although Harley was politely responsive in the sessions, Stacey didn't know that counseling was doing him much good.

She had more faith in the animals. So she'd pushed Harley to participate in the fair. His goat was a beauty in 2013. When the time came for Harley to sell her, he walked her on a leash from the goat barn up the hill through the open door of the show barn and waited his turn in the little half-moon ring. He stood there, smiling as he'd been taught to. Behind him, the auctioneer babbled *packedfullofmeat-packedfullofmeat* in a high-speed twang. At the front of the ring of red plastic chairs, Toby Rice, Range employees, and other corporate mini-titans faced off in blue jeans and brightly colored baseball caps that advertised their affiliations. Harley was too nervous to watch them bid. Better to keep his attention on the goat. In a matter of seconds, it would be over. He heard his name announced, then the buyer, Range Resources.

Harley stumbled toward the ring's steel gate, where Stacey was waiting for him. In the heat and heady ferment of yellowing hay, she thought he might faint. Harley didn't know what to do. He told his mother that Range was trying to make up for Boots after what he'd told them in his deposition.

Stacey craned to look at the audience. She could see where the Range employees were sitting and she pointed him in their direction.

Walk over there, smile, shake their hands, and say thank you, she ordered him. Pappy disagreed. He wanted Harley to cuss them out, saying, You killed my one goat and now you're buying my other. You think this makes it any better? It doesn't.

Stop, Stacey hissed at Pappy, and warned Harley not to dare. Harley steeled himself and walked over to the Range men. They handed him a royal-blue Range Resources bag with glo-sticks, a hat, a Slinky, and a certificate. He stalked back to his mom and shoved the bag at her, and she had to carry it around for the rest of the day.

Stacey wanted nothing more than for Harley and Paige to be able to move on, but the unfolding case kept them tethered to the past. Stacey was still tallying any tangible cost, along with her mounting debt. At the corner of her notebook, she calculated what they owed— $206,015.90—and went through her monthly budget once again. The only two items she could cut were the $33.80 a month for cancer insurance and the $230.51 payment on their camper. To Stacey, the cancer insurance seemed essential to cover out-of-network specialists and long hospital stays if they needed them in the future. A future of cancer was an awful thought and the coverage a gamble, but letting it go seemed stupid. Then there was the camper. It had seemed like such a good idea, back when Harley was sick and they'd had to move out of the farm, to live in the driveway behind her parents' home, rather than spend more than a thousand dollars a month on rent in addition to carrying the mortgage on the abandoned farm. But that camper had become a millstone. She took it back to the dealer in the hope that someone would see it in the lot and buy it so she could be shut of it.

"It scares me that the camper is so hard to sell," she told me. "Is God sending me a message that we're going to have to live in it again?" Now, in every struggle, Stacey wondered what God was trying to tell her. Then there was the cost of feeding the animals, which, in addition to feeding her family, came to two thousand dollars a month. There was no way her paycheck of six hundred dollars a week could cover her costs, even with the extra mowing income. So she started charging food to her credit card, racking up a twenty-nine-thousand-dollar bill while looking for additional work. Worried about their daughter's high interest rates, her parents took out a home equity loan to help pay it off. But Stacey refused to get rid of the animals; that act, like going on

antidepressants, would mean to her that Range had won. Stacey resolved to say as little as possible to the kids about their money troubles.
As someone who'd grown up plagued by her parents' worry that they
wouldn't get by, she didn't want her kids to carry that same burden.
Sometimes, though, she couldn't avoid it. Harley was still sleeping in
their half-finished basement, which he shared with the washer/
dryer and the bee suits they used for their family hives down in the
pasture. But finishing the basement wasn't simply a matter of nailing
up drywall one weekend. The project required hiring a contractor to
replace a retaining wall, and that carried an estimated price tag of
eight thousand dollars she just couldn't find. When she finally told
Harley, he said he didn't care. Later, he went downstairs and punched
in a wall.

The case was taking over Stacey's life, in practical ways and emotional ones. She had to keep taking off work to attend the ongoing depositions for her and the kids. Five days after Range paid $460 for
Harley's goat, Stacey was up crying most of the night. The next day,
Paige, now fourteen, was going to be deposed. "It's one of the hardest
things I've had to do as a mother, these depositions," she told me. "It
was just a bad day. It was just one of them days. I get like that every
once in a while. I do good for so long, and then I have one of them days
and I just cry." Paige sat in front of a battery of ten attorneys and
described sour stomachs, dizziness, headaches, nosebleeds—"some
days they would only be for a few minutes, and then other days they'd
be real long and thick and heavy." Then there was school. "I was perfectly fine focusing on the stuff, before the gas wells got put by my
house," she said. "Before the gas wells came, I had As and Bs . . .
when I was living in the house, I had Bs and Cs and Ds." Along with
sickness, loss distracted her from school. Under oath, she described
the death of animal after animal, including the toll of the wild dog
attack, for which she held Range resposible.

"Duchess and Floppy were at the house but we weren't allowed
to—we couldn't live there. So, I feel like, if we would have been able to

live there, they wouldn't have got attacked," she said. Paige hadn't imagined that these men would ask her so many questions about herself and her brother. When they asked about Harley, whom she called "brubby," she explained that she'd thought "he was going to die." That had been hardest of all, both in the living and the retelling. She broke down and went to the bathroom with Stacey on a break.

Like Harley, Paige had always wanted to work with animals. She'd dreamed of being a zookeeper, but had recently given that up in favor of working at the Prosperity general store after school. At school, she was struggling mightily. She was failing tenth-grade English; her reading level was stuck at fifth grade, the year that Harley'd gotten sick. Stacey thought the overlap of her arrested development at school and Harley's illness was no accident. Paige was trying, but she didn't seem to make the necessary progress. In an effort to make Paige feel better, Stacey had finally bought her Take the Money and Run. Already so deep in debt for costs she couldn't control, Stacey decided buying him, and feeding and boarding him at a nearby farm, was worth it. She'd picked up more time on call at Washington Hospital and started taking shifts at Advanced Surgical Hospital. She'd even found a job teaching nursing students. Now she was working three jobs to pay for a horse called Money.

Her own deposition began on September 24, 2013. At the end of the seven hours, Stacey felt she'd done pretty well, holding up for the most part, except when she spoke about the robbery.

The farm was lost to her now, and so was the hopeful young woman who'd lived there, so sure that hard work would yield her the life she dreamed of. Now, much like her parents, who were often jobless workaholics, Stacey no longer believed that hard work yielded anything other than exhaustion.

One November afternoon, when she went to check on the house, she could see that the piece of blue cardboard she'd left in the doorframe to alert her if anyone had been inside had been moved. She peered into the basement and saw that the last of the wiring and pipe had been ripped out of the crawlspaces. She left a note on the door:

TO THE IGNORANT MOTHERFUCKERS who keep breaking into my house: it's bad enough that my children and I have been homeless for 2 and a half years but now I have to deal with this. Your greediness has cost me over $35,000 in damages and the bank has put a forced insurance of $5000 on my mortgage, so as of jan 1, my mortgage payment goes up $500 a month. I hope you feel good about what you have done and I hope you know that the contamination in this house causes cancer, so keep coming back you fucking losers. I hope you rott with cancer!!! And when your spending all your scrap money I hope you think about what you are taking away from my children.

25 | A SPECIAL AGENT

The day after Stacey spiked the note on her door, she went shopping at Walmart. She was pacing an aisle when Kendra called and asked if she could come to the office right away. Jason Burgess, a special agent from the criminal division of the Environmental Protection Agency, was hoping to meet her. By now, Stacey had encountered three different divisions of the federal agency. First there was Martin Schwartz of the criminal division, the bald ex-cop who'd vanished. Then there was Troy Jordan from the EPA's civil division, who'd gone to work for Chesapeake Energy. And finally, there was Rich Wilkin of the ongoing nationwide drinking-water study, which didn't seem to be going anywhere. But Burgess seemed different: he wanted to launch an official criminal investigation, Kendra told her. She thought it was worth taking the meeting, so Stacey sped up the highway from Washington to Southpointe and pulled onto Technology Drive. When she walked in, Beth and John were already in the conference room sitting across the table from the young-looking special agent and eyeing him coldly. He looked pretty green. Yet Burgess reassured them that he was nearly forty and had been doing this work for almost fifteen years. He'd also been quietly following this case for three months on his own already.

Stacey asked Burgess why they should cooperate with him. She meant no offense, she said, but the EPA had let them down before. All of these interviews cost her shifts at work and time away from Harley and Paige. She didn't want the kids being poked at or having to retell traumatic stories that weren't going to lead anywhere. By now, she had no problem being blunt. Excuse me for saying this, she recalled saying, but we have been shit on by our government, both state and federal. Everything we've done has been nothing but disappointing.

Burgess explained what had happened. Martin Schwartz, the criminal investigator, had indeed launched an initial investigation, called a lead, but he'd been transferred to New Jersey and that's why he'd disappeared. For Schwartz, now retired, Stacey's plight, like that of others in Washington County, stuck in his craw, alongside an unsolved double homicide in New Jersey years back. He still wished he'd been able to do more. Now Burgess believed that he could. That past July, three FBI agents, two other EPA criminal investigators, an assistant U.S. attorney, and the Washington County assistant district attorney had met with John and Kendra Smith. An EPA analyst had examined Kendra's own analysis to confirm that she was drawing the correct conclusions, and assess if Kendra had it right. After that meeting, Burgess was assigned to the case. Based on all of this data, Burgess thought he could move forward. In addition, he'd been given a green light to pursue the investigation at a very high level. Despite government cutbacks, he'd been told he'd have the money and agents necessary.

If I can't make a conviction in this case, I will hand over my gun and my badge to you, he'd told Kendra. That didn't mean it would be easy or even safe. Taking on a powerful industry could be dangerous. He asked the Smiths if they owned a handgun and had a remote starter in their car.

Stacey left the Smith Butz office unconvinced. The next day, Burgess called to ask if he could come out to Amity. Standing in her kitchen, Burgess told her a personal story. Growing up in New Jersey and around Philadelphia, he knew what it was to live next door to environmental catastrophe. He went sledding and played baseball as a child in a toxic waste dump that sat three houses away from his home.

One day guys came in hazmat suits and put up a chain-link fence and air monitors. Ten-year-old Burgess asked the men in white suits what they were doing. As long as you stay on your side of the fence, you'll be okay, they told him. Even at ten, he realized their claims about his safety made no sense: it was the same air on both sides of the fence. Since then, he'd wanted to do this kind of work, he told Stacey. When other kids played Cops and Robbers, Burgess played Cops and Polluters.

While Stacey listened, she thought that even if Burgess had good intentions, and he probably did, she'd lost faith. It wasn't so long ago that the friendly federal agent Troy Jordan had come to her home making promises about justice. She'd believed him too. Then Jordan left the EPA for a better-paying job at Chesapeake Energy. She told Burgess that she had an idea for the people who'd poisoned her water. "If I had my choice, I wouldn't send them to jail," Stacey told him. "I'd send them to my house to live." Burgess seemed to understand. His earnestness that afternoon eroded her reluctance, and by the time he left she'd decided that she'd participate in this new investigation, despite her misgivings.

"I don't trust the government," Stacey told me. Her disappointment reached all the way up to President Obama, in whom she'd developed a personal mistrust. She felt he'd let her down on so many counts. First, he'd never responded to the plea for help in her letter. "I never heard a thing," she said. Second, he'd ended up selling her family out by supporting fracking.

His administration hadn't begun that way. When President Obama first took office, he'd talked a lot about protecting the environment against fracking. He'd promised to toughen Bush-era regulations and to put forward new ones that required drillers to disclose the chemicals they used. Then, with the success of the shale boom, that messaging changed. By 2013, he was touting the positive power of fracking, saying in his State of the Union address, "We are finally poised to control our own energy future . . . We produce more natural gas than ever before—and nearly everyone's energy bill is lower because of it . . . The natural gas boom has led to cleaner power and greater energy independence. We need to encourage that."

Energy, for the Obama administration, was fractious and complicated. It wasn't as simple as phasing out fossil fuels in favor of wind and solar power. Obama, like many others, saw natural gas as a "bridge fuel": a necessary step in the transition from coal to renewables. In his administration's efforts to stave off climate change, some fossil fuels seemed better than others. Replacing coal-fired power plants with those fueled by natural gas would reduce America's carbon emissions by half.

Fracking wasn't only a domestic energy solution. Exporting the technology became part of the Obama administration's foreign policy. As secretary of state, Hillary Clinton launched a new directive at the State Department, the Bureau of Energy Resources. In a 2009 cable later released by WikiLeaks, the State Department requested that its officers abroad provide "any information they could obtain about the potential for unconventional gas development in their host country." During Clinton's tenure, the U.S. government hosted conferences on fracking in Botswana and Thailand, and later, under John Kerry, they expanded to about thirty more countries, including Cambodia and Papua New Guinea. The State Department office boosted the technique around the world, even in countries that didn't want it, like Romania and Bulgaria. (Such countries may not have simply opposed fracking on environmental grounds; there were also persistent rumors that Russia paid them.)

At home, any honest assessment of the natural gas boom had to concede its benefits: enough natural gas lay beneath American soil to meet the nation's electricity needs for decades. Meanwhile, the use of new extraction techniques in the oil industry, mainly in the Midwest and Southwest, promised the end of reliance on foreign oil within less than twenty years. Before fracking technology broke through, the United States imported almost two-thirds of its oil. A decade later, that figure would drop to one-fifth. The development of domestic energy resources also played a role in bringing manufacturing jobs back to the United States, to the very same rust belt communities hardest hit by their disappearance.

Obama used his 2014 State of the Union address to call for a $100 billion investment in factories that used natural gas. At the same time, the administration sought to close coal-fired power plants and end the coal industry's leases to mine coal on public lands. Living in coal country, Stacey watched those STOP THE WAR ON COAL, FIRE OBAMA signs start to line Amity Ridge Road.

For the administration, the economic and climate benefits of fracking outweighed the possible environmental hazards. But in Stacey's eyes, Obama was sacrificing her family in favor of some fucked-up version of the utilitarian principle. The greatest good for the greatest number of people made Harley a justifiable casualty in the struggle against melting ice caps and rising sea levels wrought by climate change; against faraway despots bolstered by energy supplies; against a slump in American industry that left millions out of work, including her father. Looked at this way, human to human, it was Stacey against the Bangladeshi woman who was losing her farm to a rising sea. It was Stacey against factory workers eager for a manufacturing revival. It was Stacey against most of the world, and Stacey was losing.

For Stacey and others, energy wasn't an abstraction. Policy made in Washington, D.C., affected people's jobs, and their health. A sense of alienation grafted onto a feeling of being sacrificed to the extractive industry. And it didn't really matter what party was in power. Stacey used to tune her father out when he ranted about the federal government. Now she agreed. Her father had been hurled into the jaws of Vietnam only to return and be let down by, of all people, Ronald Reagan. When the steel mills closed, Pappy didn't think about global shifts in trade and technology. Like others, he held Reagan responsible. He'd caught me by surprise one day with his anti-Reagan diatribe: "We got one president in there said we didn't need no more power plants.

Nineteen eighty-four. Reagan. When they shut them down, they shut us down. I was in the mills for forty-five years. I lost eight hundred and fifty dollars a month in pension. I get a hundred and fifteen a month. What happened to all that money?"

As Pappy saw it, he'd given his life twice to larger American interests, first in Vietnam and then in the mills. And now his daughter and her kids were guinea pigs for American industry.

One afternoon, as Stacey ranted about these and other ills, she drove over from Amity to check on the abandoned farmhouse. She found a pink postcard in the broken door. Range was planning to come back to frack two more wells on the Yeagers' farm.

Stacey and Beth wanted the Smiths to try to stop the wells. To block the frack, John first had to convince a judge to grant a temporary injunction. If the judge agreed, Stacey and Beth would have to put up a bond of several hundred thousand dollars while a trial went forward. If they lost, they'd lose the money too. They couldn't afford to post a bond like that, so they told the Smiths to drop the idea. When the fracking began again, Stacey wrote in her journal, *They have the drilling rig set up at Yeager's with the sky lit up. We get to drive down 19 [Amity Ridge Road] and look at that every night.*

26 | FULL METAL JACKET

C ome one and all to meet God here," Pastor Dick Berardinelli
preached on a Sunday in 2013 at Lower Ten Mile Presbyterian Church. Its pews were painted the color of buttermilk
and covered with red cushions. The walls were unadorned but for a
plain wooden cross. Ordained only in his late fifties, Berardinelli
was a practical pastor who moved around the countryside minister-
ing to a couple of congregations, due to a shortage of rural clergy. He
lived eighteen miles away in an old coal patch town called Cokeburg,
and he'd grown up helping his family run the general store in a part of
town called Blackbottom. ("It's got nothing to do with your keester,"
he told me later. Smoke from the coke ovens blackened the houses.)
He knew that Harley had been awfully sick and that Stacey was fighting with a natural gas company. "Our future is in wind and solar and
our job is not to damage what we have left," he said. "I guess I'm what
you'd call a liberal." But the pastor kept his views to himself, in part
because they were fairly unusual in Amity. Mostly, however, he believed that church was no place for politics.

"Let all who are suffering find hope in this place," he went on. He
prayed aloud for Shelly, who was home sick. She and Jim were also
divorcing after twenty-five years of marriage, and Jim was moving
back to West Virginia. It was sad, but it was probably for the best.
Shelly couldn't have him on the couch anymore. She had too much life
in her to sit still beside him. Pastor Berardinelli invited the children
in church to come forward from half-empty pews to play a game of
"Stump the Preacher." A boy named Alex handed him a Q-tip.

"Stacey, can you clean your ears with this?" he called. "It's for cleaning sin from your heart."

Stacey, who'd managed to haul herself there with Paige that morning, smiled and fanned herself with a leaflet. Across its cover, it read *Ut sementem feceris, ita metes* in a bold twenty-two-point font and with no translation for the Latin. Beneath, in a tiny eight-point font, the pastor had typed, "Live it." This was the no-nonsense liturgical style of the Lower Ten Mile Presbyterian Church, which had quieted considerably since the days of Thaddeus Dod's tirades about damnation. The quote originated not in the Bible but with Cicero: As you sow, so shall you reap.

To Stacey, the maxim didn't seem to apply. Her whole life she'd worked on sowing good things, and what she was reaping was, frankly, shit. It made her think of the story of Job. To test Job's devotion to God, Satan takes the man's children and covers him with boils "from the sole of his foot unto his crown." The sores in the story reminded her of the weird rashes she and the kids had suffered from. "That kinda freaks me out," she said. Although she'd never doubted God's existence, she often wondered what she'd done to incur this much wrath. At least Job lived the good life until the devil arrived. "Unlike Job, I've never had an easy life," she said, only half joking.

Her new home on Mankey Lane, redolent of apples and bacon, was a few minutes' drive from the church, and following the service she went home to grab her Taurus and respirator before heading over to the farmhouse. Even though the animals were gone, checking on the farm had become a ritual. "Pappy wants me to carry it in case of snakes," she said, referring to the pistol. "Or creeps like the guys who stole the copper."

The FBI and EPA criminal investigation seemed to be going forward, and it worried Chris. "You get involved in all this EPA shit, people think they're going to jail and you've got to be careful," he told her. He wanted her to get a concealed carry permit. She agreed. She carried her pistol everywhere now. It wasn't just about the case. Around

Washington County, the drug problem was getting worse. At the hospital, it was making her tough job even harder. "Thanks to the drugs, the scumbags are starting to outnumber us," she repeated that afternoon as we drove over to the abandoned house. It was something a fellow nurse who owned the Prosperity general store liked to say. "When I started there twenty years ago, it was one drug addict every two weeks. Now it's four a day." All of them begged and finagled opioids. She and her colleagues were doing their best not to go the easy route and just say yes. "Patients complain when they have to wait for things, but they don't understand there's only so many of us, and we work as fast as we can."

When we reached the nearby farmhouse, Stacey found two cigarette butts and kept them for the state police to test for DNA. Maybe it was the scrap metal thieves. Someone had even stolen the tire from the tire swing. Its frayed rope swung above the yard overgrown with Queen Anne's lace.

As fall arrived, she didn't think she could face the old families at Amity's 2013 community Thanksgiving. She dreaded wandering around the fire hall, making polite conversation with people wearing their Range Resources hats and T-shirts, family members making thousands of dollars off of tainting the land and her kids' health. The idea was too much to bear. Linda wanted Stacey to appear with the kids, as she always had. She feared that Stacey risked causing rifts that could last generations. Shelly defended her sister. If Stacey didn't want to face "the gas-well-loving, church-going hypocrites," then she didn't have to.

In Amity, the divisions continued to deepen with every article published in the Washington County paper, *The Observer-Reporter*, in which Beth spoke out about Range Resources, and every time the Smiths were quoted in the *Pittsburgh Post-Gazette*, Stacey's neighbors doubted her story even more. *Everybody looks at us like we're the troublemakers*, she wrote in her journal. For Stacey, although she didn't like to admit it, the subtle ostracism became a struggle of its own. "This whole situation has changed every aspect of my life," she told me. She looked at Amity differently now, not simply as a wholesome town where people worked together to share everything, including hardship. She felt betrayed by families who didn't believe her because the truth she told went against their pocketbooks.

"Sometimes I can't even go into public because of it. I just can't deal with the greed that has come over this whole area," she said. She kept her head down, worked three jobs, and when she and Beth had a win in their case, they muted their cheers.

Occasionally there was some good news. On November 5, the Smiths scored a rare victory in *Haney v. Range*, unfolding in the Washington Court of Common Pleas. For years now, Kendra and John had been attempting to procure a full list of the chemicals used at the site, to little avail. Now Judge Debbie O'Dell Seneca ordered Range Resources to reveal all of the chemicals used there. She gave the contractors and subcontractors thirty days to make good on Range's public claim that it knew—and disclosed—every chemical they'd employed. Matt Pitzarella of Range Resources told *The Observer-Reporter*, "They're asking for and we're supplying every and any chemical used on the location."

Beth was having breathing problems. Although the Voyles spent three weeks of every month traveling to horse shows and barrel races, they had to come home sometime. On December 2, 2013, a week after the community Thanksgiving, which Stacey didn't attend, Beth's round face swelled up until her skin shined. The next morning, after a long night, John rushed her to the emergency room at Washington Hospital. Stacey didn't know that Beth had been admitted until noon the next day. After settling a post-op patient into the recovery unit, Stacey went to the bathroom at 1:00 p.m. to check her text messages. There was one waiting from Beth. *Hay* [sic] *was at hospital all morning yesterday*, it began. *My whole left side of face swelled up.*

So been on couch all nite and morning and just got up to take a
shower. Heard this big pop. Bullet come all the way through house right
above my head where I was laying. Got the bullet. Called state police
and waiting for them to come out and game commission now.

Stacey called Beth from the ladies' room to hear the story.

Two hours earlier, just after 11:00 a.m., Beth had peeled herself
off the beige couch with the boxer pillows for the first time in more
than a dozen hours. She'd been diagnosed with a bacterial infection
in an old root canal, she explained. She was pretty out of it on
Clindamycin and Percocet. She thought she'd take a shower, then decided on a bubble bath. She'd started the tub water running when
she swore she heard a hollow bang like a gunshot in the living room.
The sound was implausible, and, since she'd taken the Percocet, she
headed into the living room in a slight haze. The mark wasn't hard to
find.

Against the wall, three feet from where she'd been sitting, there
was a bullet hole the size of a nickel. She called for John, who searched
the carpet for the slug. When he found it and held it in his palm, he
realized the bullet came from a nine-millimeter, and that it was a
kind of cheap ammunition, with a soft leaden core encased in a harder
metal, usually cupronickel. The bargain bullet, called a full metal
jacket, was often used for target practice. But this was deer season.
Tradition held that, out of common courtesy, no one shot at targets
during the season, so as not to startle any hunter's prey. Beth wandered
outside to find where the bullet had entered. On the side of her house
facing the road, there was a hole the size of a bullet. The shot seemed
to have come from the direction of her neighbor Jim Garrett, on the
hill just below the waste pond. Mr. Garrett had been suffering from
brain cancer. Part of the pond sat on his land, and he was the one
who'd told Beth that he'd just drink beer if something went wrong
with his water. According to EPA test results, which Kendra procured
through a Right to Know Request, Garrett's water tests indicated
contamination with ethylene glycol. After he died, Range bought the

Garrett property for about $380,000, Garrett's son, John, told me. Range allowed John to live there rent-free. As John Voyles put it, "Range bought their own headache."

Stacey didn't know what to make of Beth's story. "Maybe they put a hit on me," Beth said. Was this a random accident, or something more ominous? "I feel like I'm not safe. I don't know what they'll do. I mean maybe it's just a freak thing." This happens in movies, Stacey thought, not in Amity, not on our road. Had someone tried to scare Beth? Had some gashole made a mistake? Stacey didn't think so. *Well that is bullshit because no one target practices in the middle of deer season*, she wrote in her journal.

The full metal jacket ended up in the possession of state troopers. Several months later, they called Beth and told her that she could retrieve it: they were closing the case without further investigation. Beth was predictably irate. At the time, I was reporting in Amity, so she asked if I'd like to go with her to state police headquarters in Waynesburg, not far from the border with West Virginia, to pick it up.

The trip took us south along Amity Ridge Road, past Dean's Laundromat and Mankey Brothers garage; past Stacey's parents' house and the old post office; past Rinky Dinks and Shelly's lawn, studded with logs holding hives of feral bees. When we reached the Ruff Creek filling station, the white-painted cinder-block hut where she and Stacey, like everyone else, came to haul water, she showed me how hauling worked. On the side of the building, a sign read WATER VENDING MA-CHINE. It was coin-operated, and next to the slot for quarters there was a thick black hose. A line of silver water tankers was turning in and out of the lot. One had the name Shipman Sanitary on the side. It belonged to the Shipman family. "That's the one that got in trouble," Beth said. She rolled down the window to yell to the driver and ask how much the water was these days. "Twenty-five cents for fifty gallons," he called back.

"Thank you!" she called. At least the price hadn't changed.

I needed to ask her about some of the rumors I'd heard over the years, about the several lawsuits in which she and John were involved, and most notably whether or not she'd shot that man in California. I wasn't sure how she'd react. Sitting together, both of us captive in her 2011 Nissan Rogue, it seemed the time to ask.

Yes, there was trouble in her past, and it began in California, where she'd fled an abusive ex-husband. Then it followed her back to Washington County, where trouble went by the name of Thomas Jeffrey Gorby, who was serving a life sentence in the next county. Gorby had been a friend of Beth's ex-husband, and when the two men had a falling-out about money, Gorby kicked down their door in Washington when Beth was home alone. He'd tried to rape her, then shot her in the head before fleeing. But the bullet only grazed her skull, she said, steering with one hand and pointing out the scar with the other. Beth's ex was also a problem, and she'd struggled to leave him. "That's why I can sympathize with people who've been abused. You get hit so many times you don't know if they're going to come back and really do you in the next time," she said. John Voyles, who'd known Beth since the two were teenagers, stepped in at first as a friend to protect her. In his quiet way, hammering horseshoe nails into crosses while sipping on beer in the garage, John had saved her. He was one of the few people who seemed to understand Beth, and he was able to withstand her ferocity, maybe even loved her for it.

When we reached the state police station and went inside, the state trooper, who looked to be smirking, told her the case was closed and handed her a plastic baggie containing the flattened ingot. Beth took the bag and left, feeling she wasn't important enough for one more official to do his appointed job. "I don't believe any government official from the DA's office to DEP to EPA and FBI to the attorney general has planned on doing anything to help us in any way on the protection of us being U.S. citizens with rights and dignity," she told me.

PART 3

THE RIGHT TO CLEAN AIR AND PURE WATER

We seared and scarred our once green and pleasant land with mining operations. We polluted our rivers and our streams with acid mine drainage, with industrial waste, with sewage. We poisoned our "delicate, pleasant and wholesome" air with the smoke of steel mills and coke ovens and with the fumes of millions of automobiles. We smashed our highways through fertile fields and thriving city neighborhoods. We cut down our trees and erected eyesores along our roads. We uglified our land and we called it progress.

—HERBERT FINEMAN, SPEAKER OF THE PENNSYLVANIA HOUSE OF REPRESENTATIVES, IN A SPEECH TO THE PENNSYLVANIA LEGISLATURE, 1971

27 | THE RIGHT TO CLEAN AIR AND PURE WATER

The people have a right to clean air, pure water, and to the preservation of the natural, scenic, historic and aesthetic values of the environment. Pennsylvania's public natural resources are the common property of all the people, including generations yet to come. As trustee of these resources, the Commonwealth shall conserve and maintain them for the benefit of all the people.

—ARTICLE 1, SECTION 27,

OF THE PENNSYLVANIA CONSTITUTION

On the morning of October 17, 2012, John Smith donned a red tie and spiked his short hair to a peak with gel. He repeated to himself the finer points of zoning law in the crowded hallway outside the courtroom in downtown Pittsburgh. Smith rarely rehearsed his arguments; addressing judges and juries didn't tend to make him nervous. On this morning, however, he would argue before the Pennsylvania Supreme Court for the first time in his career. His parents were coming to watch him, also a first. Yet it wasn't his parents' presence or the court's status that made him jumpy. Instead of speaking on behalf of a private client or a single township, he was arguing on behalf of all the citizens of Pennsylvania, explaining to the court why the new oil and gas law violated their constitutional rights. This felt like a sizable responsibility.

The hearing was scheduled to take place in downtown Pittsburgh's City-County Building. That morning, before the courtroom doors opened, the hallway was packed with observers. Most were activists carrying signs with sayings like PROTECT OUR LOCAL RIGHTS. Among those eyeing the protesters with distaste were three older women in blue jeans and fleeces.

"Anyone has the right to challenge the law," one, Elizabeth Cowden, said to me. "But I'm shocked that this is a party atmosphere." Cowden, the township supervisor from Cecil, supported the new law and opposed Smith's challenge. "Washington County is a very poor county," she said. Extraction was the necessary solution to their woes, and natural gas, in particular, offered Washington County a chance to escape a grinding downturn. "Our county is now the third fastest growing in the state. Our economy is booming." She and the two women with her were angry that John Smith had taken the case. It was Smith's fault, one of Cowden's friends told me, that the oil and gas industry was delaying paying Cecil Township its impact fee, as punishment for his action. "Cecil just lost out on a $249,000 impact fee, and our roads are deplorable," one said.

The courtroom doors opened and the rowdy crowd filed in. Amid their cheering, Chief Justice Ronald Castille looked over the courtroom from behind tortoiseshell horn-rims and ordered the activists to leave their signs outside. If they wouldn't be quiet, he barked, he'd eject them from the proceedings. Castille grew up fishing and camping as a Boy Scout and military brat on remote U.S. bases from Florida to Japan. Then he followed his father into the military to serve in Vietnam. "Vietnam is a beautiful place as long as they're not shooting at you," he told me later. "I was there before DuPont sent Agent Orange over." He lost his right leg while dragging a fellow U.S. Marine from a Vietnamese rice paddy and was awarded two Purple Hearts and a Bronze Star. The Supreme Court's panel of six justices traveled between Pittsburgh, Harrisburg, and Philadelphia and sat only six times a year. The oldest in the nation, the court dates back more than 328 years, its roots established under William Penn.

The first case that morning involved an Erie County magisterial district judge who had given the finger to a fellow driver after the Pittsburgh Steelers lost a game, then brandished a handgun out his car window.

Seamus McCaffery, a bald supreme court justice from Philadelphia best known for building a court and a jail under the Eagles' football stadium for unruly sports fans, made a joke: "Being from Philadelphia, we're used to our team losing. Could this be attributed to the Steelers' loss, which is unusual?" The activists packing the courtroom laughed. Later, McCaffery would be suspended amid a state scandal: he had sent obscene emails to fellow government officials as part of a long-standing ring of lewd jokers.

Smith had already heard much of the argument the state and the DEP were putting forth that day: the state had the right to allow drillers to drill where they wanted, and little towns couldn't block them. State rights trumped local ones every time. Legally, this was a defensible position, but Smith wasn't arguing that local rights were always more powerful, only that zoning came with certain responsibilities to protect citizens' welfare under the constitution. Act 13 would force his clients to breach them.

Matt Haverstick, an attorney hired to represent the commonwealth, stood first. He focused on the financial benefit that drilling brought with it: "the development of a natural resource that has profound economic and job promise for all Pennsylvanians, not just some, but for all." As Haverstick laid out his argument, one justice, Max Baer, took issue.

"Counsel," Baer asked, "isn't the whole purpose behind zoning to protect neighbors, protect everybody from unreasonable uses? So if you buy a home in a residential neighborhood, you're assured your government is going to protect you to some extent, stopping somebody from building a steel factory beside it?"

Smith found Baer's line of inquiry heartening. But Baer was also a liberal Democrat and not one of those Smith worried about winning over. It did seem to Smith, as he tried to gauge the responses of the justices on the bench, that the others also seemed skeptical of the commonwealth's position. After three-quarters of an hour, it was Smith's turn to face the panel of judges. He boiled down his argument to its essential question: "Can I use my property in a way that's injurious to my neighbor?" That, he went on, the constitution wouldn't allow. What's more, under the law, zoning brought with it a constitutional duty for little towns to protect the "health, safety, and welfare" of their citizens, which they couldn't guarantee if a gas well could be drilled three hundred feet from a playground.

After Smith finished, Jon Kamin, the attorney who had represented South Fayette Township, in addition to strip clubs, made the case that aspects of Act 13, including the physician's gag rule, rendered the new Oil and Gas Act a "special law"—a law that applied only to a single industry. The state couldn't create laws like this, according to a constitutional amendment designed to rein in cronyism between the state and the railroads one hundred years earlier. If Act 13 was a special law, Kamin argued, then it also violated the Fourteenth Amendment of the U.S. Constitution, which mandates that everyone be treated equally.

Finally Jordan Yeager, the civil rights lawyer from the eastern part of the state, put forth his argument, that the new law violated Article 1, Section 27, of the state constitution, the Environmental Rights Amendment. This was the liberal argument dismissed by the lower court. Yeager invoked the ancient notion of public trust, that some natural resources belong to the people, and the government as custodian has a duty to protect them.

Chief Justice Castille said little that day in court. At one point, however, he turned to Smith to ask, "Did you say there's something in this act that makes the municipality have to pay the other side's legal fees?" John replied, "Yes, Your Honor." Castille told me later that he found this provision particularly egregious. Little townships would be up against the industry's expensive lawyers and looking at $800,000 bills for one small fight. As he saw it, due process was all about fairness, and that was unfair.

The argument lasted nearly two hours, which was unusually long. Afterward, Kamin took the Smiths to lunch at the Carlton, where Pittsburgh's lawyers, judges, and bankers did business over crab cakes.

On December 19, 2013, in a 4–2 decision, the Pennsylvania Supreme Court found in favor of Smith and his team of challengers. A typical supreme court opinion might run about 20 pages; Castille's went on for 162. He affirmed the decision of the lower court, agreeing with Smith that the law violated people's constitutional rights to protect their property, as well as a township's responsibility to protect the health and welfare of its citizens. He also questioned the constitutionality of the physician gag rule, sending it back to the lower court to reexamine. He did the same with the provision allowing homeowners to settle over ruined water with oil and gas companies without notifying their neighbors. Treating people who relied on private wells differently from those who had access to public water was unfair, he wrote.

Most surprisingly, Castille's argument relied on Article 1, Section 27. "It is not a historical accident that the Pennsylvania Constitution now places citizens' environmental rights on par with their political rights," he wrote. Water and air belonged to the public trust—to the people of Pennsylvania.

Castille's landmark decision went further. From timber to coal, he detailed the successive waves of industrialization that had laid waste to the commons for the past four hundred years. "Approximately three and a half centuries ago, white pine, eastern hemlock, and mixed hardwood forests covered nine-tenths of more than twenty million acres. Two centuries later, the state experienced a lumber boom that, by 1920, had left much of Pennsylvania barren."

Environmental disasters continued to harm not only the landscape but also the health of its citizens, he wrote. "The overwhelming tasks of reclamation and regeneration of the Commonwealth's natural resources, along with localized environmental incidents (such as the 1948 Donora smog tragedy in which twenty persons died of asphyxiation and 7,000 persons were hospitalized because of corrosive industrial smoke; the 1959 Knox Mine disaster in which the Susquehanna River disappeared into the Pittston Coal Vein; the 1961 Glen Alden mine water discharge that killed more than 300,000 fish; and the Centralia mine fire that started in 1962, is still burning, and led to the relocation of all residents in 1984) has led to the gradual enactment of statutes protecting our environment."

All of these disasters, he went on, helped establish the need for environmental protections and laws. In Pennsylvania, the most significant was the Environmental Rights Amendment, which passed into law in 1971 with overwhelming support from both parties. Its author was a Pennsylvania legislator and ardent conservationist named Franklin Kury. He wrote the amendment in response to the destructive legacy of coal. But he credited its success with the country's growing environmental consciousness born out of the work of Rachel Carson and her fellow Pennsylvania native Edward Abbey, the author of *Desert Solitaire* and *The Monkey Wrench Gang*. As Carson was raised in the shadow of a glue factory, Abbey grew up among farmers living alongside the ravages of coal. Abbey wrote, "A civilization which destroys what little remains of the wild, the spare, the original, is cutting itself off from its origins and betraying the principle of civilization itself."

Beyond Castille's opinion, the historical moment at which the amendment came into being bears noting. According to Kury, it wasn't only books like Carson's and Abbey's that made his amendment popular. Television also played a role in birthing an environmental consciousness in Pennsylvania and across the United States. Much as pictures of African American children cowering before hateful white mobs helped change the nation's civil rights laws, footage of mile upon mile of rust-red rivers so polluted they caught fire helped earn the Environmental Rights Amendment such widespread support that it swept through the legislature with nearly unanimous approval from both parties.

On the floor of the Pennsylvania legislature, Herbert Fineman, the Speaker of the House, spoke of its import in the argot of the times: "The measure of our progress is not just what we have but how we live, that it is not man who must adapt himself to technology but technology which must be adapted to man." Forty years on, this question applied to the technological revolution made possible by fracking: Did Stacey and her children have to adapt to technology by leaving their farm, or did fracking have to adapt to the communities that preceded it? The Pennsylvania Supreme Court came down firmly in favor of individual rights and community, over the rights of the extractive industry.

The language of the opinion stunned Jordan Yeager and John Smith. Neither had allowed himself to imagine such a sweeping success on any grounds, and certainly not on the basis of the Environmental Rights Amendment. Now, for the first time in Pennsylvania history, the amendment had actual teeth. The level of popular support was startling. One day, after the local paper published the fact that the state had spent more than $700,000 thus far in attorneys' fees to defend Act 13, Smith opened a letter and found a twenty-five-dollar check from a concerned citizen. She wanted to help compensate him on behalf of the people of the commonwealth. John sent the check back with a thank-you note. The victory also alarmed the state. Governor Corbett said, "We must not allow today's ruling to send a negative message to job creators and families who depend on the energy industry." A spokesman for the Marcellus Shale Coalition, an industry trade group, said the decision represented "a missed opportunity."

When the Smiths had the chance to read the decision, Kendra called Stacey. On page 49, Castille recounted the ordeal of "a homeowner, a nurse who leased her mineral rights." She took a minute in the break room. So much of her struggle had revolved around the fear of not being believed. Now the highest court in Pennsylvania had used her sworn testimony to strike down the law.

28 | DREAMS

Stacey counted the supreme court win as the most important accomplishment of her life, after giving birth to Harley and Paige. Although she and the kids didn't benefit from the decision financially, she clung to the public victory all the more as the cost of the battle bore down on her throughout 2013. By year's end she was $224,000 in debt, which included the cost of the camper, the two mortgages, and tutoring for Paige when she floundered in English. Stacey attributed all of these financial setbacks to the gas wells. Every day brought a fresh outrage that seemed to lead her further from the life she'd envisioned. She'd been so sure that her goodness, paired with relentless work, would yield success. In her mind, she'd set herself apart from her parents, who worked impossibly hard but still fought to secure the American dream of upward mobility. Now she, like them, was failing to rise through no fault of her own. As this core optimism crumbled, a new, painful worldview took its place. The world was against her. She muscled through her days at the hospital and managed to hold down three jobs, teaching, nursing, and working at the orthopedic hospital alongside Shelly, who was suddenly busy and ridiculously happy.

Shelly had fallen in love with the president of the Washington County Beekeepers Association. The president was an older man and a kind one. He insisted that Shelly stop living in a house where, during the winter, a glass of water left by the bed froze over. He helped her put in a furnace, and Shelly went back to church and started teaching Sunday school. For the first time in her adult life, Shelly felt taken care of. And although she worried for Stacey, sometimes she tired of her sister's sense of being wronged by the world. Shelly didn't doubt for a second the severity of what Harley had been through—she'd smelled the noxious fumes, seen the black water, and been stricken with headaches and dizziness at the farm—but she sometimes wished that her sister would try to let go of her self-righteous anger. The increasing crusade mentality risked hurting Harley and Paige by keeping them perpetually trapped in a story of victimhood.

Stacey felt utterly alone. Despite the fact that she and Chris were engaged, getting married with all of her debt seemed impossible. "I can't afford a wedding dress, let alone a wedding," she told me. She wanted to put the wedding off until the fight with Range was settled, which wasn't going to happen anytime soon. In her mind, she remained a single mom on her own with Harley and Paige, and late at night her terrors of what might come next spun out of control. Even when she managed to sleep, her dreams betrayed the chaos and uncertainty that she and the kids were still going through.

She dreamed that Paige was stuck in a tank full of frack fluid and rolling down a hill.

She dreamed that she bought a thousand dollars' worth of groceries, which were suddenly stolen. She wept knowing that she and the kids would go hungry.

She dreamed that she and the kids were wandering around an abandoned subdivision. Everything was pristine, but the inhabitants had vanished. Something had gone catastrophically wrong, but they had to pick an empty house to live in anyway.

She dreamed that they were back in their contaminated house trying to pack up and leave as quickly as possible. Paige's friend was coming to pick them up, but once they got in her car, she kept driving backward. Paige fell in a hole full of mud and Stacey tried to drag her out while Paige yelled, "I'm just trying to be a normal teenager!"

She dreamed that she had a baby. She was trying to get animal pens ready when she realized she hadn't fed it, and it had shriveled to nothing. She tried to give the baby a bottle, then an IV. She forgot its name.

She woke night after night with her heart raging against her chest. Half-awake, she was caught between gasping for breath and fearing the air. So much was out of her hands: What if one of her new neighbors signed a gas lease and one morning she woke up to a well site? What if she or one of the kids contracted cancer; would their cancer insurance actually cover the cost? Her mouth tasted of ash—cortisol, the aftermath of adrenaline. Overwhelmed with catastrophic fantasies, she went to see Chuck Porch, the counselor who'd seen Harley. Chuck wanted her to start taking the Zoloft he'd prescribed. But Stacey continued to refuse. "If I have to take that, Range wins," she told him again. Now he diagnosed her with post-traumatic stress disorder, which made her self-conscious given what she'd seen as a girl of her father's violent Vietnam-soaked nightmares.

Stacey was thirty-six and long moved out of the house by the time Pappy finally got help. After one particularly rough night in 2006 when Pappy woke up and saw the bruises he'd made around Linda's neck, he decided to go to the VA Hospital in Morgantown for help. He spoke to a counselor who diagnosed him with PTSD. Attending sessions with fellow vets, he realized how isolated he'd felt for decades. A crack shot before he went to Vietnam, Pappy was awarded three Purple Hearts but accepted only one of them. "A lot of boys were like that," he'd said. Pappy found that talking made him feel better. He drove down to West Virginia for group therapy, and Linda went along for her own sessions for wives. Traveling in their camper, they attended festivals selling military hats, shirts, pins, and flags. They also made a practice of greeting young soldiers returning from Iraq and Afghanistan to thank them for their service. That kind of welcome, Pappy thought, would have served him well all those years ago when he came home with feet too rotten to go back to work in the steel mill. Among his most prized possessions was a set of dog tags that read *Never again will one generation abandon another.*

Whether he liked it or not, Pappy's life revolved around Vietnam, much as Stacey feared hers would spin around the gas wells forever. Every life seemed to have a central event—a marker of before and after. This would be hers. Still, how could she have contracted PTSD? The diagnosis seemed so extreme. She'd never been shot at. Chuck Porch wanted her to see a specialist, which she resisted at first. The co-pay was twenty-five dollars.

I just don't want another expense, she wrote in her journal. *Maybe it will get better.* It didn't. Eventually, the night terrors drove her to see a therapist in Washington. Using a method called eye movement desensitization and reprocessing (EMDR), the therapist led her to recall the worst of her fears—the idea was to help her body integrate trauma while awake, she explained to Stacey. In addition, she tried to help Stacey accept what she couldn't control. She couldn't control whether a well site sprang up near their new home. She couldn't control what was in the air. She couldn't control cancer. Instead of focusing on the sores in the book of Job, she could practice being grateful for the resources to fight back against feelings of rage and self-pity. She tried to spend more time thanking God for what she and the kids still had.

On Thanksgiving in 2014, she wrote: *We have so much to be thankful for. Our home and our health improving. Our clean air and clean water and safe place to live. We have each other and our family. I thank God every day. We are thankful for John and Kendra and their family and staff with the sacrifices they have made. We are thankful for our pets that survived with us. And having everyone in one place again. We are thankful for all the good people we have met that helped us along the way. I thank the Lord every day.*

The only person who could get her to laugh at herself, and even at her dreams, was Chris. In one odd nightmare, she'd dreamed that a dog with a rocket strapped to its back was poisoning Amity. She shouted something to that effect in her sleep, and Chris overheard her. When things felt particularly grim, Chris would tease her, saying out of nowhere, "It's a dog with a rocket strapped to its back!" and Stacey would crack up despite herself. But such interludes were rare.

One evening late that fall, Stacey got a call from Beth. The Voyles had lost yet another horse that year, Zee, who'd reared up in fright when a truck driver used his jake brake on the hill by Justa Breeze. Zee'd struck a fence and nearly severed her leg. When the Voyles put her down, Ashley struggled to function, and throughout 2014, she'd plunged into a deep depression. Now Ashley had just called Beth from Burke's stables, where she was grooming horses, hysterical, threatening to kill herself.

I've lost everything, Cummins, Jodi, Oakie, the farm's worth nothing, I've got nothing to live for, she told her mom.

Ashley had a new boyfriend who worked in industry, as locals called it, meaning oil and gas, and he was proving to be aggressive. Beth, given her own fraught history with abuse, was overwrought. Listening to Beth, Stacey felt sick. She knew what Beth was going through.

Get all of the guns out of the house and call your family doctor, she told Beth. The next day, Beth drove her daughter to Washington Hospital and Ashley signed herself into the psychiatric ward. *Ashley admitted to 3A*, Stacey noted in her journal. Ashley wanted to leave right away, but the doctors convinced her to stay. Talking to people doesn't help me, she told them. At five foot six, she had already dropped to a hundred pounds; the three days she spent in the hospital, she refused to eat. Finally, Ashley signed herself out and came home with a prescription for Xanax, which she took once a week, and an antidepressant she quit taking within months. Maybe it was living in a community ravaged by drug abuse, she told me, but Ashley, like Stacey, felt that taking medication to dull emotional pain meant she'd lost and Range had won.

29 | CLOSING DOWN THE PONDS

In June 2014, Range's stock price hit an all-time high of ninety-three dollars per share. The abundance of accessible shale gas was exceeding even the wildest predictions, and Range was first in terms of production and acreage in the Marcellus. The company dominated its sector, and analysts often rated Range best in its mid-size class.

To Kendra and John, it came as a shock that September when Range got hit with the largest penalty in Pennsylvania history to date. The DEP was fining the company $4.15 million for eight leaking waste ponds and ordered Range to close five of them for good. All were in Washington County, and the Yeager pond was one of them. For the Smiths, this extraordinary news arrived while they were preparing Buzz's fight for clean water. Privately, one Range attorney told the Smiths that if it weren't for their doggedness in bringing Buzz's case, the leaks would never have come to light.

If Act 13's being struck down proved their largest constitutional victory, then closing the waste ponds felt like their biggest practical win. But closure was proving tricky. In order to shut down the site, the company had to demonstrate they'd successfully cleaned up the remaining contamination, yet test samples showed elements of BTEX, oil, grease, and chlorides. Kendra could see them clearly in the ongoing remediation reports that came to her from the DEP. At least Range was now publicly admitting to trouble at the Yeager site. "We recognize that we've had some issues at the location, which can occur in our work," Range's Matt Pitzarella said. The record now reflected a history of spills, leaks, and a failed cleanup half a mile up the road from Buzz. The DEP had found as well that a number of the chemicals leaking at the site were the same ones in Buzz's water.

By September 2014, John Smith hoped that all of these public findings against Range would give Buzz's case a better shot as it came before the Environmental Hearing Board. The EHB was a trial court that functioned like a court of appeals: people and businesses argued in front of a judge against findings issued by the DEP. To the Smiths' knowledge, however, no one in Pennsylvania had ever brought a case before the EHB in which a landowner charged that oil and gas had contaminated his water and that the DEP had gotten it wrong. The term of art for their challenge was "a case of first impression." As such, *Kiskadden v. DEP and Range Resources* was likely to garner a lot of local attention.

Of all the judges they might have drawn, Thomas Renwand, the diminutive and fiery chairman and chief judge of the Environmental Hearing Board, seemed like a lucky selection. Since he was appointed in 1995, Renwand had established a long record of standing up to the DEP, and under his guidance, the EHB had agreed to hear the Kiskadden case, which the Smiths saw as a good sign. Even hearing the case required courage. John Smith believed they had a chance at getting Buzz clean water. Kendra, the skeptic, was less certain.

"I don't think the court has the guts to go our way," she told me. To find in Buzz's favor could open up a flood of angry citizens alleging that the DEP had made mistakes with their water also.

The twenty-day trial was held downtown in Pittsburgh's Piatt Place, a swanky office complex only an hour's drive but a world away from Buzz's junkyard. On one side, Michael Heilman, the DEP attorney, sat next to John Gisleson, a skilled litigator working for Range. The company had asked to join the suit to defend its interests, and Gisleson was there, as he saw it, to dismantle the Smiths' case. By discrediting Buzz's claims, Gisleson hoped to call into question the fundamentals of the Smiths' larger suit against Range. And although the agency had recently issued sanctions against Range, the DEP wasn't changing its position regarding Buzz's contaminated water. Heilman was there to argue that despite the now-established fact that the Yeager waste pond had leaked, and despite the contamination in Buzz's well, there was still no proof that Range Resources was responsible. What's more, Heilman began, to meet their burden of proof, the Smiths had to establish a definitive link between the site and Buzz's water, and that they couldn't do. There was no "silver bullet," he argued in his opening statement. There was not enough evidence to prove that Range's actions had contaminated Buzz's water. He continued:

> Your Honor, this is a nostalgic time for me, late summer, early fall. Because we think back on our lives, this is the time of transition, the time when we move—we do different things, move onto new different adventures. And so, I realized last month, it had been thirty-eight years since I enrolled as a college freshman at Notre Dame. Amazingly, I still remember things from back then. I remember the football national championship with my good friend, Joe Montana . . . Even more incredibly, I remember some stuff that happened in class . . . that coincidence is not causation . . . And in preparing for this case, thinking of this hearing, this vignette came back to me and back to me because no matter the bar, it seems that the appellant's case is based upon evidence, introducing evidence of coincidences and conflating them with causation . . .
>
> Let me be clear though, the Department is not here to argue to the Board that the Department has regulated this well site as effectively as we could have. We haven't. We are not here to argue that Range Resources is in full compliance with the law or its permits and regulations. It hasn't done that. We are not even here to argue that Loren [Buzz] Kiskadden has great water quality, he doesn't. What we are here to say is even if all the coincidences [advanced] by the appellant are true, it does not follow that gas well activities polluted appellant's well. Coincidences of that are just coincidences.

In response, Kendra laid out the specific timeline of how problems at the site affected her client's water. To underscore her facts, she called the DEP's Vince Yantko to the stand and walked him through a litany of mishaps—from the leaks and spills, to the holes in the liners, to the fact that the leak detection zone was designed incorrectly. She laid out the DEP's failure to enforce its regulations—how it hadn't taken the leaking pond out of use or examined its liner for rips. She also detailed the large-scale, failed remediation that removed 2,125 tons of soil. Then she demonstrated to the court how the soil test results had been manipulated, altered to read to a lay observer as though there had always been contaminants in that field, when that wasn't the case.

She walked Yantko through Carla Suszkowski's decision—against his own advisement—to flush the contaminated drill cuttings pit with thirty thousand gallons of water. She returned Yantko to his notes, in which he'd called the action "intentional and reckless." Yantko himself had said that her flush could drive contaminants deeper into the earth and the groundwater. Two weeks later, Kendra insisted, three known constituents of frack fluid, which had been in the drill cuttings pit, ended up at the bottom of the watershed in her client's water.

It wasn't enough, however, for the Smiths to prove that Ron Yeager's field was still contaminated, or that the DEP had relied on doctored water tests to determine that Buzz's water wasn't polluted by oil and gas. Each of these facts were already a matter of record, and the DEP had already admitted failure in overseeing the Yeager site.

Heilman had been correct in his opening statement: in order to meet their burden of proof, the Smiths had to make a definitive case for how the industrial chemicals at the top of the hill, at point A, flowed half a mile southwest to the valley bottom, where Buzz lived, at point B. The crux of the argument lay in how water moved underground. As the weeks of the hearing went on, a DEP hydrogeologist argued that the water flowed north and away from Buzz. The Smiths' experts argued

the opposite. The underground springs on the hillside flowed downhill and to the southwest. What's more, after the pond had leaked, the
DEP had mandated that Range install monitoring wells. Those results
showed that ethylene glycol had somehow penetrated the ground west
of the waste pond to a depth of eighty-two feet. Not only did that
serve to indicate evidence of contamination, it also proved which way
the water was moving. And the contaminants weren't only moving underground. The poisoned springs also ran into a stream that belonged
to the commonwealth called Tributary Number Four, according to the
Smiths' experts. This stream ran past Beth and Stacey, and then
down to Buzz.

Range's attorney, John Gisleson, called the Smiths' expert findings
into question. It was too simple to say that if chemicals were found at
the site and in their clients' water, that was definitive proof of contamination, he argued. Furthermore, the ratios found in Buzz's water were
different from those up on the hillside. And when it came to oil and
gas contamination, particularly in regard to salts, those ratios mattered. There were also plenty of other potential sources of contamination lying around Buzz's junkyard at the Bottoms. Buzz's water may
have been undrinkable, but that wasn't Range's fault. Gisleson took
aim at Stacey and Beth's case too, arguing that if the same water
flowed downhill past their houses, then why were the chemicals different in all three homes?

The Smiths paid little attention to Gisleson's questions about
Stacey and Beth. They thought he'd proven nothing—simply revealed
more of what he didn't know. At one point, according to the Smiths,
he'd had to ask Kendra for help in reading test results. And as the
lengthy hearing drew to a close, the Smiths felt it had gone well. Still,
given the stakes involved for the state and the possible flood of cases
that would follow a court decision in their favor, Kendra wasn't so sure.
She was also cognizant of the costs. She'd raced her experts through
their testimony, trying to get them off the stand as quickly as possible, since most charged by the hour. The Smiths were never going to

be paid back for what Buzz's trial cost them, since victory in that suit wouldn't come with damages. This was also true of their case against the DEP on behalf of Beth Voyles. Victory for the Smiths would mean, simply, getting Buzz clean water. There were also advantages other than money to winning these suits; they helped the Smiths gather evidence for *Haney v. Range* and garnered public opinion in advance of their case.

At the end of the trial's last day, John and Kendra carried their stacks of files out of Piatt Place to the parking lot in darkness. It was nearly 8:00 p.m. by the time they finished loading, and there were no other cars in the indoor lot. Under the green fluorescent lights, Kendra started to cry. After twenty years of marriage, John had never seen her cry at work. Not once. But Kendra felt in her marrow that they were going to lose, and Buzz wasn't a railroad or another corporate client. He was an indigent man dependent on the state for help that the state refused to give him. John put his arms around Kendra.

Did we do enough? she asked him.

We tried the best case we could try, he replied.

One of the common tactics employed in corporate defense is to simply drag out an expensive case, rendering it too costly for plaintiff lawyers relying on settlement fees to continue. But the Smiths did continue, year after year, and that raised suspicions on the other side. Once, when John walked into one of the near-weekly hearings related to the Kiskadden case, he overheard a DEP attorney ask an attorney from Range, *Who is paying them?*

While the Smiths were still awaiting the Kiskadden verdict, Range Resources filed a motion asking the court to order the Smiths to reveal who was funding their suits. By now, the Smiths had been fighting in three separate cases against Range Resources and the DEP for three and a half years, and there were those at Range who found it hard to believe that the Smiths hadn't received a dime. In their September 2014 motion, Range's attorneys cited the fact that the Smiths often brought two lawyers—John and Kendra—to depose witnesses, which constituted an unnecessary expense. This was true: John often went with Kendra to take depositions in Harrisburg. First, he wanted to learn about these characters, to strategize about how to approach them on the stand. Second, after the level of hostility rose, he didn't want Kendra to go alone. It wasn't that he felt he needed to protect her, exactly. Kendra could take care of herself. She just might need a witness for some of the antics she was growing tired of enduring.

Since the Smiths' clients were poor, Range's attorneys argued that they'd developed "a good faith belief during the course of discovery that one or more third parties may be directly or indirectly paying the litigation costs associated with the Plaintiff's prosecution of the case." The Smiths responded by stating in legal documents that the motion was based on "mere apparitions and surprising paranoia."

"Are Washington County residents expected to have less advocacy or access to our judicial system due to their financial positions?" they asked in their response. Poor people had as much right to protect their health and property as rich people did. This was the cornerstone of environmental justice: a legal concept that had striven since the 1980s to balance environmental benefits and burdens between wealthy and impoverished communities. John Smith scoured legal history to find an ennobling argument about poverty and equal justice. He found this from the retired U.S. Supreme Court justice Lewis Powell Jr.: "Equal justice under law is not merely a caption on the façade of the Supreme Court building, it is perhaps the most inspiring ideal of our society. It is one of the ends for which our entire legal system exists . . . It is fundamental that justice should be the same, in substance and availability, without regard to economic status."

At the Washington County Courthouse, Judge Debbie O'Dell Seneca called the company's allegations "offensive." Soon, however, O'Dell Seneca became embroiled in a scandal of her own. Accused of altering transcripts in a murder trial and eavesdropping on colleagues in the Washington County Courthouse, she was forced to step down, leaving the Haney case orphaned.

Range continued its efforts to dig out the source of the Smiths' funding, seeming to believe that the Smiths' legal challenges were being secretly funded by the Heinz Endowments, a family foundation that focuses on environmental health, among other social causes, in southwestern Pennsylvania. The charge was fairly incendiary: it accused a well-respected civil society group of engaging in subterfuge. The Heinz Endowments had met with Stacey and Beth once, but Range threatened to issue subpoenas to every member of the Heinz family, including Teresa Heinz Kerry and her three sons. The attorneys also subpoenaed other small civil society groups funded by the Heinz Endowments, including the Southwestern Pennsylvania Health Project, which had worked with Stacey and Beth while conducting a study on fracking-related illnesses, and the Center for Coalfield Justice. "We've never given Smith Butz any money," Veronica Coptis, the executive director of the Center for Coalfield Justice, told me. "But when we checked our books we found that in fact, they'd given us a two-hundred-dollar donation."

There was another working theory among Range employees as they searched for a money trail leading to the Smiths: the money was coming from Russia and being funneled through a foundation like Heinz in an attempt to disrupt the U.S. energy industry. After all, there was credible evidence to suggest that Russia was funding the fight against fracking abroad. But there was no evidence to suggest that Russia, or anyone else, was funneling money to the Smiths.

In October 2015, the Smith Butz firm found itself the subject of an audit by the state of Pennsylvania. The auditors wanted to see the Smiths' records related to sales tax, which was odd. Other than buying office supplies, law firms are exempt from paying sales tax. However, if the firm had received some money that wasn't a straight legal fee, say for consulting or lobbying, that money would be subject to tax and would certainly appear on an audit. Although there was no way to prove it, it seemed to the Smiths that the state of Pennsylvania was singling them out for scrutiny as a result of their suits against the DEP and Act 13. It wasn't a hard leap for the Smiths to make: the auditor said he was looking for income including "lobbying services." But the audit turned up no such income.

The Smiths said little about the pressure they were under to Beth and Stacey, who were still facing their own ongoing health issues. For a decade, since long before the gas wells arrived, Stacey had suffered from an underactive thyroid. The condition, called hypothyroidism, was more of a nuisance than anything else; she was always cold.

Still, every six months, she visited her endocrinologist's office, where she saw a nurse practitioner named Donna Gisleson. The two women were friendly, and Stacey recognized in Gisleson a sympathetic listener and an experienced professional. On one visit that February, while Stacey perched on an examining table, Gisleson ran her fingers over Stacey's neck and listened to her chest with a stethoscope. What happened next is contested. According to Stacey's version of events, Gisleson was gently poking at her when the nurse practitioner started up a conversation about Buzz Kiskadden. His case had been in the newspaper, and Donna Gisleson knew what Stacey had been going through with the gas wells, so the first few beats didn't seem out of the ordinary. But Stacey grew uncomfortable when she heard Gisleson calling Buzz's story into question. As Stacey recalled it, Gisleson said that she didn't believe him. She wagered the junkyard he lived in had likely contaminated his water. What's more, as Stacey listened, the nurse went on, saying Buzz didn't have a pre-drill, so there was no way for Buzz to prove contamination anyway.

When Stacey heard the word "pre-drill," she started. The word was fairly technical and so deeply embedded in the opposition's case that she wondered how Gisleson knew it. The nurse explained that her husband, John, was one of the lead attorneys facing off against Buzz. John Gisleson was a big gun, Stacey recalled her saying, and

Range had brought him in because he was well-known for being a tough litigator. According to Stacey's version, Donna said her husband had been looking at medical tests as part of discovery when he saw his wife's name and asked Donna if Stacey was one of her patients. Yes, she said. She'd seen Stacey for years and Stacey wouldn't make up symptoms. Stacey recalled Donna saying breezily that she knew that Stacey didn't have a pre-drill either. It would probably be smarter for her to settle than to risk trial. As Donna pressed delicately on her throat to palpate her thyroid, Stacey felt her gorge rise.

Oh, we're not looking to settle, she remembered replying. We've got plenty of evidence.

Stacey called the Smiths on the car ride home. John Gisleson was indeed a lead attorney for Range on Buzz's case and on hers. As a nurse living and working in such a close-knit community, Stacey was accustomed to treating her neighbors for all manner of ailments and saying nothing to anyone about who and what she'd seen. To guard against any infraction, she stringently followed the rules of the Health Insurance Portability and Accountability Act (HIPAA), which she believed made it a violation to talk about confidential patient issues with anyone, let alone your husband, an attorney. The Smiths thought what Donna Gisleson had said sounded pretty unusual, but they didn't handle such matters. They recommended that Stacey retain an attorney who dealt with HIPAA issues.

So Stacey signed on with Jon Kamin, who brought a case against Donna Gisleson, arguing that the nurse broke her professional code of conduct, and the law, by discussing Stacey with her attorney husband. The Gislesons denied the violation, responding in legal documents that Donna had in fact said something nice about Stacey— that she wouldn't "make up" symptoms. The allegation, they argued, was an attempt to blacken someone's name. And furthermore, Stacey had waived her right to privacy when she signed off on *Haney v. Range*, in which she was named plaintiff, rendering her medical records available to opposing attorneys. Eventually, when the case came before a judge, Donna Gisleson's lawyer asked him to throw it out. Her husband was sitting in the courtroom. To his thinking, this suit was nothing but retaliation. He was a lead counsel working for Range, so he figured the Smiths were punishing him by embarrassing his wife, and trying to get him removed from the Haney case. The judge disagreed. *Haney v. Gisleson* was moving forward. (Donna Gisleson's attorney, while declining to comment on litigation, said the claims are "completely false and are denied in total.")

After Jon Kamin won the argument and prepared to leave, Mr. Gisleson approached him. Kamin, an aggressive attorney in his own right, was accustomed to confrontations on behalf of his clients. But the degree of heat that ensued in their exchange was unusual. The two men disagree on what was said next. Gisleson recalls telling Kamin that John Smith was a liar, and Kamin remembers Gisleson saying, Tell John Smith I'm coming for him.

30 | CHASING GHOSTS

By 2015, the Smiths had been fighting for two years to try to make Range obey the court order and hand over a definitive list of chemicals—from soap to cyanide—used on the Yeagers' hillside. But the company refused to disclose, and there was good reason for that. Range wasn't simply being obstructionist; it was likely the company didn't know, since some of the products its subcontractors used were proprietary, and their contents were secret.

Range had a problem. If they admitted this fact, it could put them in violation of their very public claim that they *did* disclose all the chemical additives used in a frack and were the first company to have done so. When John Smith deposed Ray Walker, Range's chief operating officer, he pushed this point of full disclosure. "So the qualification is you'll tell the public everything you know?" "Everything we know, yes," Walker replied. "But there are things you don't know?" Smith asked. "Of course," Walker said. The Smiths believed that this admission had legal and financial ramifications: since Range had touted its full disclosure to investors as demonstrable fact, this could prove a violation of the Securities and Exchange Commission law.

In the absence of this list, Kendra did her own sleuthing late at night, her legs curled beneath her on the porch's red couch, with hundreds of pages of material-safety data sheets, which a company is legally required to keep to list the harmful side effects of its products. Although the data sheets were helpful, they weren't definitive by any stretch. The companies weren't required to divulge secret ingredients;

they could simply use the word "proprietary." When identified, most of the chemicals were listed only by numbers and letters, which Kendra was learning to decipher. "MC" stood for Multi-Chem, the chemical company now owned by Halliburton, which had supplied the chemicals used up at the site. "MX" stood for experimental. Then there was "T."

What "T" stood for was anyone's guess. There was no definition on Multi-Chem's products or website, so Kendra surfed other industrial websites for clues, including that of Halliburton, which had bought Multi-Chem in 2011. Halliburton did indeed list products that ended in the letter "T"; they were tracers, the chemical and often radioactive signatures used to mark exactly where a frack and its fluids went. Kendra remembered what the DEP attorney had said during the Kiskadden trial about the lack of a silver bullet. What was a tracer, she wondered, if not a silver bullet?

Through deposing a Multi-Chem employee who wrote data sheets, Kendra learned her supposition was right. "T" did mean tracer. The first tracer she discovered turned out to be one of thirteen used at the Yeager site.

She found the others by accident. From the beginning of discovery, Kendra had been asking Range to produce sign-in sheets from companies entering and leaving the site. It was the easiest way to find out who'd worked up there. Range responded that these sheets had been destroyed. Then one day a sign-in page blew down the hill and into Beth and John's yard. Beth gave it to the Smiths, who sent it back to Range without reading it to make a point. The next time Kendra caught sight of one of these sign-in sheets, it arrived in a stack of discovery documents from Universal Well Services, the company that conducted the frack. On it, Kendra saw the name of a company called ProTechnics, and during a deposition, she asked a Universal Well employee if he knew what ProTechnics did.

ProTechnics was a tracer company, he explained. They manufactured both chemical and radioactive tracers. For each of the eight stages of the frack, the company had used a different tracer to map where the fluids and fractures went. ProTechnics pumped the chemical tracers into the frack fluid. It also encapsulated its radioactive tracers in the ceramic pellets used to prop open the fractures in the rock and allow the gas to flow back up to the surface.

The Smiths took their new evidence of tracers—and the fact that Range had failed to disclose them for years—to the court. They asked the new judge assigned to the case, William R. Nalitz, to compel Pro-Technics to divulge the names of the specific elements in their chemical and radioactive tracers. It was probably too late to find the radioactive tracers, which had likely decayed, but maybe not the chemical ones. If Kendra could find one of these signature chemical tracers in her clients' water, she'd be able to prove that Range had contaminated their water. "I just need to find one," she told John, "and we've got a slam dunk."

To determine whether or not Kendra had the right to learn what was in both kinds of tracers, among other issues, the judge held a hearing. On the stand, a ProTechnics executive refused to tell Kendra what was in the chemical tracers. Doing so would render their trade secret public and might ruin their business, he argued. He did, however, disclose the contents of their radioactive tracers, which contained Iridium 192, Antimony 124, and Scandium 46. They were marketed under the label ZeroWash® and made in a process that was supposed to seal the radioactive substances so that they couldn't be washed out of the ceramic pellets. In a scientific study conducted by Texas A&M, the pellets released only a "negligible" amount of radioactive isotopes. But Kendra contended that a negligible amount could be a concern, even if their half-lives were short, as these three elements' were. A half-life can be misleading; technically the term describes the amount of time it takes for half of a radioactive substance to decay. For each of the tracers, within three months, half of their radioactivity decayed. But what about the other half?

And even if the radioactive elements in the tracers proved to be harmless, Kendra was learning about other issues related to radioactivity at the site. Fracking could also bring naturally occurring radon from miles underground to the earth's surface. Radon is a known carcinogen and a leading cause of lung cancer in the United States.

Searching for potential violations, Kendra began to investigate the laws surrounding the use of such material. Tracking radioactive tracers turned out to be particularly difficult. Since radioactive material was hazardous and fell under the Nuclear Regulatory Commission, its use required a permit from the DEP. When Kendra went looking for one, the DEP told her that it was classified as a matter of national security. She also found that the DEP knew that radioactive tracers had been setting off landfill radiation alarms in Pennsylvania for years.

The first had occurred in the eastern part of the state on December 22, 2009, the same month ProTechnics pumped radioactive tracers into the Yeagers' hillside. It struck her as contradictory: on the one hand, these radioactive tracers were allegedly so harmless they could be used at the top of the watershed a few hundred feet from people's homes; on the other, they were so dangerous that disclosing information about them was a threat to American national security. A terrorist might use such material to build a dirty bomb, the DEP responded to the Smiths in an affidavit. An amount as small as "a pencil eraser" could cause a radioactive cloud that endangered people and heightened their risk of cancer. To Kendra, this sounded ludicrous. Which was it? Were these materials harmless or potential agents of destruction? The DEP seemed to want to have it both ways.

Kendra wasn't the first person to try to gather information about the industry's use of tracers only to hit wall after wall. Robert Jackson, chair of the Earth System Science Department at Stanford University, had been studying tracers used in horizontal hydraulic fracturing for years. His team conducted the first studies examining fracking and drinking water. "Chasing tracers is like chasing ghosts," he told me. They weren't only proprietary; they were elusive.

Range's failure to disclose the use of tracers seemed bad enough to

Kendra. But she found it harder to stomach what the DEP had done. At one point, she and John got so frustrated that they started asking state employees under oath if they knew the Pennsylvania DEP's mission statement: *To protect Pennsylvania's air, land and water from pollution and to provide for the health and safety of its citizens through a cleaner environment.*

"For me, the greatest injustice is that FBI and EPA and the U.S. attorney haven't moved on this," Kendra said. Instead, Special Agent Burgess, the EPA's environmental crimes investigator, along with his FBI counterpart, had gone silent. But as an EPA criminal investigator, Burgess didn't have the authority to bring charges; he could only build the best case he could before turning it over to the U.S. Attorney's Office in the hopes they'd see fit to prosecute. Kendra didn't understand why the EPA and the U.S. Attorney's Office didn't want to move forward; she'd spent days with them explaining the case, and they'd independently confirmed her findings. She thought their passivity betrayed a lack of courage to take on a complicated case.

"Beth, Stacey, and Buzz aren't perfect plaintiffs," she told me. "You'll never have a perfect case. You'll always have something cutting against you. But so what? You prosecute someone and you lose."

Finding the tracers wasn't the only one of what Kendra called "her geeked-out bombshell moments." Through studying the data sheets, she also found that despite its public statement to the contrary, Range and its subcontractors were using diesel in the frack fluid up at the Yeager site. That was a violation of federal law, and of the Halliburton loophole in the 2005 Energy Policy Act, which stated that although most chemicals related to fracking weren't subject to federal regulation, diesel still was. It was simply too dangerous to inject in the ground without government oversight. Universal Well Services, the company that conducted the frack at Yeager, along with thousands of others, had written to Congress to say that it didn't use diesel in its frack fluid, but on those data sheets, Kendra found that Universal Well Services had used diesel. She checked the product ID numbers against those on a federal registry that detailed the elements of diesel fuel, like kerosene, among others. They matched. She had them "dead to rights," as she liked to say. Substantiating the presence of diesel took her two weeks of work at ten hours a day. She'd have been happy to hand her results about this violation over to federal investigators, yet the investigators were nowhere to be found.

When the EPA finally published the first draft of its study in June 2015, its findings regarding Stacey, Beth, and Buzz's water were inconclusive. The EPA couldn't definitively determine whether the drilling process had affected their water, despite the presence of fuels, arsenic, 2-butoxyethanol, iron, and manganese, which differed from house to house. For the EPA, the problem with making such a determination was twofold. First, Washington County had been subject to so many industrial uses over time: "past coal mining activities, agriculture activities, industrial operations, waste disposal . . . and oil and gas development," the study argued. All of these uses rendered it impossible to determine whether shale gas development was the culprit. Second, neither Stacey, nor Beth, nor Buzz had a pre-drill. So there was no clear picture of what was in their water before and after drilling. Ron Yeager, however, did have a pre-drill, which Kendra had helped the EPA procure. Based on that pre-drill and the DEP's finding, the EPA study determined that the Yeagers' water was contaminated.

The conclusion that the Yeagers' water was contaminated but their neighbors' wasn't mirrored the study's initial draft conclusions. Although fracking may contaminate water, the EPA said, it didn't lead to "widespread, systemic impacts on drinking water resources in the United States." As soon as the EPA published its draft study, the oil and gas industry touted its findings. *Energy in Depth* ran an article under the banner headline "Long-Awaited EPA Study Finds Fracking Has Not Led to Widespread Water Contamination."

But the EPA's Scientific Advisory Board, an independent review panel of scientists examining the draft findings, took issue with this conclusion. The use of phrases like "widespread and systematic" wasn't based in science or supported by evidence, they argued. These were political words that misled the public.

A year and a half later when the final report was published in December 2016, the EPA removed the phrase "widespread and systematic" and the agency altered its conclusions. Thomas A. Burke, the EPA's science advisor and deputy assistant administrator of the agency's Office of Research and Development, told *The New York Times* that the new report "found evidence that fracking has contributed to drinking water contamination in all stages of the process: acquiring water to be used for fracking, mixing the water with chemical additives to make fracking fluids, injecting the chemical fluids underground, collecting the wastewater that flows out of fracking wells after injections, and storing the used wastewater."

Although the drinking-water study was the largest and most ambitious effort by the EPA to study the effects of fracking, any important conclusions were lost in the fray as activists and the oil and gas industry argued over what the study really meant. "Fracking," as a word, had become politicized and polarizing.

"I wish we had never used that word because fracking is now slang for everything bad associated with fossil fuels," Ray Walker of Range said. Industry had a word for those who condemned extraction near peoples' homes. The opposition used to be called NIMBY, for "not in my backyard." Now the term was BANANA: "build absolutely nothing anywhere near anything."

31 | "THE JUNKYARD PLAINTIFF"

On June 12, 2015, Buzz lost his case. In his verdict, Judge Thomas Renwand wrote that despite "extensive evidence of leaks and spills," he couldn't rule out the possibility that the rotting hulks of cars, boats, and school buses in the junkyard, as well as the horse farm across the road, had contaminated his water, not Range Resources. Tom Shepstone, a blogger for *Energy in Depth*, concluded that the verdict "once more proves the junkyard is [the] best final resting place of not only cars, but also of false fracking accusations." The Smiths appealed right away, but their appeal was denied.

Even still, the court had hard words for Range. "Range's reckless business practices, combined with its repeated failure to report problems at the Yeager Site are irresponsible to the extreme, bordering on reprehensible. The list of leaks and spills at the Yeager Site is troubling," the appeals court wrote in their decision not to hear the case. "Although there is little dispute that the activities at the Yeager Site impacted the environment and contaminated the soil and adjacent springs, the issue before this Court was whether Range's activities impacted Kiskadden's water well." And on that specific issue, six out of seven judges affirmed Renwand's decision. There were simply too many potential sources of contamination at the junkyard to be sure where the chemicals had come from. Furthermore, the Smiths hadn't proven a definitive connection between the Yeagers' hillside and Buzz's home. There would be no retrying the case. One judge on the appeals panel, however, disagreed. The Smiths had established the necessary link between the two sites, she argued in her dissenting opinion. They'd presented what she called "volumes of empirical data showing a highly positive (if not nearly perfect) correlation." In doing so, the Smiths had met their burden of proof: a preponderance of evidence clearly showed that Range Resources was responsible for contaminating Buzz's water. But as only one judge among six, she held a minority opinion.

"I'm up against more than the law here," Kendra said in response. "There is no legal reason why this should be denied. If this was an uphill battle before, now it's Everest."

After Buzz lost, he renounced whatever small purchase he'd had on the world. "No one's going to stop this," he told me one afternoon when he agreed to leave the cement-block room where he slept in his mother's basement to speak to me. Often, when I showed up, he simply refused. His mother, Grace, was wary too. For them, there was no advantage in talking, especially now that Buzz had lost his case. Still, Grace was polite and patient enough to entertain my visits, and sometimes she was able to coax Buzzy, as she called him, from his bed.

"They're making too much money from it," he said when he finally arose. "That's what it's all about: money. Greed."

He'd stopped raking a razor across his stubbled chin, and his long beard and white mane gave him the look of a prophet. The methane levels in his trailer, and the lack of water, made it impossible for him to live down in the hollow, so he'd moved up the ridge into his mom's while he was undergoing chemotherapy for his leukemia.

"I'm depressed. I don't go nowhere unless I have to," he said. When the leukemia looked to be claiming his life, he'd wanted to stop the treatments. "About gave up on the doctors," he said. Yet in the end, he persevered, and that perseverance led to good news: the blood-borne cancer had gone into remission. Buzz didn't really think it was the doctors who'd done it—he thought it was God. But instead of feeling gratitude, he felt defeated. Even after he was given a clean bill of health, he didn't return to the things he'd loved, riding dirt bikes and fishing. He didn't even watch TV. He just sat in his room in the dank basement.

His old girlfriend Loretta Logsdon had recently died, but Buzz was still close to her grandson, Junior. Buzz had angered Junior's mother by forcing her to move out of the trailer too. "I made them move out because I didn't want them to get sick the way I did. They didn't understand it. I don't want anyone living there." The issue had driven a wedge between them, and now he didn't get to see Junior anymore, which deepened his hopelessness.

"DEP can't get me nothing," he said. "Hauling water now. Me and my mother pay the water. Right now we're getting it at Walmart." With Buzz still weak and Grace turning eighty, the sheer weight of hauling water was just as much a concern as the cost. They had to buy one-gallon jugs, instead of five, because neither could lift the heavier ones. Grace, who still relied on dandelion tea as a cure-all, was trying to get Buzz to eat natural foods.

"My mom is trying to get me to eat broccoli raw. I can't eat that shit. I don't have no teeth," he said. He no longer believed that the system could be changed. In fact, he'd never thought the Smiths would win.

On another afternoon, when Buzz refused to get out of bed and I sat waiting for him in the basement, Grace spoke to me of her disappointment.

"I can't understand how we had papers proving what was in our water, and we still lost," she said. "I feel we've been done an injustice. I'm not against the U.S. making progress, but not at the price of ruining our water. Water is the most precious thing we have." But that was the way it went now in America. The forces they were up against were simply too big. This wasn't a matter of fixing the political system. "According to the Bible, we're not supposed to vote. God puts who he wants on the throne. God permitted this to happen because the U.S. has gotten so far from him."

As Grace Kiskadden saw it, this was the beginning of the end of the world, as foretold in the book of Revelation.

"The water will become so poisoned, you can't drink it," she said. In Revelation 8:11, God embitters a third of the rivers with wormwood, and the men who drink this water die.

"I just hope we're raptured out of here," she said.

32 | DIVA

U p the hill at Justa Breeze, Beth hadn't wanted to risk breeding dogs since she'd lost those two litters in 2011. But now that the DEP had ordered the frack pond closed, Beth figured it was safe to try again. By the late summer of 2015, her boxer Diva was expecting, and one warm day in September, Diva gave birth to a litter of eight puppies in the Voyles' basement. Afterward, Beth led her down to the stream behind the show ring to cool off. The stream was Tributary Number Four, which flowed from the underground springs on the Yeagers' hillside down past Beth's and Stacey's houses, then on to Buzz's place down in the Bottoms. Diva splashed and played for an hour while Beth talked to John, who was building a deer blind nearby. Then Beth led Diva back up the hill and into the blue plastic pool in the basement where the puppies were waiting to suckle. Beth lined each up by a teat to nurse, rotating them as she'd learned to do as a breeder.

By the next day, something was wrong. The white sheet lining the blue pool was stained with blood. Diva couldn't stand. The puppies were bleeding from their mouths and their rectums, and over the next three days, six of the eight died. Diva recovered, or seemed to, for the next several months. Then she struggled to walk again. One evening, Beth was at the stove in the basement cooking the dogs' dinner when she looked up and saw Diva collapse while trying to climb onto the couch. Minutes later, Diva died. Beth called Kendra to ask if she should have Diva or the puppies autopsied, but Kendra told her not to bother. None of the animal testing had proven conclusive, and they still didn't know what chemicals to look for.

John Smith made a policy of not contacting the federal investigators working on the case—"Let them do their own jobs," he said. But when he saw videos of Diva's puppies dying, he forwarded them to the EPA criminal division and called Jason Burgess. He asked Burgess to spell out the difference between what had occurred at the Yeager site and the situation in Flint, Michigan, where by early 2016 protesters were carrying signs that read WATER IS A HUMAN RIGHT. To Smith's thinking, the two cases bore marked similarities. The story in Flint involved a government cover-up as well as lead poisoning. Why was the EPA willing to move on Flint and not in Washington County?

The difference was public versus private water. If there had been forty houses below that leaking pond, and if Stacey, Beth, and Buzz relied on public water, which, unlike their private wells, was subject to regulation, then they'd have a winning criminal case. As it stood, the investigation hadn't been closed, yet by the time 2016 began, Smith surmised it wasn't moving forward. He knew that investigators had summoned Carla Suszkowski to Pittsburgh for an interview. She'd flown up from Texas, where she now lived and worked for Southwestern Energy. The statute of limitations on any violations she might have committed at the Yeager site was approaching. If the federal government didn't bring charges against her soon, it would be too late.

To the Smiths it seemed clear that all of Burgess's promises to their clients—his talk of handing over his gun and his badge—were going to be for naught. Kendra felt that speaking to him any further was a waste of her time. But Burgess had cause to be frustrated also. What looked to Kendra like a slam dunk in her civil arena was in fact much harder to prove as a federal environmental crime.

Beth wasn't going to let the federal investigators fade away so easily. She suspected she knew what had killed Diva and her puppies: some unknown chemical remaining in the waters of Tributary Number

Four. The stream was fed by the Yeagers' springs, and there was no dispute that Range's actions had contaminated them.

To keep her dogs safe, Beth had been giving them bottled water for more than a year, but it never occurred to her that the little stream flowing behind her house might be dangerous. Now she wondered if Tributary Number Four was contaminated and whether Diva had splashed around in something, then passed that on when she nursed the puppies. Beth wanted answers, and she wanted to know why the EPA hadn't made a single indictment in their case. For months, she'd been calling Jason Burgess once a week to leave messages. In June 2016, she called the office of Nelson Cohen, the assistant U.S. attorney who'd been assigned to their case, and demanded to find out what had happened. She also left a message for Samantha Bell, an FBI analyst. Together, Cohen and Bell called her back. Beth had questions written down for the conference call: *What about the labs altering test results? Isn't that conspiracy and fraud? What's happening with your investigation into Carla Suszkowski?* Beth found Cohen's answers frustratingly vague. About all he would say clearly was that the investigation was still ongoing. Beth didn't believe him. She knew enough by now about the laws regarding water to know that Tributary Number Four belonged to all the citizens of Pennsylvania. That's what it meant to be a water of the commonwealth. Even if their private wells weren't subject to regulation, polluting the stream should count as a violation of the law. But her argument didn't seem to make any difference. After the call, she phoned Stacey to commiserate.

Stacey was finished with the federal government. She was also tired of waiting for the case to come to trial. She worried about the toll that living in limbo was taking on the kids. Emotionally, Paige seemed intact. Despite her troubles with school, she kept herself busy playing lacrosse, raising her 4-H pig, and planting flocks of plastic flamingos in people's yards to raise money for a local boy with cancer. Informal fund-raisers were common in Amity. When people were hit with high medical bills that insurance didn't cover, neighbors often hosted spaghetti or pancake dinners to help out. Stacey was more and more concerned about Harley growing older down in the basement. Thanks to cyber school, he'd finished eleventh grade virtually, without leaving his room, then returned to Trinity for twelfth, walking across an actual stage to get his diploma that past June. Triumphant about his graduation, she sent out photo announcements: four pictures of Harley Austin Haney leaning against pickups, riding a four-wheeler, standing against a weathered barn.

For work, Harley was running the lawn care business he'd taken over from Cousin Mike. He'd renamed it Harley's Lawn and Tree Service, LLC. The work was physically challenging and he was feeling up to it. He'd even gotten insurance to do high tree work, which involved dangling from a trunk with a live chainsaw. That was his favorite part; the rest bored him a bit, and the money was terrible, since he had to pay two young boys he'd hired as summer helpers before he paid himself.

He'd like to do something else, but what? Getting a job with FedEx or UPS would be ideal, since those jobs came with benefits, but they were nearly impossible to procure. Coal miners made a great living, but mining jobs were even harder to get. Other than yard work, that left little else but installing gas pipeline or working in the gas fields, which he didn't want to do. He'd tired of hearing people say, "You should just go get a job with the gas wells!" and "Oh, the gas wells are paying pretty good." It was annoying but it wasn't their fault, he said. "Yeah, a lot of the kids I know will end up with the gas wells. It's not that they want to, it's just what's going to end up happening." They were the only jobs. Harley didn't talk much to his handful of friends about the lawsuit. "About all my friends will say, 'That's still going on?' I say, 'Yeah, we're still dealing with it every day.'"

Harley turned most to his girlfriend, Ciarra. She was from Washington, and her family was better-off, solidly middle-class. She'd known Harley since middle school, but not well. "I never really talked to

Harley in middle school," she said. "I just knew him as the sick kid in school and he was never there." In high school, they'd friended each other on Snapchat and now they were inseparable—at least until Ciarra went to college at the University of Pittsburgh that fall to study international business. Harley wasn't pleased about her leaving. "One of the hardest parts is his trust issues," Ciarra told me. "He doesn't want to go anywhere and he thinks that things are being hidden from him."

For Harley, now that he'd graduated, whatever anyone wanted to say about his life, they could keep to themselves. This included his pot-smoking. "Everyone smokes weed," he told me, irritated that I still asked. "Even country songs talk about smoking weed."

Although Stacey didn't like Harley's smoking marijuana, she'd seen far worse at the hospital and elsewhere in Washington County. A few months after Harley graduated, during the 2015 fair, eighteen people in Washington County overdosed on opioids and three died. Stacey wasn't sure of the cause of the crisis; likely there wasn't just one. She kept hearing different things: doctors were writing scripts too easily; Washington was so near major highways that it was a convenient place for dealers; out-of-town oil and gas workers either brought in drugs themselves or created a market for dealers.

Drug-related deaths in Pennsylvania spiked by 23 percent, with some of the highest rates occurring in Washington County. Inmates from Washington County Jail and from the federal prison inflicted horrible pain upon their bodies in order to get medication. They'd taken to swallowing things and inserting objects into every possible orifice. Toothbrushes, hunks of mattress, and whole apples—the hospital had spent hundreds of thousands of dollars fishing them out of esophagi, stomachs, and rectums. But the prisoners kept hurting themselves, hoping for fentanyl, despite orders to doctors not to give it. Stacey had learned to be tough with addicts; she wasn't going to be part of the problem of too-easy access to medication.

"These are God's ways of telling me, Stacey, you've had enough," she told me. Through with emergency nursing, she learned there was an administrative position opening for which she might be qualified. As a quality assurance nurse analyst, she'd serve as a kind of ombudsman, making sure patients received a high standard of care. Becoming a watchdog appealed to her.

"This is a really big promotion, but you know what? I've put in twenty years," she said. She got it. The job's hours ran from 7:00 a.m. to 3:30 p.m., Monday to Friday. Working forty hours, she'd be making as much as she did as a nurse working forty-five to sixty hours.

One day before she left the ward for good, Stacey received a text message from Linda. Cousin Davy Hull was going to be on TV again. Recently paroled after serving seven years of his twelve-year sentence, he was appearing on *Dr. Phil*. Still on probation and unable to leave Kentucky, Hull joined the show by satellite. Stacey switched on the TV and stood among her fellow nurses to watch. The KKK leader's twenty-year-old daughter, Peyton, had recently had a baby with an African American man, and Hull refused to acknowledge the child or the fact that he was a baby: "One drop of nonwhite blood, it ceases to be human," he said.

Peyton told Dr. Phil that growing up, she hadn't really understood who her father was. "All I knew of the cross burnings was I just thought it was pretty, you know, like a big candle," she said.

Then Hull preached to Dr. Phil about the biblical sanctity of the Aryan race and furnished pictures of himself brandishing a pistol in front of a Confederate flag. Stacey and her colleagues couldn't believe he was allowed to say some of those things on TV.

By the summer of 2016, Trump fever was raging through Washington County. It bred strong feelings on both sides. One local high school teacher found himself under fire from parents for asking students wearing Trump gear to leave his classroom. But such opposition to the Make America Great Again moment was rare. Given its history of energy extraction, Washington was one of the places where Trump's promises of reviving coal and bolstering the natural gas industry against attack by federal regulators were particularly resonant.

David Wayne Hull also supported Trump. Hull, like Stacey, had grown up amid the industrial collapse of the eighties. "I would've pulled out two of my back teeth to get a mill job," he told me over the phone. But there was no such job to be had. This was why he said he stood behind Donald Trump, attending rallies to drum up votes. "He wants to give white men jobs and we want to work," he told me. Still, Hull preferred Putin to Trump, calling him "a man's man—he rides black bears for God's sake, swims in ice water. If he spoke English I could hang out with him."

In Amity, Trump's antipathy toward the EPA was popular, along with his promise to cut the federal agency's budget by $2.6 billion. Beth Voyles welcomed Trump's message. Given her feeling that the federal agency had abandoned them, she cheered the gutting of the EPA. She was less sure about his silence on other protections for the environment, and emailed the Trump campaign numerous times to ask for specific positions on air and water, but no one responded. She decided to vote for him anyway, as did John Voyles. That fall would mark the first time in his life that he'd voted. Later, she came to regret her decision. "Unfortunately I did bite as always with not good choices," she told me.

Stacey didn't buy the Trump craze from the start. Although she'd watched federal regulation fail her family, that didn't mean she believed in obliterating the EPA. She was even more skeptical about his belief that fracking could save Appalachia. "I think probably no other business has been affected by regulation more than your business," he told oil and gas employees. "Federal regulations remain a major restriction to shale production." When she heard his empty messaging—"The shale energy revolution will unleash massive wealth" in America— she scoffed. He was just one more politician pandering to those with the deepest pockets.

But Stacey was no fan of Hillary Clinton's either. Stacey thought she was corrupt, and when it came to fracking, she was just as bad as Trump, if not as vocal. So Stacey decided that come November, she'd vote for the Green Party candidate, Jill Stein. Stein was farther to the left than anyone Stacey had voted for in her life, but one of Stein's slogans was "Protect Mother Earth," and Stacey decided she'd support her for that saying alone. She would be one of 16 people out of 1,861 voters in Amity's township of Amwell to vote for Stein. Trump carried 1,336.

Outside the goat barn, Harley glanced around uneasily as he waited for Paige to clip Cashew onto a lead. "Coming to the fair drives me crazy now," he told me. We were standing a few hundred yards uphill from Cowley's lemonade stand. The scent of funnel cake was mixed with diesel. At twenty, he'd finally aged out of competition, and he was glad of it. His anxiety spiked in social situations, and none more so than the Washington County Fair. On this August evening, among pithy T-shirts like HILLARY FOR PRISON, FARM-RAISED, and LIFE IS BETTER IN THE COUNTRY, all around him there were royal-blue and white baseball hats, shirts, and banners emblazoned with the Range Resources logo. Even the mini water bottles that a girl was handing out read "Range Resources," and that struck Harley as ironic: Range handing out clean drinking water.

"I don't even want to go walk around. I feel like everyone is looking at me, judging me," he said. "Everyone has something to say." But no one said anything. He no longer felt like part of the community he was raised in, and that was hardest for Stacey, since a sense of belonging was one of the few advantages she'd thought she could give her kids. For Harley, however, it wasn't all bad to be able to see beneath the surface of things. "It matures you faster," he said.

"Grow up and realize what's going on in the real world. The whole Range Resources deal. It pretty much ran my life, having to move so many times. We don't talk to Mr. Yeager now, period. I saw him at a dinner one time and I didn't even like being at the same church dinner."

Stacey still remembered the night at Rinky Dinks a few years back when Toby Rice, the CEO of Rice Energy, talked to her about "a black mark" hanging over Harley. Stacey still felt it. "We didn't do anything wrong, but we feel like nobody likes us because we're not on the same bandwagon with everyone else," she said. "It's worse at the fair because so many fair people are gas well people." She was right. The gas money had helped save many small farms, paying for much-needed equipment and barns like the one Stacey herself had wanted. She was also correct that the black mark still hung heavily over the family, perhaps even more so with the lawsuit dragging on and, with it, their claims of sickness. Over the past five years, Rice's attitude about Stacey and the kids had changed as well. Standing in the arena's sawdust, bidding on animals, Rice now doubted that Harley had been poisoned by gas production. He thought that Stacey was out for a payday. "Everyone who complains isn't making any money," he told me. It was always the small landowners who had trouble, like Stacey, never the larger ones, like Ray Day. It all boiled down to dollars. Soon Rice would sell his company to a competitor, EQT, for a reported $6.7 billion.

A Rice Energy ice cream truck sat in a large barn nearby. Shows of corporate largesse were everywhere, and over the past decade, Range had raised $1 million for the fair. "It's kind of the Super Bowl for them, right?" Mike Mackin, the soft-spoken Range spokesman, asked me later. It wasn't just good PR, he went on. "We're talking about the future of this region and the future potentially of our workforce," he said. A new generation of jobs would go a long way here, and he was especially proud that amid the recent downturn in the price of natural gas, accompanied by a precipitous drop in drilling activity and revenue, Range hadn't cut back on its presence at the fair or corporate giving. Beyond the fair, Range Resources had helped to raise $10 million for the communities where it operated. That money, donated through events like golf tournaments, clay shoots, and chili cook-offs, sustained the United Way of Washington County, supporting, in turn, CASA for Kids, Inc., which helped abused children; Domestic

Violence Services for Southwestern Pennsylvania; the Washington Health Systems Children's Therapy Center; and the Greater Washington County Food Bank. Range Resources was the largest donor to hunger-related causes in the county. Since 2011, the company had also paid more than $3 million in impact fees to Amity's township and spent nearly $3.3 million on roads and infrastructure there. No matter what the long-term burden of abandoned wells and other public costs would prove to be, these were sizable contributions; one township supervisor, Wayne Montgomery, called them "a godsend."

To Harley, all of the above was blood money. "I hate them for what they did," he said. Range's seeming support for farming and agriculture was nothing but hypocrisy. Look what they'd done to their animals. Lately, he'd been constantly scolding Paige about how little care she took of her goats and pigs. Paige was staying overnight in her grandparents' camper for the week on her own for the first time, managing Cashew and a pig named Ohmar. With Paige alone at the fair, Harley grew fearful for her. The past five years had bonded them closely in good ways and bad. Harley was crazily overprotective, wanting to keep her safe from the world that had hurt him so. Stacey had had enough of his temper, which was often directed at her shortcomings, especially when they'd been at the fair, where farm families were put under the microscope—everyone could see who had ribbons and bows, rhinestone-studded cowboy boots and belts, who was doing a better job at raising kids country.

"You know, Har, I'm the only single mom up there," she said. "After everything we've gone through, I think I've done pretty well."

Chris and Stacey were still engaged and still putting off the wedding. Stacey felt she couldn't handle the expense, or the emotions, in the midst of the ongoing suit. Waiting was hard for Chris. He wanted their life together to officially start, and frankly it felt weird to him that he wanted to get married while Stacey didn't. They'd been engaged so long now. Chris was proving to be as stalwart as he was quiet. He was coming that evening to the fair with Linda and Pappy to watch Paige and Cashew walk in the goat sale. When they arrived, Linda called Stacey, who was standing outside the goat barn with Harley and Paige, a few steps from the lemonade stand. As she took the call, Stacey waved at Beth Voyles, who was coming down the hill toward the exact same spot where, six years earlier, she'd told Stacey that Cummins was dead. Beth was wheezing fiercely. She'd been diagnosed with asthma, as had her dog Diesel. He'd had an allergic reaction to the albuterol used to treat asthma and died. Although it was the medication rather than the asthma that killed Diesel, Beth blamed Range for the underlying cause. Dogs didn't get asthma. Now she was also having trouble with her heart.

"I have to have a heart catheterization," she told Stacey. "There's some kind of bundle in my heart."

"Oh, that's okay," Stacey reassured her. "Lots of people have bundles. It's just a block."

That afternoon one of the defendants in *Haney v. Range* had called to talk about settlement. Five, in all, had initiated discussions, but the figures they'd offered were low, so talks had gone nowhere. And settlement, in general, was like a game of chicken: no one wanted to flinch first. These conversations were also highly confidential. John had admonished Stacey and Beth to talk to no one outside their families about settlement. If it got out that defendants were willing to offer money, it would make them look guilty. That's why if they ended up going to trial, settlement talks couldn't be used in court: they were potentially prejudicial to the defendants, and their disclosure could also harm the plaintiffs if it shut down their prospect of settlement.

Over the past four years, *Haney v. Range*, which began with seventeen defendants, including two water-testing labs and two individuals, had passed through the hands of three judges. In the endless shuffling the case seemed doomed to undergo, it would soon circle back to the judge who'd first heard it. From the start, several defendants had attempted to get out of the suit by arguing that in Pennsylvania, under the terms of strict liability, they bore no responsibility to Stacey, Beth, Buzz, or their families. This was the argument Halliburton and others had advanced during preliminary objections.

In 2012, that argument hadn't won over the first judge to hear it, Debbie O'Dell Seneca. She'd found that even if the families were not the intended endusers of their products, the companies did bear a responsibility to them. In 2016, the third judge assigned to the case, William Nalitz, reversed O'Dell Seneca's earlier decision. He allowed several defendants out of the case—including a chemical manufacturer and one of the two testing laboratories. The other testing laboratory had succeeded in getting out of the case too, but on different grounds. The suit alleged that the company, Test America, had committed conspiracy and fraud by allowing Range to alter test results through its computer system. To support this claim, Kendra argued that in Test America's user manual, there was a section called "Hiding Results" that walked a user through how to do exactly that. This, along with the fact that Range was paying Test America's legal bills under an indemnity clause, Kendra argued, was enough to demonstrate that Test America had committed both fraud and conspiracy. But Judge Nalitz found otherwise, ruling that neither of these charges applied, so Test America was soon out of the case as well. So were the two engineers included in the original complaint—Scott Rusmisel, who'd designed most of the site, and Carla Suszkowski. Both had been released from the case on the grounds that their respective employers bore responsibility for any possible misdeeds.

It was disappointing to Stacey and Beth to watch the number of defendants shrink from seventeen to eleven. Range and ten other defendants remained. They worried that this exodus didn't bode well for their case and that momentum might falter even as Range weathered a local scandal that spring. A Range executive named Terry Bossert had been caught at a large meeting saying that Range avoided drilling near "big houses," where wealthier people might be able to challenge their practices. Two environmental organizations were present, and they went directly to the state's Office of Environmental Justice to demand an investigation. Bossert apologized and said he'd been making a joke.

At the time, Range was facing its largest fine to date: $8.95 million for contaminating water with methane near Williamsport, Pennsylvania. But soon afterward, the case took an odd turn. John Quigley, the DEP secretary who'd levied the fine, was fired and escorted out of the Rachel Carson building after he'd sent an expletive-laden email out to environmental groups, berating them for their lack of support amid all the pressure he felt from industry. The next day, Quigley learned the state of Pennsylvania rescinded the impending fine against Range Resources, which he discovered by reading the newspaper. The governor's office claimed that the reversal had been in the works for months and that Quigley had in fact been briefed about it. For Quigley, it was the final straw in a long and maddening fight against the power of the oil and gas industry. "When you finally see in its full flower how corrupt the world of the DEP actually is, it's nauseating," he told me.

Yet these small skirmishes in Pennsylvania meant little on Wall Street, where Range was facing more significant challenges. Range's stock price had plummeted from its high of ninety-three dollars a share in 2014 to a low of seventeen dollars. Most of that collapse was sector-wide: natural gas was under pressure from fracking's own success. Thanks to technology and to warmer winters, there was a gas glut in the Northeast. Range had once been able to corner the Marcellus because their wells were so productive and their drilling costs low. But so many wells had come online so fast, there was now more gas than anyone knew what to do with, and that drove down profits.

Beth and Stacey didn't think much about Wall Street. They thought about their case, and they wanted it to end. Since it kept dragging on with delayed trial dates and appeals stretching on indefinitely, *Haney v. Range* looked more and more likely to settle out of court. Harley had no idea what settling entailed.

"Will the FBI and the EPA keep investigating if we settle?" Harley asked.

"They will no matter what," Stacey reassured him. Stacey didn't tell him that the FBI and EPA seemed to have vanished. Harley still hoped the cavalry was coming, and Stacey saw no reason to dash that hope too. Instead, she reminded Harley and Paige of the Pennsylvania Supreme Court victory. Their family had helped make that possible, she said.

"With Act 13, we know they will never be able to do what they did to us to anyone else."

Over the loudspeaker, the fair announcer called Paige's number, fifty-nine. Wearing her rhinestone belt and her holey pig socks, Paige led Cashew up to the show barn. Beth Voyles went to find John in the bleachers, where Chris, Linda, and Pappy waited for Paige to enter the ring with Cashew.

Sitting on the cold steel bench, having eschewed the giveaway Range Resources seat cushions, Pappy was in a terrific mood. For the seventh time in the past eight years, his butternuts had won first place. He'd also recently received two small and unexpected windfalls. First, after decades of disturbing dreams and health concerns, he'd been awarded compensation from the U.S. government for his exposure to Agent Orange. And he was now making money off the gas boom: he'd recently signed a mineral lease. Between the two sources of income, the Hillberrys were doing better financially than they ever had. "It's much more money than we had when we were working," Linda said. "It's more than we've had in our life."

Pappy had often groused about the loss of his family farm to the coal company, which had bought the property years ago. Now it turned out that although Pappy didn't own the land, he still, without realizing it, owned a portion of his mineral rights. Toby Rice had leased his land for about ten thousand dollars, then swapped the lease, which was now held by Range. Although Pappy loathed Range, he focused on what he could do for others with the money. He could be generous with his grandkids in a way he'd never been able to be with Stacey and Shelly. He and Linda loaned Shelly's son Judd money to buy his first truck. Judd needed to drive to his new job as a contractor installing natural gas pipelines in residential neighborhoods. They also loaned Harley twenty-five hundred dollars to buy a trailer to haul the mowers for Harley's Lawn and Tree Service. Yard work looked like Harley's most plausible future. It was an uncertain career path that Stacey didn't love, but she didn't know where else to steer him. Most days, Harley woke early, went to work, came home, and stayed in the basement.

Linda and Pappy wished Harley's life was turning out differently, and although they, like Shelly, didn't doubt that he'd gotten sick on account of the gas wells, they too wanted Stacey to stop allowing the case to hijack her future, as well as that of the kids. Her family's desire for Stacey to move on made her feel maligned, misunderstood as she'd been as a child. It brought up more of that same feeling that she was alone in a fight against everyone else in the world, beginning with her own family. These old wounds opened some nights during screaming phone calls between sisters.

Yet, under the happier exterior of the fair, these raw places remained invisible. Despite Harley's reluctance for the family to be there, 2016 was shaping up to be a good year for Paige. Her goat, Cashew, won second place, and her best friend's dad bought her for four dollars a pound. Stacey noticed that neither Toby Rice nor Range Resources placed a bid. In the show barn, the announcer said fairgoers should thank anyone wearing a shirt with a Range logo. This year the company was doubling its donation to every child involved in 4-H from one hundred to two hundred dollars. Every year, the donation arrived by check following the fair. And every year, Stacey bought thank-you notes for the kids to send to Range. In 2016, as a simpering fuck-you, she chose cards ringed with purple violets that said, *What a wonderful world this would be . . . if everyone was as nice as you.*

After the fair, Chris decided that Stacey needed to get away. Still broke, they could afford only an hour's drive east over the Pennsylvania border to Friendsville, Maryland. That weekend in September, the weather was terrible, the rain constant, and hiking proved impossible. As Chris drove them around the countryside, Stacey watched the rolling, deep jade hills, which reminded her of Amity and Prosperity. Through the rain-smeared window, she kept seeing signs that read DON'T FRACK MARYLAND and wondered what was afoot. When they stopped for breakfast, Stacey went searching the rack of pamphlets for something they could do on a rainy Saturday. She spied a brochure for a local winery called Deep Creek Cellars. She checked Google Maps. It was only seventeen minutes away. When Stacey called to make sure it was open, the owner, Nadine Grabania, glanced at the caller ID before answering. She saw the name STACEY HANEY but thought little of it. There must be lots of people with that name. She told Stacey that Deep Creek opened at eleven and asked if she was part of a group. No, Stacey said, just a couple.

In the basement tasting room, paneled with blond wood, Nadine and her husband, Paul, had tried to keep the feel as humble and mom-and-pop as possible. Paul's idea was to hang a shingle out front like small wine producers did in Italy. They were the only winery in the area, and their aim was to be friendly and unpretentious. As she wandered around the tasting room, Stacey spied information sheets on a table about Pennsylvania's air and water quality and the effects of fracking.

She told Grabania she was really glad to see them. She was from

Pennsylvania, and she and her kids had gotten into a big mess with a drilling company. They'd lost their animals, their water. Their air was contaminated and they'd had to leave their house about three years earlier.

The vintner was quiet for a minute. Are you Stacey Haney? she asked. Stacey started to sob. I didn't mean to upset you, Grabania said gently. She came out from behind the wooden counter and put her arms around Stacey. She said she knew everything about Stacey and her kids. Everyone in Friendsville did. For the past six years, Grabania had been reading everything she could about fracking. Back in 2010, a leasing boom had scared her and some of her neighbors into trying to get involved in the issue. "We became instant activists," she told me later. Grabania was born in Washington County and grew up along Ten Mile Creek. After reading Stacey's story five years earlier, she'd decided to help lead the effort to place a moratorium on drilling until the state could determine whether or not fracking posed "unacceptable risks." Now the moratorium was about to expire, and the state faced a fight: whether to drill or ban fracking outright. Your story has helped us a lot here, Grabania said. She insisted on giving Stacey two bottles of wine, which made Stacey uncomfortable.

Stacey didn't want people giving her things; accepting charity wasn't the way she was raised. Back in the truck, Chris could see she was embarrassed by the gift. He teased her, Why don't we see if we can use your celebrity for more free wine? She laughed. From the truck, she called the kids to tell them what had happened. It was one more sign that what they'd lived through had some greater purpose. She felt that God had sent her there more for Nadine Grabania's benefit than her own. "Maybe she needed to see that we're real people," she told me.

EPILOGUE: WHITE HATS

When Maryland banned fracking in 2017, Stacey celebrated quietly. It might be too late for Amity and even for Pennsylvania, but not for other states. In addition to New York and Maryland's decisions not to frack, four out of Canada's ten provinces had bans in place. France and Germany were also rejecting fracking out of concerns over large-scale industrial problems—the trucks, leaks, and spills at the surface—occurring next door to people's homes and farms. The global pushback against fracking called into question the notion that natural gas must serve as a necessary "bridge fuel" between coal and renewables. Europe was proving it possible to jump over the bridge. The advance of technology was such that a growing number of countries were able to run their power grids for more and more hours of the day on wind and solar power. Even China was moving slowly on fracking. In the global energy market, much of the fastest growth was happening in renewables; even investors who cared nothing about the environment were betting on renewables, because that's where the action was.

Stacey felt relieved and also proud when news of fracking bans reached her. She imagined herself in the middle of a worldwide fight between good and evil. It was how she made sense of the world: to place herself at the center of things and believe that her story was helping to change things far away, since closer to home their future was bleak.

Settlement talks had collapsed; the sides were too far apart to find a way forward. In the Washington County Court of Common Pleas, the case seemed to be going nowhere. After waiting for more than a year to argue in front of Judge Nalitz, the Smiths petitioned the court for a new judge, and the case was reassigned, to Katherine Emery, president judge of the Washington County Court of Common Pleas. Judge Emery wanted both sides to attempt mediation.

The Smiths urged the Haneys and Voyles to move on with their lives as best they could while struggling to do so themselves. One Saturday morning in October 2017, after Kendra finished coaching an early soccer game, she and John sat at the granite-topped farm table in their kitchen taking stock of the enormous and unexpected costs this case had entailed. It was turning out to be more personal than they'd imagined. The Smiths had received threatening letters sent to their home. They pulled one out to show me. It was typed on a tiny piece of paper and read "I pronounce a curse on you, mouthpiece of satan, in the name of Lord Jesus Christ." The Smiths had never told the kids about the letters.

At one end of the table sat a fat white Haney binder full of test results, which Kendra had been reading late the night before. They were still working the case seven days a week. Outwardly, they were putting on a stoic face, but inwardly they were flagging. The need to support each other bound them together. Although their marriage had always been strong, it was now stronger than ever.

"People ask me how I can work with my husband so closely," Kendra said. "But the truth is, I don't know how we'd do it any other way." What other partner would understand why she could never put down a document and have a glass of wine or talk? She had to keep going. John Smith, usually unflappable, wasn't sleeping, which he didn't like to admit.

"No one sees the toll," Kendra said, referring delicately to John. He was still mirthful and fun, ever positive, but the glint in his eye was clouded by worry. He didn't want to dwell on his insomnia, however, and was still quick to point out advantages. They'd learned more about new areas of the law than they could've imagined needing to use six years ago.

"We're better lawyers because of this," he added. For Kendra, the hardest thing to accept continued to be Buzz's lack of clean water. The only thing she could get Stacey, Beth, and the kids was money. And money would never make them "whole," in legal parlance. She'd been at this for too many decades not to know that money was never the cure-all people imagined it to be. Water was something different. To Kendra, the right to clean water was about one of the most basic rights an American should have.

"You hear about this in third-world countries, but when someone comes to you and says, 'Here's my basic necessity in life. Can you get it for me?' I couldn't help someone get something I take for granted every day. How is that even possible in the United States?"

The Smiths had taken their challenge against the DEP all the way to the state supreme court, which ultimately refused to hear Buzz's case. Tom Shepstone, the pro-fracking blogger who'd followed the case for *Energy in Depth*, wrote on his new blog, *Natural Gas Now*:

Loren [Buzz] Kiskadden, the junkyard plaintiff from Southwestern Pennsylvania, the serial litigator used by some trial lawyers and the fractivist special interests as a poster child for their cause has finally lost for good . . . The Environmental Hearing Board, the Commonwealth Court, and now the Pennsylvania Supreme Court, all looked at the evidence and concluded Loren Kiskadden had no case. It's over. Range Resources won and fractivism lost "bigly" as some New Yorkers say.

Kendra also worried about the precedent their failure set. "Never again will a poor person like Buzz be able to challenge the DEP," she said.

Under state order, the waste pond had been closed, along with the drill cuttings pit. Yet, as Beth stayed put on Justa Breeze, her health problems continued. On May 17, 2017, Beth made a trip to the Washington Hospital emergency room, where she was diagnosed with chemical burns on her cheeks and in her nose and throat. Range denied that anything unusual was happening up at the site, but Beth had the blisters to prove exposure. The ER doctor at Washington Hospital had put her diagnosis in writing and instructed Beth that she couldn't return home until the DEP checked that it was safe, so now she was occupying a park bench. "I'm fucked up the ass with no Vaseline and against my will and I'm not a happy camper right now," Beth told me as she sat in Washington Park with nowhere to go. She'd just called John Smith and threatened to go up to the Washington County Courthouse and stand out in front yelling about what Range had done to her.

"I don't care if I go to jail," she told me. "At least I'll have clean air to breathe."

John Smith calmed her down, and she went to the Kopper Kettle instead. This time, however, Beth and her family weren't the only ones to experience the fumes. A new neighbor, Rick Loar, had bought an old abandoned farm across McAdams Road from their home and just next to the Garretts'. A thirty-nine-year-old wireliner who mapped preexisting wells at fracking sites, he now lived there with his nine-year-old daughter. He'd paid only $10,000 for a property estimated to be worth $150,000. The old couple who'd owned the place had passed away. At first, he'd thought that the surviving family didn't want to be bothered with cleaning out the house, but now he wondered if the gas wells had driven them off. On the day Beth ended up in the hospital, Loar smelled the chemicals and saw the trucks before the Voyles did. He came down with a horrible headache and burning eyes and throat. He thought he recognized what he was smelling; he'd worked at remediation sites cleaning up after this smell for more than a decade. To him, it smelled like pit gas, which could indicate there had been some kind of release at the site, where there were now three active wells. "It's pretty nasty stuff. It's basi-

cally all the carcinogens of oil and fluid all mixed in," he told me. Beth
had said the overwhelming smell was that of electric poles treated
with creosote, a preservative that can be derived from either coal
or shale. Loar had looked out his window and watched triaxle trucks,
what Beth called "Dumpster trucks," heading up the access road.
From his window, he could see inside: they were carrying fresh gravel.
Later, however, one triaxle headed back down McAdams. Covered
with a tarp, it was leaking something oily that stained the road. "You
only go to that kind of effort to cover a truck with a tarp that fully if
there's something inside," he told me. Loar called Range. The company told him nothing had gone wrong; that truck was empty. When
I inquired, Range also sent me the DEP inspector's report that read
"At no time did I notice any kind of odor in the air resembling that of
creosote, any other industry associated odor or anything out of the
ordinary."

Six days later, Range Resources took me out to the Yeager site. At
9:00 a.m. I met two Range Resources employees, Mike Mackin and his
colleague Mark Windle, in the lobby of their Southpointe Headquarters.
Fox News was playing on a large flat-screen TV and the cafeteria,
run by a local outfit, the Hopewell Diner, was serving barbecue
chicken burritos for lunch. Two thousand seventeen marked Range's
ten-year anniversary in Southpointe, and the company celebrated by
placing paid articles in *The Observer-Reporter* that chronicled Range
employees sampling Lenten fare at local fish fries every Friday,
among other community activities. Everyone was wearing jeans for a
charity day. The friendly atmosphere reflected a softening in public
messaging. Matt Pitzarella was gone, and Mike Mackin, a quiet
father of two in his thirties who'd previously worked at the Heinz
History Center, had taken his place. In addition to handling reporters, Mackin worked with communities on their local drilling ordinances. Since Act 13 could no longer be used to override zoning,

Range had an incentive to keep each township as friendly to drilling as possible.

We donned hard hats and protective glasses before heading south on I-79 toward the Amity/Lone Pine exit in a gray, unmarked Jeep. Mackin and Windle were locals. In their thirties, both had grown up in the shadow of industrial collapse—"post steel," Windle called it. They were thoughtful young men: smart and looking forward to long careers in oil and gas, ideally at Range. Despite Range's dismal stock price, Mackin and Windle were optimistic about the company's future, and that of natural gas in general. For the first time in two years, Range had reported a quarterly profit that April. The hottest shale play was elsewhere now, down in Texas and Louisiana in the Permian Basin, where Range had recently spent $3.3 billion acquiring a Louisiana-based driller. Unlike the Marcellus, the Permian promised a ready market nearby, the Gulf's petrochemical belt, and the pipeline to reach it. Yet Range was late to the new play, and the Permian boom brought problems too: most operators in the Gulf were drilling for more lucrative oil. For them, the gas that flowed out of the ground wasn't valuable; it was nearly free. On Wall Street, although most analysts argued that natural gas was ready for a comeback, others, who were watching the growth of renewables, problems with pipelines, and a disappointing global gas market, weren't so sure.

To secure its future, Range was betting on ethane—used to make ethylene, for everything from antifreeze to plastics to ripening fruit. Ethane was a liquid cheap and easy to derive from natural gas, and Range was the first U.S. company to export ethane to Europe in a boat custom-built by the Chinese. An hour away, where Windle grew up in Beaver County, Shell was building a huge ethane cracker plant not far from Pittsburgh International Airport, which had also leased nine thousand acres to oil and gas. Appalachia was hoping to build similar plants elsewhere, to create a petrochemical belt of its own supplied by the natural gas of the Marcellus. Even though it wasn't open yet, the new plant was changing attitudes and fortunes in Beaver, Windle said.

"When I grew up, you were—my grandparents were teachers—you were either a teacher in my town, or you worked for US Air, or you worked for FirstEnergy down the street." Windle went on, "Things haven't changed there in twenty years, up until about a year ago when Shell started moving dirt. Just, you know, commerce—things have totally changed, the Chamber of Commerce out there has totally reshaped itself, so it's pretty exciting. Everyone is really excited." Windle's siblings were also employed by the industry. His sister was Range's in-house attorney, and his brother worked for the opposition research group FTI Consulting.

We passed the Lone Pine truck stop, which, in addition to the Subway franchise, was now home to Washington County's largest beer store—boasting five hundred brands on the banner tied to a chain-link fence in front of an RV graveyard. We took the back route past the Days' farm toward the Yeager site.

We'd agreed that day to talk about Range's current practices, and what had changed over the past few years. We got out of the Jeep and walked around the well pad. Then we stood knee-deep in the field of alfalfa where the frack pond once sat and peered over the edge of the hill and across the road to the barn roof at Justa Breeze. "It's no secret to you, we've had some challenges on this location," Mackin told me. "We've learned from these challenges, and we've developed a better way to practice."

The better way to practice involved abandoning drill cuttings pits, which had been decommissioned since 2011. With the downturn in natural gas prices, Range, like others, had found ways to cut drilling costs, which had the simultaneous advantage of reducing the well pad's surface footprint. Sand silos now stood vertically as opposed to horizontally so they took up less room, and instead of building new pads, Range returned to existing sites to drill more wells as technology allowed. Where there had been three or four, on average, per pad, there could be upward of a dozen.

Range now recycled 100 percent of its fracking wastewater by using it to frack again, Mackin said. Although that cut down dramatically on the withdrawal of water, there was still the problem of where to store the liquid between fracks. The company continued to operate impoundments in Washington County. But the liners Range now used were double the previous thickness. Instead of two layers of liner, Range now used five, placing clay and other protective soils between them. Range had finally adopted the long-discussed "closed loop" system, Mackin further told me, in which all kinds of waste—flowback, drilling muds, cuttings—were now stored in containers, not in open ponds. But that made no sense to me. He'd just said there were two open ponds in Washington County. That wasn't a closed loop as I understood it.

We drove on a few miles to an active site to watch a seventy-five-foot-high white Pioneer rig drill successive horizontals for four new wells. A Range Resources flag that read TOP DAWG fluttered from the roof of a trailer. Squat gray tanks belonging to Halliburton waited by the rig's base; inside them were the elements needed to shoot cement to seal the casing of the well. Nearby sat red Adler tanks filled with water to mix the cement for the casings. Mackin pointed out the berm that covered most of the site. If anything spilled, it spilled on that tarp and not on the ground, he stressed. That was a major change in itself.

Mark: "I can't speak to how other operators do things, but we've always just gone the Range way. The white hat guys . . . from the country western movies, doing things the right way."

Mike: "It's not outward-facing, necessarily, but internally, be the white hat guy, do the right thing. Even if things are—even if you're facing tough situations, you gotta do the right thing."

The white hat guys doing the right thing—I knew they believed it. Yet I knew that Beth, Stacey, their families, and the Smiths never would. It was nearly impossible to think how one small patch of earth could contain such disparate stories. Later that day, I stopped by the Voyles'. John was out on his tractor, a light beer in a cup holder, mowing the yard. "At least you know we're not crazy," he called, stopping the mower as I pulled in the driveway. "You saw the vapor, you smelled it." Beth came out of the house trailed by a boxer named Titan. She still had blisters on her face. "I've never had so much hate in my heart. We're not supposed to feel that way, but I do. There are so many people out there who know what's going on, but they're not affected so they don't care," she said. She was grateful, though, that her daughter was doing better. Ashley was working as a highway laborer pouring concrete for road crews, a difficult job that helped prepare her to become a heavy machine operator. Someday, she wanted to be able to drive a bulldozer, crane, and backhoe. The work would pay well, although it would take years of training. It was also something to look forward to.

"I'm tired of everything being so negative," Ashley told me. She still lived at home and ran a small horse training business out of her mom's barn. But the trouble with the gas wells in such a small community had left some of the same psychological scars on her that it had on Harley. "I'm worried about what the world thinks of me," she said. "I'm so quiet and bland. I'm boring. I'm down all the time." The sense of indignation that Beth and Stacey had focused outward in their ongoing battle, Ashley and Harley had turned inward upon themselves. "Instead of having the rage, it has just backed me down a hundred times worse," Ashley went on. Despite everything that had occurred up at the Yeagers' farm, she still hoped to build her own home close by. She'd spoken to Stacey about the possibility of buying her abandoned farm, and Stacey promised to consider it, although she didn't want Ashley bringing up kids in the contaminated house. But Ashley, like her mother, was hell-bent on staying on McAdams. She wasn't so scared of the air; what she feared for was their water. Ashley was hoping that as part of a settlement, the defendants would pay to run the city water line all the way to Justa Breeze, and to Stacey's. As a parting gift, Beth handed me a jar of the honey they'd been spinning the day before.

I drove on five miles to Mankey Lane and was sitting at the kitchen table when Paige came in from school with an envelope in hand. In a few days, she would graduate from high school. Gone was the gangly eleven-year-old, and in her stead sauntered a tawny teenager in ripped jeans and a skin-tight tank. She tossed the envelope on the table. In 2012, a teacher had had her write a letter to her future self. *Dear Paige*, it began, *Hey Cutie! How are you doing? How is the gas well situation?*

Five years later, there was still no answer, although the case's demands kept coming. Range's attorneys wanted to depose Linda and Pappy, as well as Stacey's ex, Larry. Stacey thought that the company wanted to see how they'd hold up as witnesses in a trial, and that was fine by her. Stacey believed that if they did have to go to trial, Range would lose. When a jury of her peers heard about Harley's trips to the ER, the altered test results, and the fact that she believed Range employees had lied to her face, telling her the water was safe to drink, the people of Washington County would side with her. All that righteous indignation didn't matter much, however. Stacey didn't want to go to trial. She wanted to settle. She couldn't take the stress, let alone the time away from work. A jury trial would last for weeks, maybe months. Stacey could never take all that time to attend, and her absence might hurt them. Even the family depositions were costing her time and emotional energy.

Mam did okay under oath, but Pappy railed against Range. During discovery, Range had gone so far as to subpoena Stacey's journals. She wasn't sure how the company even knew they existed. During Pappy's deposition, an attorney had read a passage in which she'd written of her feelings that her parents had never really been there for her. Pappy replied under oath that she'd been a difficult child. Afterward, Stacey scolded Pappy, telling him that Range could use his testimony against her. Pappy felt awful, but the truth was he'd said very little. Larry, on the other hand, was a greater concern. It had been ten years since he'd left in 2007, and he and Stacey didn't speak. He felt that she'd chased him out of Harley's and Paige's lives, and she felt he'd abandoned them. She had no idea what he'd say under oath, if he'd use a deposition to get back at her for ten years of acrimony. But he didn't. Stacey was right, he told Range's attorneys. When he'd lived at McAdams, the water had been pure, and as he'd watched his son sicken, albeit mostly from a distance, he too had believed that Harley was suffering from chemical exposure. For once, she grudgingly admitted that Larry had done the right thing.

Harley now understood that neither the FBI nor anyone else was coming to save them. He felt that the only way Range would have to truly pay was if there was negative publicity, and that required a trial. And since he was a named plaintiff in the suit, and now an adult, his vote mattered.

One afternoon, he fought over the issue with his mom. "Let everyone see what they've done," he said. Stacey was trying to support him while pushing the kids along in their lives. Like Stacey, Harley couldn't afford to sit in a courtroom for weeks, she told him. He'd lose his job. Harley had decided to give up on lawn care and go to work installing residential gas pipelines. There was a spot available on his cousin Judd's three-man crew, and he was taking it. Stacey was pleased. She wouldn't have to help run his business anymore or worry about his falling out of a tree.

"Harley, you have to move on," she told him.

"I'll never move on, Mom, they've ruined my life," he said. Ciarra sat next to him, holding his hand.

"Well, Paige and I are getting better and we need you to move on too," she said.

"I can get better, I am doing better," he said. "But that doesn't mean I will ever move on from this." Harley and Ciarra got up to head to the basement, where Ciarra now lived with Harley. They rarely emerged, except to eat late at night when everyone else was asleep. They left crumbs around, and Chris had taken to calling them "the mice." To spend more time with Harley, Ciarra had left the University of Pittsburgh and her degree in international business to come home and attend Washington & Jefferson, a liberal arts college. Because of

Harley, she was studying psychology now. She wanted to understand his anxiety and depression.

Stacey was filling blue Ball jars with baby's breath for centerpieces for Paige's graduation party. They were hosting the party at Cross Creek Park, where, after developing gas wells on the public land, Range had donated playground equipment and a handicapped-accessible dock.

While Stacey prepared for Paige's party, Harley went outside to rock on the weathered rocking bench next to the fire pit—the spot where he'd sat over the years as I asked him uncomfortable questions about his strained friendships and his pot-smoking. He seemed different now, more comfortable in his skin. He even looked me in the eye when I followed him out to ask how he was doing.

"Today was my last day of mowing," he said. "It's like I can feel the stress dropping off of me." He looked forward to getting out of the basement every day, to seeing other people, to watching the world change beyond the backyard and the county fair. The job came with benefits, and Harley was glad to have them. It also fit his moral code: this suburban gas line ran under towns and through populated places. "What they do has to be done," he said. But where country remained pure, he wasn't going to put a hand toward ruining it.

POSTSCRIPT

The following winter, on the evening of January 18, 2018, Beth cooked spaghetti and meatballs for Ashley and the dogs. She and John were too anxious to eat. Finally, after nearly six years, settlement talks in *Haney v. Range* were scheduled to begin. To prepare for the meeting with Range and the ten other remaining defendants, Beth had invited two friends to come pray with her. Together, the women read aloud from Luke 1:37—*For with God, nothing is impossible*—and called in to a prayer hotline. Afterward, for a few hours, Beth felt better. Then she sat on the leather couch in her basement to read the expert reports that Range had filed in the case. Their doctors maintained that neither Beth nor any of the other plaintiffs suffered from chemical exposure, which made Beth furious.

Whatever came of the talks, Beth feared being silenced. What if settlement required signing some kind of gag order? What if they weren't allowed to speak about what had happened to them? Confidentiality clauses are meant to protect all parties and aren't unusual in such settlements. But for Ashley also, the possibility of having to sign one was troubling.

"My dogs can't talk," she said, sitting on the floor next to her mom, a plate of spaghetti in her lap. "Neither can my horses. I'm the only one who can speak for what happened to them."

For Ashley, there was one bright spot in the potential settlement: Stacey had agreed that once it was over, she'd sell the abandoned farm to Ashley. It didn't matter anymore that it had been Stacey's great-grandfather's; Stacey wanted to be rid of it and would sell it for as little as possible since the house was unlivable and there was no running water. Ashley still wanted to draw a water line from Amity. But it turned out that wasn't going to be cheap. According to an engineer the Smiths hired as an expert, the cost of bringing city water to the Haneys', Kiskaddens', and Voyles' farms would be $1 million per home. Meanwhile Range's experts held that even if all the chemicals the plaintiffs alleged were actually in their water, the cost of treating the water would be only $11,000 to $13,000 per household. And furthermore, the plaintiffs' water was not atypical for Washington County. "All inorganic constituents are naturally occurring and have other possible sources," one expert wrote. The Environmental Hearing Board had confirmed this finding in *Kiskadden v. DEP.*

Buzz's defeat in court was likely to hurt all the plaintiffs. And two other more recent court decisions weighed against them. John Smith had lost his motion to challenge the definition of strict liability and argue that in Pennsylvania, bystanders like Stacey, Beth, and Buzz should be allowed to claim injury even if they weren't the intended "end users" of the products in question. Most important, the Court refused to sanction Range for not complying with a court order. The company never provided the plaintiffs with a definitive list of all chemicals used at the site. Range, Judge Kathleen Emery held, had tried hard enough to find out.

Stacey, like Beth, feared these decisions didn't bode well for settlement. She too was anxious about the upcoming talks. Each night that week leading up to the Friday meeting, Stacey struggled to sleep, and when she finally managed to nod off, she did odd things just as she had during the worst of her PTSD. One night, Chris woke to Stacey picking at his beard; another, she was swatting at his face.

"Should I wear a helmet tonight?" he asked her as they crawled into bed the night before the settlement talks began. She laughed. She didn't know what she'd do without Chris's humor. He was so good at gently poking at her, changing her mood. On the morning of January 19, when her alarm went off at 5:15 a.m., she wasn't sure she'd slept. She got up, put water on for tea, and ducked into the bathroom to shower in advance of the kids. Since their home on Mankey Lane had only a single bathroom, on days like this when they all had to leave the house at the same time, they followed a schedule. Paige would shower at 6:30 a.m. and Harley at 6:45 a.m.

No one wanted breakfast. Stacey didn't know what to expect, which made it impossible to prepare the kids for how events might unfold. To guard against disappointment, she explained that talks could last from five minutes to twelve hours, and still achieve nothing. If they did succeed in settling, whatever amount each family was awarded, the Smiths would take 33 percent from the adults and 25 percent from the children. "No matter what happens, we'll be okay," she told the kids that morning in the kitchen. Reaching a settlement would at least mean she and Chris could afford to get married.

"It'll be a destination wedding," Paige joked. "Alaska." She packed a plastic bag full of Pringles and beef jerky, along with a coloring book full of inspirational sayings. Stacey tucked a picture into her purse of Harley and Paige at eleven and eight, smiling and holding Phantom the rabbit between them. She wanted the judge to see who the kids were before all this mess began.

Harley was doing remarkably better. Ciarra was proving a loving and steadying influence, and Harley was excelling at work on the pipeline. He had the opportunity to train as an electrician. Still, on the verge of these talks, he was struggling mightily with anxiety. He'd been talking to his counselor for weeks about this day. She'd taught him a technique to ground himself that involved repeating to himself the sequence of his daily routine. On this morning, he'd wake up, brush his teeth, take a shower, and put on his best pair of dress jeans. He'd drink orange juice and leave the house with his mom and sister by 7:30. Then the list ended and the unknown began.

The talks were scheduled to begin in Southpointe at 8:30 a.m. They were taking place at the Smith Butz offices, and Stacey, Harley, and Paige were meeting Grace there, along with Beth, John, and

Ashley. Buzz was home sick. The seven would wait in a separate room while the mediator, Gary Caruso, a well-respected retired judge, tried to work out a deal between the defendants' attorneys and the Smiths. By days' end, they'd either reach an agreement or head to trial.

In the conference room at Smith Butz, John Smith negotiated alone. Kendra was in a hospital back in New Jersey caring for her ailing father. She stood by his hospital bed waiting to call in to the negotiations as needed throughout the day. At 9:30 that evening, after thirteen hours of talks, the parties managed to reach a settlement.

Although Stacey and Beth weren't allowed to discuss the terms of the agreement with anyone, the amount they received left both of them feeling angry and defeated. Yet settling, they recognized, also offered some relief. It was a chance to move on, whereas continuing to fight could have meant years more in court and endless appeals.

Stacey and the kids drove home from Southpointe in silence. She woke on Saturday, January 20, and didn't want to leave the house. Chris coaxed her with all of his fun-loving tricks—he took her out to throw beer bottles at signs along Amity Ridge Road, and down to the Anawanna club to register for a raffle. But she couldn't stop crying. In contrast, Harley was feeling a palpable relief. He put away a picture from Paige's coloring book—the single page he'd worked on for most of the previous day, which read *Don't Give Up*. He made a plan to go bowling with Paige and, that Saturday afternoon at 3:30, when Stacey wanted to crawl back into bed, he suggested they all go out to eat at the Kopper Kettle.

Stacey knew she had to keep moving, so she joined Harley, Ciarra, Paige, and Chris. They were midway through dinner when she spotted the Voyles coming through the door. She went over to speak to them. Beth rose to hug her. Holding each other, they refused to cry, and said nothing about the day before, out of fear of being overheard and accidentally violating the gag order.

When Chris finished his burger topped with onions and pierogis, he joined them. He brought along a scratch-off card, a lottery ticket he'd bought for ten dollars from the Kettle's vending machine. The families shared a tradition. One night at the Kettle several years earlier, Chris had borrowed John's penknife to scratch off just such a card and won four hundred dollars. On this Saturday night, Chris thought a small win might cheer them, but Beth didn't want to play. She wasn't feeling lucky, she said. The card was a dud.

Beth and John thanked Stacey for agreeing to sell her farm to Ashley. Stacey was happy to do it, she said, but she warned them again that the contamination from chemicals and mold had made the house unlivable. It would be dangerous for Ashley to have kids in there, she reminded Beth. Then there was the issue of water. Since there was no way that the Voyles could afford to run the line from Amity, Beth told Stacey that Ashley planned to rig up a system using gutters to catch storm water and fill a cistern.

It's how I grew up, Stacey thought to herself. But she didn't say anything to the Voyles. It was too sad to think that Ashley would become one of a new generation waiting for rain.

A NOTE ON SOURCES

This book was born in Nigeria in 2007 after a bridge collapsed. I was riding across a river on an empty oil drum thinking about Minneapolis, where the I-35W bridge had recently fallen into the Mississippi River, killing thirteen people. So many of the problems of collective poverty plaguing Africa and Asia were becoming more evident in America. I decided it was time to come home, to turn my attention to how we tell stories about systemic failings here in the United States.

In Nigeria, as elsewhere in the Global South, some of the poorest people in the world live on some of the most resource-rich land. Yet this phenomenon, sometimes called the Resource Curse, applies to America also. I wanted to examine how it applied—and how it didn't—to the new gas rush striking Appalachia. I wanted to tell a story about people who were paying—and getting paid—for America's energy, and to look at how that experience fed not only poverty but also a deeper sense of alienation.

Over the past seven years, beginning in March 2011, I traveled to Western Pennsylvania thirty-seven times to follow the stories of forty-five people involved in four intertwined court cases. The mystery of what was happening to Harley Haney and to his neighbors' animals began in 2009, nearly two years before I arrived, and I have relied on recollections of that period from those I've spoken with. In several cases, individuals involved declined to be interviewed, particularly those in active litigation. In these instances, and others, I've relied on public court documents, trial transcripts, affidavits, and depositions. These records include extensive statements and testimony from Range Resources' current and former employees, chemical manufacturers, waste haulers, fracking companies, tracer companies, liner manufacturers, and laboratory technicians, as well as officials at the Pennsylvania Department of Environmental Protection. In the text of the book, I have used direct quotation marks only when I was present and recorded what was said or when the material came from court depositions, hearings, or trials.

The Smiths' case *Haney v. Range* was filed in May 2012. The initial complaint was 182 pages with 1,734 pages of exhibits. These included incident reports, trucking manifests, site plans, internal emails, construction documents, news sources, personal journals, professional field notes, water test results, medical records, aerial photographs, and state-issued notices of violation. Over the past five years, through the discovery process, this public record has expanded greatly and could now fill a room.

In addition, my reporting has included extensive interviews with confidential governmental and corporate sources, energy analysts, specialists in regional history, experts in exposure-related illnesses, and specialists in state and federal law.

In Amity and Prosperity, in order to gather perspectives beyond the primary characters with whom I regularly communicated, I attended and listened to proceedings at town meetings, county and state fairs, church services, the covered bridge festival, and court hearings. Some of these gatherings were highly contentious, as reasonable and intelligent people disagreed passionately over what was best for their town, for the country, and for the earth.

Five years into my reporting, just over 60 percent of voters in Washington County cast their ballots for Donald Trump. Reporters flooded rural America to profile the Trump voter, an enterprise that risked reducing sophisticated points of view to sound bites and missing the larger story of a complex American landscape. This is the story of those Americans who've wrestled with the price their communities have long paid so the rest of us can plug in our phones.

Some feel that price was worth paying; others don't.

NOTES

A NOTE

5 *Exploiting energy often involves exploiting people*: For an excellent historical overview of resource extraction farther south, on Appalachia's Cumberland Plateau, see *Night Comes to the Cumberlands: A Biography of a Depressed Area* (Jesse Stuart Foundation, 2001) by Henry M. Caudill.

2. WHEN THE BOOM BEGAN

26 *The companies also paved back roads*: To enumerate the public costs of oil and gas production in Western Pennsylvania, I relied on two sets of data. The first, primarily related to social costs, comes from *Measuring the Costs and Benefits of Natural Gas Development in Greene County, Pennsylvania: A Case Study* (Pennsylvania Budget and Policy Center, and Keystone Research Center, 2014) by Stephen Hertzenberg, Diana Polson, and Mark Price. The second lays out the private costs transferred to public infrastructure: "Estimating the Consumptive Use Costs of Shale Natural Gas Extraction on Pennsylvania Roadways" (*Journal of Infrastructure Systems*, 2014) by Shmuel Abramzon; Constantine Samaras, A.M.ASCE; Aimee Curtright; Aviva Litovitz; and Nicholas Burger, and published by the American Society of Civil Engineers.

3. THE MESS NEXT DOOR

29 *trees "as old as America"*: For a historical portrait of Ron Yeager's farm, see
Louise McClenathan's letter to the *Pittsburgh Post-Gazette*, "Long Before
the Yeager Impoundment Became a Source of Controversy, the Site Was
Part of Louise McClenathan Family's Peaceful Homestead," published on
September 7, 2014.

5. AIRBORNE

52 *"Undoubtedly, these shortcomings have eroded the public's trust"*: The best
analysis of the DEP's struggles to keep up with the oil and gas industry's
lies is the Pennsylvania auditor general's report, "DEP's Performance in
Monitoring Potential Impacts to Water Quality from Shale Gas Development, 2009–2012." The full text is available at www.paauditor.gov/Media
/Default/Reports/speDEP072114.pdf.

7. "ONE HEAD & ONE HEART, & LIVE IN TRUE FRIENDSHIP & AMITY AS ONE PEOPLE"

63 *Ten Mile Creek was also a dangerous place*: There are many fine histories
of Washington County. The two I found most useful were Boyd Crumrine's
*History of Washington County, Pennsylvania: With Biographical Sketches
of Many of Its Pioneers and Prominent Men*, published in 1882 by L. H.
Everts & Co.; and Harriet Branton's *Washington County Chronicles:
Historic Tales from Southwestern Pennsylvania*, published in 2013 by the
History Press.

63 *This was part of the legacy of William Penn*: For the larger historical landscape of the frontier, I relied most on two excellent books, Kevin Kenny's
Peaceable Kingdom Lost (Oxford University Press, 2009) and William Ho-
geland's *The Whiskey Rebellion* (Simon & Schuster, 2010). There are also
two rich local sources: *Rural Reflections* (1977), a four-volume series by
the Amwell Township Historical Society regarding the local history of
Amity's township of Amwell, and *The Reverend Thaddeus Dod: Frontier
Teacher and Preacher*, written and published by the Reverend Rawley
Dod Boone, S.T.M.

8. DOUBTERS

71   *from 2007 to 2012, the gas boom brought fifteen thousand industry-related jobs*: This statistic comes from the Pennsylvania Bureau of Labor Statistics. In Pennsylvania and elsewhere, employment statistics regarding the natural gas boom are contested. Studies produced by those who oppose drilling and those who support it make contesting claims, which are often used to judge whether or not the costs of industry are worth paying.

75   *the average age of local farmers climbed to fifty-six*: The fact and other context related to the plight of Pennsylvania's farmers comes from "A Devil's Bargain: Rural Environmental Injustices and Hydraulic Fracturing on Pennsylvania's Farms" (*Journal of Rural Studies*, 2015) by Kathryn Teigen DeMaster and Stephanie A. Malin. This study also provides an overview of the complex relationship between the state's farmers and the oil and gas industry.

9. HANG 'EM HIGH

82   *Rachel Carson, the legendary environmentalist, grew up against the backdrop of this devastation*: Linda Lear's definitive biography *Rachel Carson: Witness for Nature* (Mariner Books, 2009) provides a brilliant account of Carson's life and times.

83   *"beneficial use"*: For more on the law surrounding "beneficial use," and how it is that oil and gas industrial waste can be spread on farmers' fields, see www.dep.pa.gov/Business/Land/Waste/SolidWaste/Residual/BeneficialUse/Pages/default.aspx.

83   *earthquakes*: Fracking has been definitively linked with earthquakes in two different ways. First, injecting wastewater into deep underground wells was shown, beginning in Oklahoma in 2014, to cause earthquakes. Second, by 2017, in Pennsylvania and elsewhere, the unconventional drilling process itself was demonstrated to cause earthquakes. Reid Frazier of NPR's *StateImpact* broke the story; see https://stateimpact.npr.org/pennsylvania/2017/02/18/pennsylvania-confirms-first-fracking-related-earthquakes.

10. BLOOD AND URINE

85   *Dish, Texas*: The full history of the Dish, Texas, battle with the oil and gas industry has been reported in full by Reeve Hamilton in *The Texas*

Tribune. For further information on drilling in North Texas, Saul El-
bein of *Texas Monthly* has also written an account, which can be found
at www.texasmonthly.com/articles/heres-the-drill.

93   *benzene, a chemical compound*: For the potential illnesses related to oil and
     gas industrial exposure, I relied on the following environmental and medi-
     cal studies: At Duke University, Christopher Kassotis's work on endocrine
     disruption "Endocrine-Disrupting Activity of Hydraulic Fracturing Chemi-
     cals and Adverse Health Outcomes After Prenatal Exposure in Male Mice"
     (*Endocrine Society*, October 14, 2015); "Dangerous and Close: Fracking
     near Pennsylvania's Most Vulnerable Residents" (PennEnvironment Re-
     search & Policy Center, September 2015) by Elizabeth Ridlington, Tony
     Dutzik, and Tom Van Heeke (Frontier Group) and Adam Garber and David
     Masur (PennEnvironment Research and Policy Center); "Association Be-
     tween Unconventional Natural Gas Development in the Marcellus Shale
     and Asthma Exacerbations" (*JAMA Internal Medicine*, 2016) by Sara G.
     Rasmussen, MHS; Elizabeth L. Ogburn, PhD; Meredith McCormack,
     MD; et al. Although to date no peer-reviewed studies have examined the
     potential health effects of bacteria in waste ponds, Paula Mouser at Ohio
     State University has studied the issue. In 2014, she, along with Maryam A.
     Cluff, Angela Hartsock, Jean D. MacRae, and Kimberly Carter, published
     the study "Temporal Changes in Microbial Ecology and Geochemistry in
     Produced Water from Hydraulically Fractured Marcellus Shale Gas Wells"
     (*Environmental Science and Technology*, 2014).

12. "MR. AND MRS. ATTICUS FINCH"

109 *"Mr. and Mrs. Joe Schmo at 10 Cash-Strapped Lane"*: The fight over frack-
     ing in Mount Pleasant Township was the subject of "Game Changer," an
     episode of NPR's *This American Life*, which originally aired on July 8,
     2011.

13. MUTUAL DISTRUST

125 *"It's the right thing to do morally and ethically"*: Range's announcement that
     it would disclose all of the chemicals used in the fracking process was orig-
     inally reported by Russell Gold of *The Wall Street Journal*, whose book
     The Boom: How Fracking Ignited the American Energy Revolution and

Changed the World (Simon & Schuster, 2014) provides an excellent look at the early days of the gas rush.

18. INSURGENTS

156 *"Download the U.S. Army/Marine Corps Counterinsurgency Manual because we are dealing with an insurgency"*: Sharon Wilson took her recordings from the Houston oil and gas conference first to Don Hopey at the *Pittsburgh Post-Gazette*. Hopey broke the story of Range's use of psy-ops tactics and closely followed many of the local legal proceedings discussed in this book, and I'm indebted to his excellent environmental reporting. Sharon Wilson writes more about this conference and her opposition to fracking on her blog, www.texassharon.com.

20. POLICING THE STATE

171 Salus populi suprema lex esto: For a definitive history of the concept of public welfare in the United States—*salus populi suprema lex esto*—see William J. Novak's *The People's Welfare: Law and Regulation in Nineteenth-Century America* (University of North Carolina Press, 1996).

21. WHAT MONEY DOES

177 *In Pennsylvania, from 2007 to 2016, tracing the arc of the gas rush*: In Pennsylvania, Marie Cusick of StateImpact, a collaboration among several NPR affiliate stations, has traced the migration patterns of state environmental employees into the private sector; see https://stateimpact.npr.org/pennsyl vania/2016/01/21/where-are-they-now-track-top-state-officials-with-pennsyl vanias-blurred-lines.

22. RUIN IS THE DESTINATION TOWARD WHICH ALL MEN RUSH

196 *"We don't know how much is in the bank and we keep giving away"*: Rose Reilly, the U.S. Army Corps of Engineers biologist, explained that the amount of water a driller can legally take from a public stream is expressed in the formula $(Q \times 7) \div 10$. Q represents a stream's lowest daily flow as recorded over the past ten years. Under the law, drillers are allowed to take

10 percent of a week's flow at that level, but there's no mechanism in place to enforce legal limits on withdrawals.

197 *Tragedy of the Commons*: For more on Elinor Ostrom's Nobel Prize–winning work related to the commons, see her *Governing the Commons: The Evolution of Institutions for Collective Action* (Cambridge University Press, 1990).

23. REMOTE PEOPLE

201 *the DEP was testing for twenty-four different metals, yet it was reporting results for only eight*: Jon Hurdle of *The New York Times* broke the story of the controversy surrounding the DEP's use of codes in "Pennsylvania Report Left Out Data on Poisons in Water Near Gas Site," November 2, 2012.

24. IGNORANT MOTHERFUCKERS

211 *Cyber schooling was a growing trend*: Cyber school is becoming increasingly common in Pennsylvania, where one of every fifty students attends a cyber charter school, a publicly funded online-only form of homeschooling. To learn more about the challenges cyber school presents, see Kevin McCorry of NPR's Philadelphia-affiliated WHYY: https://whyy.org/articles/temple-prof-pa-cyber-charters-turning-huge-profits-sending-tax-dollars-out-of-state.

25. A SPECIAL AGENT

222 *In a 2009 cable later released by WikiLeaks*: To read more about the Obama administration's efforts to help export fracking technology, read Mariah Blake's work for *Mother Jones*, as well as the original State Department cables from WikiLeaks at https://wikileaks.org/plusd/cables/09STATE111742_a.html.

27. THE RIGHT TO CLEAN AIR AND PURE WATER

241 *"The measure of our progress is not just what we have but how we live"*: In his landmark decision, Chief Justice Castille quoted extensively from a speech given by Herbert Fineman. Fineman was Speaker of the House in the Pennsylvania legislature in 1971 when the amendment passed almost unanimously.

33. FAIR 2016

282 *"big houses"*: Terry Bossert of Range Resources apologized for his comments about not placing gas wells near "big houses." He left Range Resources shortly afterward for a Pittsburgh law firm, where he counsels oil
and gas producers on navigating regulations and compliance. The former
Pennsylvania governor Tom Ridge defended Bossert in the *Post-Gazette*,
saying, "Terry made a mistake for which he has publicly apologized. It
would be a disservice to his decades of good work to allow one ill-advised
comment to distract from what has been an exemplary career of service to
our commonwealth."

283 *"When you finally see in its full flower how corrupt the world of the DEP
actually is, it's nauseating"*: John Quigley, the former secretary for the DEP,
fired from his job by Governor Tom Wolf in 2016, left state government for
academia. He's currently a senior fellow at the Kleinman Center for
Energy Policy at the University of Pennsylvania.

ACKNOWLEDGMENTS

Extraction isn't only a matter of resources; it relates to stories. Without the generosity of Harley, Stacey, Paige, Beth, John, Ashley, Grace, and Buzz, along with their patience and willingness to welcome me into their homes over six difficult years, this book wouldn't exist.

I am also obliged to the people of Washington County. To name only several, Shelly Pellen, Linda and Larry Hillberry, Alice and Park Burroughs, Veronica Coptis, Ray Day, Rick Baker, Jason Clark, Bill "Willard" Mankey, and the late Bill Hartley—along with countless others—were generous, open, and fair, and for that I am grateful. In Allegheny County and beyond, I'm grateful for the wisdom and hospitality of Amy Weiss, along with Greg Scott, Lisa Orr, Luke Lozier, and Dorothy Bassett.

Kendra and John Smith allowed me to follow their work and their lives as they built not one but four complex cases. I thank them, along with Dakota, Sienna, and Ainsley, for sparing even more of their parents' time and attention.

Behind these pages, there are also the remarkable individuals whose professional support was invaluable. All books are collaborative efforts, but none more so than this one. I am humbled by the singular enthusiasm and fierce attention of Tina Bennett, of WME. The editorial superpowers of Alex Star at FSG have honed a complex series of legal cases into far more than the sum of its disparate parts. Also at FSG, the faith and encouragement of my mentor and friend Jonathan Galassi have carried me through some very dark days. I am also indebted to the fabulousness of Jeff Seroy, the legal prowess of Henry

Kaufman, the diligence of Dominique Lear, and the raptor eye of Lenni Wolff. There are so many others who have been generous to this work, including Emily Stokes, Nick Trautwein, and David Remnick at *The New Yorker* and Sheila Glaser and Kathy Ryan at *The New York Times Magazine*.

For investigative research, there is no one more dogged than Kelsey Kudak, who brought both brains and heart to the project, along with Heather Radke and Max Siegelbaum. I am also thankful for the Guggenheim Foundation, the Rockefeller Family Fund, the Fund for Investigative Journalism, Harvard Divinity School, and Stanford University's McCoy Family Center for Ethics in Society, which introduced the book to early and expert readers.

The support and guidance of the following friends demands a resounding and unending *thank-you*: Larissa MacFarquhar, Katy Lederer, Amy Waldman, Suzie Kondi, Michele Conlin, and Robert Hammond. I have also benefited from the support of a host of colleagues and experts, including Carolyn Kissane, Terry Engelder, Ed Morse, Jon Hurdle, Leif Werner, Neela Banerjee, Don Hopey, Marie Cusick, Rose Reilly, Seamus McGraw, Myron Arnowitt, and Joel Tarr. There are also those who can't be named: thank you for your courage in speaking to me.

For my family, Phoebe and Frank Griswold, Hannah, Louisa, and Georgina, I owe you gratitude and many, many dinners. The same goes for my wonderful new family, Susan, Paul, Ally, Rory, Emma, John, Max, Katie, and Sarah. To Robert, for enduring those endless hours in your car seat on the Pennsylvania Turnpike.

And to Steve, thank you for reading *Frog and Toad* more times than any human being should withstand, and for our life, which is more than I dared to hope for.

A Note About the Author

Eliza Griswold is the author of *The Tenth Parallel: Dispatches from the Fault Line Between Christianity and Islam*, which won the 2011 J. Anthony Lukas Book Prize. Her translations of Afghan women's folk poems, *I Am the Beggar of the World*, was awarded the 2015 PEN Award for Poetry in Translation. She has held fellowships from the New America Foundation, the Guggenheim Foundation, and Harvard University, and in 2010 the American Academy of Arts and Letters awarded her the Rome Prize for her poems. Currently a Distinguished Writer in Residence at New York University, she lives in New York with her husband and son.